The World & Christ's Prophecies:

God's Great Reset

December 2015 – March 1, 2024

By Tiffany Root & Kirk VandeGuchte

Table of Contents

Introduction

Jesus said, **"But when He, the Spirit of Truth, comes …**
He will tell you what is yet to come" (John 16:13 NIV).
When the Holy Spirit tells us things to come, it is called
prophecy. He sometimes does this through "words." Other
times, He brings visions and dreams.

Sometimes these prophecies are things the Lord wants His
people to pray about or declare. Other times, the
prophecies are "set in stone" so to speak. In other words,
they are definitely going to happen no matter what. This
book contains both kinds of prophecies, the ones that we
need to pray about and the ones that will definitely
happen or have already happened.

As you read, listen for the voice of the Holy Spirit. Ask Him
to read with you. He will bear witness to the truth because
He is the Spirit of Truth who leads us into all truth.

In a prophetic word given on August 12, 2019, entitled
"The End is Near and Not Far Off." The Lord begins by
referencing Revelation 6:12-14 (NIV).

I watched as He opened the sixth seal. There was a great
earthquake. The sun turned black like sackcloth made of
goat hair, the whole moon turned blood red, and the
stars in the sky fell to earth, as late figs drop from a fig
tree when shaken by a strong wind. The sky receded like
a scroll, rolling up, and every mountain and island was
removed from its place.

The Lord then said, *"Kirk, the end nears, and is not far off as some believe. As that day comes close, look up, for your redemption is close by. Some might say that it seems as if you and Tiffany have been teaching the very same thing over and over, which is to listen to the Holy Spirit. Yes, like training a one trick pony. But soon this hearing will not be optional, but very necessary. Your enemy knows this. Steer clear of deception! The deceiver is hard at work and will deceive many seasoned believers. With each one who will believe his lies, he is emboldened and empowered, and his fury at those who stand firm or who turn from his lies is great! As I have said, there will be deep darkness, but the light will overpower the darkness! Do not fear!*

Look to Me to see the signs. I will show you what is happening in the heavens and on earth. Listen to My voice. I do not lie and am not deceived. Your hope is in Me alone! Test My words among yourselves because deception creeps in undetected otherwise, a little here and a little there. Keep watch. Help each other. The times are evil, and spiritual pride is a great trap of the deceiver. Lastly, never fear! I AM with you, and I AM for you. You cannot lose!

Amen and Amen!

A few notes:

Some of the prophecies you will read here can also be found in our *Trump Prophecies* book. All of our books can be found on Amazon.com by searching under "Tiffany Root."

The prophecies are listed in the order in which we received them, starting in December of 2015 and ending at the beginning of March 2024. The Holy Spirit continues to tell us things to come, which can be found in video form on our YouTube Channel – Seeking the Glory of God Ministries and on our Rumble Channel – Seeking the Glory of God (Prophecies). If you are interested in daily devotionals, we have two devotional channels as well: SGGM DEVOTIONALS on YouTube and Rumble. These devotionals are excellent tools for discipleship as they contain deep revelation.

May the Lord bless you and give you His vision for the future as you read what He has prophesied regarding the world and His church. Amen.

2015-2019

ISIS Done December 2015

Isaiah 16:13-14

This is the word which the LORD has spoken concerning Moab since that time. But now the LORD has spoken, saying, "Withing three years, as the years of a hired man, the glory of Moab will be despised with all that great multitude, and the remnant will be very small and feeble.

The LORD is saying that ISIS will be nothing, or practically nothing within three years from December 2015.

*This prophecy was fulfilled. At the time it was given, Obama was sitting in the President's seat. But when Donald J. Trump came into office, he obliterated ISIS, and they were definitely done, or practically so, by 2018.

Woman on the Supreme Court – September 27, 2018

The Lord had me (Kirk) read Judges 4 about Deborah. I believe the Lord is bringing up a woman to be seated on the United States Supreme Court. I'm not sure if she will come in place of Brett Kavanaugh or later, after him. (This was during the time when Brett Kavanaugh was being vetted for the SCOTUS.) She will be a follower of Jesus and a prophet, holding the office of prophet. Her name might be Deborah, and she will dominate the SCOTUS. Her ascent into this position will look like Deborah's in Judges.

Democrat Party Few & Feeble – November 1, 2018

The same Scripture that the LORD applied to Moab and to ISIS, He also applied to the Democratic party. He said within three years of November 2018 they would be few and feeble.

*This prophecy was fulfilled. Though it has not necessarily looked like the Democratic party was few and feeble by 2021, we know that they were. The 2020 election was stolen, not just from Donald J. Trump, but from many of the MAGA candidates, and the election of 2022 was stolen on an even larger scale. For example, in Michigan, the people turned out in numbers we've never seen before to get rid of a trifecta of evil, among other things on the ballot. However, not only did an overwhelming majority of seats turn "Democrat" but all three evil proposals on the ballot "passed." All of this was a complete lie. The Deep State cheated to get what they wanted. In this example, we have been told for a long time Michigan is a Democratic state, but that is not true.

We will see that this prophecy has been fulfilled, the more things are exposed in time to come.

The Church Like Eli & Sons – November 22, 2018

The account of Eli and his sons in 1 Samuel is prophetic of the church and its leaders.

Angels Coming from the East – December 7, 2018

The Lord said, "Look to the East." So, I did. He said, "What do you see?" I wasn't really seeing anything. He said, "It's the Angel coming on the bright star in the East." So, I looked again, and saw a bright star. He said, "Behold He (Jesus) comes with healing in His wings and to make war against the darkness of this world." I said, "How will this be, Lord? What will happen?"

He said, "The battle lines have been drawn, and I will prevail. Look up! Your salvation comes. Don't despair! I, the Lord, am coming in power. I will not be turned away or misled, and I will not relent! I have heard your prayers, and I will have My victory."

I can see the angels coming, swords drawn. They glisten in the morning sun. The angels are excited for battle, empowered with fresh power and faith. They too have been waiting for this day!

I also see the demons in fear! They are complaining and arguing with the Lord – complaining of unfairness and any other argument they can come up with.

Increase of Revelatory Knowledge Among God's People – December 21, 2018

"Now the boy Samuel ministered to the LORD before Eli. And the word of the LORD was rare in those days; there was no widespread revelation." (1 Samuel 3:1).

"And it shall come to pass in the last days, says God, That I will pour out My Spirit on all flesh; Your sons and your daughters shall prophesy, Your young men shall see visions, Your old men shall dream dreams." (Acts 2:17)

Of these two verses, the Lord God of all says, "That was then; this is now."

"But you, Daniel, close up and seal the words of the scroll until the time of the end. Many will go here and there and (through the scroll) knowledge [of the purpose of God as revealed by His Prophets] will [greatly] increase." (Daniel 2:14, NIV/AMP)

The Lord says He is increasing understanding, wisdom, and knowledge among His people.

"Revelatory knowledge! It will come through the Apostles and Prophets. There will be **no** other source. Nothing like this outpouring has ever happened before, and the academia and intelligentsia will be aghast. For even the foolish who believe shall easily outwit them. There shall be knowledge and understanding of things never seen and imaginations of solutions which only I, the LORD, could know of alone. Then the world shall know that 'I AM' is the Lord!"

False Teachers & Prophets in the Church Losing Power

– June 13, 2019

A word to Kirk and Tiffany, but also to the church at large.

"Because with lies you have made the heart of the righteous sad, whom I have not made sad; and you have strengthened the hands of the wicked, so that he does not turn from his wicked way to save his life. Therefore you shall no longer envision futility or practice divination; for I will deliver My people out of your hand, and you shall know that I am the LORD." (Ezekiel 13:22-23)

"Kirk, I just want to say that there are false prophets and false teachers everywhere! You and Tiffany are not included in this group, however. I know you already know this, but I want to be clear on this."

Father is saying how it hurts His heart that He is misrepresented.

"The individual lies of theology and doctrine (religion) are many, and also there are those who claim to know Me, but do not. But power forces a decision, and in these days of the latter rain, I AM pouring out My Spirit to force people to decide. They will be forced to seek the Giver, or in their pride, be forever separated. And I AM especially speaking of church leadership. I AM removing the 'power' of their lies. Logic will be meaningless, and hype will be overshadowed by real power. They will come against My true followers, and even the weakest in My kingdom will be ten times their strongest strength."

Vision Coming to Jesus as a Child – June 15, 2019

I (Kirk) was listening to the Lord and thinking about how Tiffany has been able to go up to the throne room of God. I asked if I could too. I then heard, "Come up here," and I did.

I found myself standing in front of a huge pyramid, and in front of me was a door. It looked very heavy and large. I heard a voice like thunder, which I knew came from a seraphim. It said, "Put one hand on your heart and place the other on the door because only those with a pure heart may enter."

So, I did. I put my left hand on my heart and my right hand on the door. I heard an unlatching noise and the door popped open slightly. It was very heavy and big and moved open with difficulty. I entered, and in front of me was a long stairway. The roof of the stairs was angled as if it followed the contour of the outside of the pyramid. At the top I could see a light.

I went up and when I got to the top there was a sort of landing area, and I walked a ways and then turned to the right to enter a huge room. The room was flooded with white light and smoke. I walked into it and made a slow turn to the left. Then I saw Father with Jesus at His right hand. I thought about how the other times that I was in the throne room I had felt so reverent. This time was different.

All I could think to do was run full tilt, like a child, to Jesus. So, I did, and I jumped in His arms. He said, "Oh good. You've come to Me as a child!"

Prophecies of Destruction are not Final – June 24, 2019

"Then God saw their works, that they turned from their evil way; and God relented from the disaster that He had said He would bring upon them, and He did not do it." (Jonah 3:10)

The Lord says, "When My prophets prophesy destruction, it is not a done deal. Just as in Jonah's time, I watch to see if people turn from their evil ways, and if they do, I may relent and not do the thing which I had threatened. I don't simply bring destruction on people. They will get a warning first."

The Drumbeat of the Religious Prophecy –

June 27, 2019

Isaiah *66:3b-5 (TNIV) They have chosen their own ways, and they delight in their abominations; so I also chose harsh treatment for them and will bring on them what they dread. For when I called, no one answered, when I spoke, no one listened. They did evil in My sight and chose what displeases Me. Hear the Word of the LORD, you who tremble at His word: Your own people who hate you, and exclude you because of My name, have said, "Let the Lord be glorified, that we may see your joy!" Yet they will be put to shame.*

Jeremiah 6:16-19 (TNIV) This is what the Lord says: "Stand at the crossroads and look; ask for the ancient paths, ask where the good way is, and walk in it, and you will find rest for your souls." But you said, "We will not walk in it." I appointed watchmen over you and said, "Listen to the sound of the trumpet!" But you said, "We will not listen." Therefore hear, you nations; you who are witnesses, observe what will happen to them. Hear, you earth: I am bringing disaster on this people, the fruit of their schemes, because they have not listened to My words and have rejected My law.

"Kirk, listen to the drumbeat of the religious! Listen to them drone on and on about how they have 'figured out' the right way. They make great speeches and practice the 'perfect' delivery of them. Their sheep are so impressed with their mastery of history, the Bible, Hebrew, and Greek! Their hunger for ever more sheep is insatiable! As is their desire for more money, bigger buildings, and more programs. Their long, flowing prayers are like honey to the hearers' ears; all the right religious words are used perfectly. Their booming voices crackle with boldness and authority so that even they believe that they know Me! Their sheep are weak, however, and don't know Me. Their leaders know Me even less. The leaders and their sheep look around them and see success as measured by the world. They see what they have built with their hands. They look over the crowded venue over which they preside or to which they belong and proudly declare that God is with them!

But My justice will be swift, and none shall escape it! Kirk, pray that these will give up their fools' gold and fake silver, and turn and humble themselves, so that they may desire the true riches of My kingdom! For those who will not turn, the time of their disaster is near and will not wait forever. I will not be mocked, and neither shall My chosen! I will repay, says the LORD! The time of the latter rain is here. My Spirit is being poured out. Pray for the latter rain! He will fall on all who are willing to carry Him. The darkness shall increase, but the Light shall increase more. Those whose focus is on the darkness shall be overcome by it, but those who walk in the Light shall never be in darkness. Therefore, set your face toward the Light and not toward the darkness! If you have died to the darkness, you will never die again! If not, there will be no end to the death you will die."

2020 Prophecy – December 9, 2019

The Lord says that the year 2020 will be a year of "unlocking," a year when the promised things are unlocked.

It will also be a year when a great lurch to the right shall happen, so much so that even some of those on the right will be made uncomfortable.

"My Trumpet shall be loosed and be constrained no more! In 2020, the 2024 election will be decided.

The Great End Times Harvest shall have its roots in the year 2020! The time of the youth shall begin, and as it matures, it shall be greater than the earth has ever seen.

The age of the 'church' will soon be forgotten. Indeed, the 'church' as it is will be looked at as a bad memory, and the buildings which house it will be viewed as monuments to a failed system. The churches that survive shall be looked on as pariahs, houses of fools. My glorious ones, however, will shine with a brilliance never before seen!"

2020

Leave the Intellect, and Go into the Deep –

January 17, 2020

Jesus was teaching by the Lake of Gennesaret. He got into one of the boats belonging to Simon and taught from the boat.

When He had stopped speaking, He said to Simon, "Launch out into the deep and let down your nets for a catch." But Simon answered and said to Him, "Master, we have toiled all night and caught nothing; nevertheless at Your word I will let down the net." And when they had done this, they caught a great number of fish, and their net was breaking. So they signaled to their partners in the other boat to come and help them. And they came and filled both the boats, so that they began to sink. (Luke 5:4-7)

The Lord wants us to know that Peter in this account learned that he must leave logic, reason, experience, and also a failed attempt at fishing. Additionally, he needed to go out into the deep. Of course, Jesus could have done this same thing in shallow water, but the added toil and faith that it took was necessary. Peter also called for help because the blessing was more than he could handle.

Jesus is calling us now. He's saying, "Go out into the deep! Leave the comfort and ease to which you have become accustomed. You will find your blessings to be more than you can even imagine in the deep water. I desire to bless you extravagantly, more than you will ever find in the shallows! Go with what I'm asking, against your 'better'

15

judgment, deeper than your shallow prayers, deeper than logic and reason. Leave the moorings of the letter. Dare to believe! I cannot resist faith! It may seem to you to be foolish, and it will require labor, but these things will be quickly forgotten in the glory of the blessings you will find in Me!"

Line Between Those the Lord Loves and Those Who Have Attracted His Wrath – February 4, 2020

G od is jealous, and the LORD avenges;
   The LORD avenges and is furious.
   The LORD will take vengeance on His adversaries;
And He reserves wrath for His enemies;
The LORD is slow to anger and great in power,
And will not at all acquit the wicked…
Who can stand before His indignation?
And who can endure the fierceness of His anger?
His fury is poured out like fire,
And the rocks are thrown down by Him. (Nahum 1:2-3a, 6)

The Lord asks me (Kirk), "Isn't this what you and your Apostle want to know? This anger and judgment is My reputation, isn't it? You (Prophet) have said that I AM not in heaven with a lightning bolt in My hand ready to zap someone, and yet, is this not My reputation? Does not My wrath rest on those who will not receive My Son? Therefore, My son, My wrath is justified. I do not change, says the LORD!

My love, however, is infinite. For those who have turned their hearts to Me shall never die! My Son has turned His affection toward them and loves them, and My heart is always for them and *never* against them, for these who have received Him are Mine.

In these last days it shall be shown who I love and also those who have attracted My wrath. There shall be no doubt regarding this."

God's Anger & He's Raising Up Others Like Trump –

February 11, 2020

The LORD says His anger is aroused like it was in Isaiah's day (Isaiah 3). He reminded Kirk of a time several years ago when He had shown him His anger. As a witness to that event, I (Tiffany) can assure you it was not a pleasant experience for Kirk. He was visibly shaking and tearful and said he never wanted to see the Lord's anger again.

After this reminder of His anger, the Lord took us to Isaiah 11:11.

It shall come to pass in that day
That the LORD shall set His hand again the second time
To recover the remnant of His people, who are left,
From Assyria and Egypt,
Pathros and Cush,
Elam and Shinar,
From Hamath and the islands of the sea.

The LORD God says, "In My wrath I will again deal with the workers of iniquity, those who reject My Son. And again, I will also have mercy and express My love and favor on the ones that I love!

I want you to know the times and seasons. Therefore, open your eyes to see and incline your ears to hear. Watch My anointed one, the one who always holds My trump card and plays it wisely. Watch as this party is in its early stages. Watch for the best wine to be served later! See! The wedding party is in its early stages, the bride is being vetted and will be presented without spot or wrinkle. The Bridegroom has been ready and will not be made to wait much longer. The enemies of the bride and the Bridegroom are being pushed to the outside of the party and will be marginalized even more. Do not fear them. The only power they have is lies, fear, and intimidation. Their wrath will become great, but in their frenzy for power and lust for relevance, they will eat their own and see mass defections. Receive their defectors with love, and they will also be loved by Me.

Son, the time of shaking is at hand. Those whose foundation is the Rock shall find themselves to be fearless, even to death, because they have already died! They will find themselves rooted and grounded in the word of God, nourished by the Latter Rain, and with their eyes looking only upward!

Open your eyes and ears and take notice that I have others whom I, the LORD, have anointed, and they too will rise up in their countries, and the pattern of My Trumpet shall be repeated over and over as My people who are called by My name are vindicated and My wrath will be satisfied. So be it says the LORD."

Coronavirus Judgment Word – March 15, 2020

"Kirk, the coronavirus is a judgment of the Lord. I AM is NOT the author of sickness and death. However, I set the boundaries and amplitude of everything that I allow to happen. Further, all who are Mine are already judged to be 'in Christ,' and to the degree of their faith in what He has done for them, they will not be judged (affected by this judgment).

So, Tiffany, look around you, and look at those who are affected. You will see through My eyes and pronounce My judgment back to Me, and it will be so.

When either of you hear differently about this, it will be a lie. I AM is not speaking anything different to anyone, and most are hearing nothing.

My anointed will be lifted up because of how the distribution of this sickness works out, and it will be clearly seen where My favor lies. The end of this judgment shall come as quickly as its beginning, and due to fear, some will suffer great loss, and others who look to Me will be blessed. I AM has spoken."

Billion Youth Movement Prophecy – March 15, 2020

Jesus is showing me (Kirk) that the great harvest of a billion youth has begun. Every world event, the weather, every sickness, every true follower – all things are working together toward this event.

"Now, look at how a car is built. First the screws and bolts are made, then the metal is purified and formed into the needed parts. These parts look nothing like a car. They need to come together in perfect order to make the mold and form desired.

The pieces of the movement that will be the billion-youth movement are still in pieces. You can only recognize and guess at how and what these pieces will form. This is what you see in the natural, but I have shown My servant Bob Jones My dream, and have now given you and Tiffany this same dream. It was never Bob's, and it is not your dream either. It is My dream, and I AM has invited you both into it! Dream with Me, therefore!"

Vision of Jesus as Elder Brother – March 17, 2020

I (Kirk) have a vision of Jesus standing in the throne room. I walk up to Him and put my arm around Him. I was thinking of Him as my Elder Brother. Then I drew back my arm because it occurred to me that He is Lord of all, God, Savior, Master, and I should not be so casual with Him!

Then tears come to my eyes because yes, He is all of these things. He is King of ALL, but He sees me as a child of the Father too. He sees me as a friend. He loves me and calls me to do what He did on the earth! To be Jesus on the earth if that were possible. And then He says that I will do MORE than He did!

He knows who He is! He is not threatened in His Lordship or in His divinity by my desire to be like Him. In fact, that's what I am called to! It saddens Jesus when we pull back because we have been told that our relationship must look a certain way. The world and religion say, "Well, you are not Jesus after all."

So, He is calling us to be BOLD, act as if we are Christ in this world! As He is, so are we in this world! The Lord says, "Come on! Stop drawing back and putting limits on yourself! You are in Christ! Live your life as I lived Mine!"

Coronavirus Vaccine Dream – March 22, 2020

I (Tiffany) dreamed this morning that the U.S. government was injecting people with something. It was killing them, making them crazy, and opening them to the enemy. I was the only one in my dream who didn't do it (didn't take the injection). I saw what people were being put through, and I couldn't believe so many people were agreeing to this. Even a well-known prophet was doing it. Close family members did it. I couldn't figure out why everyone was volunteering for it. It's like it wasn't mandatory, but people were doing it because the government wanted them to. I got really mad at what the enemy was putting people through. It was like he was making them crazy or something. I went outside the building to pray and use my authority. I met a man who must have also had the Holy Spirit because he would listen to God. I was talking to him and walking my new dog (a larger dog with short hair).

Interpretation from the Holy Spirit:

The Holy Spirit says this dream is prophetic. The government will come out with a vaccine against Coronavirus, but it will be tainted. This will not be deliberate on their part, but when it comes out, we need to stand against it and warn people that it is not good.

* Obviously, this dream did come to pass. Some people in "authority" knew it was tainted and others not. Interestingly, even the large dog with short hair came to pass, and that was definitely not on the radar!

Coronavirus Reaches Its Boundary Prophecy –

March 24, 2020

"Kirk, look around you. Look at the fear! Did you see the pictures of those who, in panic, were standing in line at the Jenison Meijer? The store shelves were completely emptied of product!

But where is the fear of the Lord? Where are those who will stand together to pray? Where is the one who has faith?

Therefore, mighty warriors, now is time, while it is still called Today! Call out, ask, petition the LORD your God! As it says: a thousand will fall at your side and ten thousand at your right hand, but **IT** shall not approach you. The Lord your God is calling you to action now, today! Therefore, pray as instructed, and watch the hand of the Lord as He moves on your behalf!

Therefore, command life! Your Savior is the Way, the Truth, and the LIFE! Declare it, command it, and it will go out from you as you speak. This judgment has reached its boundary, and I AM is calling on those who only bow to His name to action. Praise Him whose judgments are good, and whose mercies go on forever! Amen!"

Greeting from the LORD – Lift Up Your Eyes –

March 26, 2020

"Grace, mercy, and peace will be with you from God the Father and from the Lord Jesus Christ, the Son of the Father, in truth and love." (2 John 3)

This is the greeting from the Lord this morning! The Lord is full of joy this morning! He is imparting MORE grace to those who are in the light! Yes, He sees you! You know who you are! He sees His joy in you. He knows your heart. He calls you "the light!" Is there darkness in the world? He's asking because otherwise "the light" (yes, you) might not notice!

Mercy and peace are your calling cards, and you pass them out freely now. Yes, you see yourself actually walking as He did. In your wake and always following you are Truth and Love.

Now, lift your eyes and receive! Come on! It is time to shine in all of your brilliance, the very Son of the Living God living in you by His Spirit! You can't help but shine! Lift up your downcast eyes. Look at the Truth. Look into His eyes. You cannot be downcast. Listen to His voice and LIVE!

You are His and He is yours! You are KNOWN by God! Amen!

Rejoice! Justice is on the Way! – April 1, 2020

" If anyone comes to Me, and does not hate his own father and mother and wife and children and brothers and sisters, yes and even his own life, he cannot be My disciple... So then, none of you can be My disciple who does not give up all his own possessions." (Luke 14:26, 33 NASB)

"Tiffany, it has always been important to listen and follow. I know you already understand this. The verses regarding the winnowing fork are speaking of the last days. (Jer 15:7, Mat 3:12, Lk 3:17, Is 41:16) So yes, I will clear the threshing floor and gather in the wheat. I Am is separating the wheat and tares as well."

Father is saying: "I love My Son and I love those who are His! The cup of My wrath is nearing its limit and will soon be poured out. They have rejected Him, therefore Me, and the blood of the saints calls out to Me every minute. My wrath and My justice will not wait forever! I Am Love! Rejoice! Justice is on the way!"

Shaking Taking Longer – April 3, 2020

The Lord says, "COVID will end as quickly as it began. The shaking, however, is taking longer than I intended." (The backdrop to this was that people were not praying in faith, but in fear.)

Trump Signals End of COVID – April 4, 2020

Trump will do something that will be amazingly bold, even for him. It will be around the time of the Passover and will signal the end of the COVID-19 "pandemic."

Know Jesus as I AM – April 6, 2020

In Revelation Chapter One Jesus is standing among the lampstands in all His glory. With this image in mind, He is saying that until now He has appeared to us as He was on earth. But now He will be appearing to us as He IS. We are to prepare our minds and hearts for this. His appearance as He is will, or could be, a very fearful time for us. We are to keep in mind that nothing has really changed; only in appearance has He changed.

"Kirk, I will not appear the same as when I left. You will have to get used to Me as I AM. The world, when it sees Me as I AM, will tremble and be shaken. You also will now begin to present Me as I AM, not how I was. Look directly into the fire in My eyes, see the sword that cuts both ways, look at Me! I AM Jesus. I AM the Lamb. I AM Love. I AM also King of kings and Lord of lords. The world has not known Me as King of kings and Lord of lords, but they will.

They will see Me as I AM and faint, fall down, cry, and in their great fear, they will know the Truth! You, however, you will only see Me in your love for Me, because you are in Me. You will stand because I also love you and will make you to stand. You have already died. Therefore, what does a dead man have to fear? Come, look Me full in the face! I love you! Do not fear! Certainly, perfect love casts out all fear."

Fear of God Prophetic Word – April 9, 2020

When His disciples James and John saw this, they said, "Lord, do You want us to command fire to come down from heaven and consume them?" But He turned and rebuked them, [and said, "You do not know what kind of spirit you are of; for the Son of Man did not come to destroy men's lives, but to save them."] And they went on to another village. (Luke 9:54-56 NASB)

"Kirk, My Son did certainly come to save men, and not to destroy them!"

Then in a vision, I see Jesus getting whipped, yes, taking the stripes whereby we are healed. Then I see Him on the cross. I see how He saved us from certain death in our sins. I see that the atonement did everything for us. We are saved, healed, and delivered by what He did. Yes, and also the whole world as well, potentially everyone! Father is saying that He would never do anything to in any remote way minimize what His Son did at Calvary.

I then remembered Ananias and Sapphira who lied to the Holy Spirit. I also saw that the Holy Spirit can be grieved and also quenched. Jesus Himself said that blasphemy against the Holy Spirit is never forgiven – both in this world and the next. The Holy Spirit is held in such high regard that even the cross, the very blood of the Savior of the world cannot take this sin away.

Blasphemy (Merriam Webster) *1. The act of insulting or showing contempt or lack of reverence for God.*

It was said of Jesus that He did what He did by the power of Beelzebub – yes that Jesus was demon-possessed! (Might be a bit insulting to the Holy Spirit).

I was telling the LORD that it was my desire to never offend the Holy Spirit in any way. Then I heard the gentle voice of the Holy Spirit say: "Kirk, you could never offend Me. Those who are 'in Christ' cannot offend Me."

I asked the LORD if what appears to be happening is actually happening right now? Is everything tightening up for Christ-followers? (I don't know what to ask exactly).

The Lord is saying, "Yes, you are seeing the beginning of the Latter Rain right now. During this time those who are in Christ are expected to shine brightly. Less and less accommodation for behavior which is less than Christ-like will be tolerated. Just the same, those who will come to the light will not have the generous time to come as before. They will, however, receive more grace to come. There will again be fear of the Living God upon the earth. People will be drawn, but they will also be fearful because of the holiness of the Lord in the 'Church.' When the light shines brightly, the deeds done in darkness are exposed. There are fearful times to come, but never for those who have died already."

How the Last Days Church will Come into Being –

April 17, 2020

The Lord says, "For understanding regarding how the last days church will come into being, simply look to Nehemiah and also to Zerubbabel. Times of great faith before the rulers of your time, yes and a time to put your hand to the plow in human labor in the Spirit of the Lord. Temptations and trials, mockers, perseverance in labor and in holiness and rejection of things creep in. Build the Temple and the Wall! Refute and cast down the detractors and traitors. Only go forward by My Spirit. I Am is with you. Do not fear, but cast it out! Fear is a liar! Go!"

No Economic Downturn – April 25, 2020

There was a headline in the Wall Street Journal saying that the Coronavirus would trigger the worst economic downturn since the 1940s. But the Lord says about the Coronavirus triggering an economic downturn: "There will not be an economic downturn because 'they' don't know My anointed one (Trump). He did it before, and he'll do it again!" (He'll make the U.S. economy awesome.)

Trump Will Play the Trump Card Wisely – April 29, 2020

Regarding the Coronavirus, the Lord says, "When I said those who are in fear would lose, and those who remained in faith would gain, you thought I meant monetarily, and that's true. However, do not limit your thinking on this. There is much more to it. The losses and the gains will be breathtaking. The conspiracy: Yes, there are some who are conspiring! Again, rejoice! What have I said regarding the wisdom of the wise? My Trumpet will play the Trump Card wisely at just the right time. Watch for it. You won't be able to miss it. My enemies will see it and know that I AM is God. Fear will turn to anger!"

A Sign and a Wonder – April 29, 2020

A sign and a wonder. A sign in the heavens and wonder on earth. The sign will appear first. Look for it. Soon after wonder will make itself known on earth. This will be the beginning of the things to come. It is the beginning of the end times harvest. Prophetic compression. Latter rain. Power for the faithful. Deep darkness for those who cannot come to the light!

The Winds of Change Angel – May 10, 2020

Today I saw an angel on a white horse coming toward me from the West. He was bright white like light and the horse was too. As he approached, I saw that he was covered in armor, and the horse had armor on it too. The armor was very bright, like polished silver. The brilliance of it all was blinding. The helmet of the angel had a rather small slit for him to see out of, and he carried a large, two-handed sword in a scabbard. I wondered why someone as powerful as he obviously was had to wear so much defensive armor.

Then I heard a Voice say that he gets attacked a lot. I also wondered what his name was. The voice said that he was named the "Winds of Change."

As he drew near, I saw that he was very large! And the horse too! The Voice said that he was almost always opposed in whatever he did because people dislike change and did whatever they could think of to keep things from changing.

The Voice continued... "The Winds of Change never loses. He is even more powerful than he appears. He always accomplishes what he is sent to do. I, the LORD, empower him."

So, I asked in my mind what he was sent to do this time? Why am I seeing him? Then I heard the LORD of Heaven's Armies say, "Look around you, Prophet. Things are about to change in a very significant way – even more than they have already. Do not fear! Embrace the change! Pray for the 'Winds of Change' to do his job well."

I asked to see what these changes looked like, and I understood that I would see more later.

Later …

The LORD says that the Winds of Change takes care of his friends. (Like those who pray for him.) I again asked what sort of change was afoot.

The LORD says that the Winds of Change is here to facilitate the removal of those of the political class who oppose what is right. Yes, Democrats, but more than that. This moment in time involves the USA, but it also involves the world. The strong wind WILL uncover, yes, blow the lid off from corruption. The world will be appalled at what the wind uncovers. Justice WILL be served. The wicked will get what they deserve, and if not for the Lord stopping this movement for justice, it would go too far.

The Winds of Change has Taken Hold of the Hand of the Lord's Anointed – May 12, 2020

*T*herefore, *IF you have been raised up with Christ, keep seeking the things above, where Christ is, seated at the right hand of God. Set your mind on the things above, not on the things that are on earth. For* you have died, *and your life is hidden with Christ in God. When Christ,* who is *our life, is revealed, then you also will be revealed with Him in glory. Therefore, consider the members of your earthly body as dead to immorality, impurity, passion, evil desire, and greed, which amounts to idolatry. <u>For it is because of these things that the wrath of God will come upon the sons of disobedience</u>, and in them you once walked, when you were living in them. (Colossians 3:1-7 NASB)*

The LORD is simply saying that His wrath rests on those who reject His Son, Christ Jesus. He says, "The political class have only done evil in My sight. They even have the gall to use My name as they convince the people to follow their evil. They love evil and don't feel any shame as they advertise their adulteries and sell them to anyone who will listen. They are bald faced liars and are not capable of doing good in My sight, says the Lord. But My Trumpet...

The Winds of Change has taken hold of the hand of My Anointed. Cyrus of Antiquity knew the Winds of Change, but not like My Anointed does. Just as Cyrus was seen, so My Anointed will be seen, and more so because he declares My name as he goes. He will not take prisoners because doing so would be below him. He takes in freedom those who can see and hear. They will never leave him because they know Me. Just as freedom followed in the wake of Cyrus, so shall freedom follow the call of the Trumpet."

Believe You Hear God – He's Calling You into Things You've Never Imagined – May 17, 2020

I (Kirk) was praying/listening, and I heard a verse to look up. When I looked at it, there was really nothing about it that struck me, and I wasn't hearing the Lord say anything about it either. This happened a couple more times, and then a verse came that didn't exist. So, I stopped asking and just prayed. I told Him that I didn't care how many times it didn't work out, I was still going to look up the verse I heard, and I was still going to believe that I had heard correctly.

Then I heard John 3:12 *NASB "If I told you earthly things and you do not believe, how will you believe if I tell you heavenly things?"*

The LORD has been talking about having faith for what we hear. Immediate faith. He has also spoken to us about getting rid of all doubt. He said, "Kirk, if you cannot believe that you've heard a simple verse, how are you going to believe things (concepts and ideas, situations for which you have nothing to compare) of heaven? Do you believe that you must make sense of things? Will you reject mysteries as crazy or false simply because they do not follow your logic? I am calling you and Tiffany into things that no human has ever imagined. Can you both die to self to the extent that you will follow Me wherever I desire to take you?"

The Lord is calling us into more faith! Believe Him!

The Doors of Heichal (Hekhal) are Open Prophecy –

May 19, 2020

Kirk was reading about some massive golden doors called the doors of heichal or hekhal, which formed a second barrier to the Holy of Holies besides the curtain, which was torn in two when Jesus gave up His Spirit. Reportedly, a number of things began to happen around 30 AD. One of those things was that these doors began to open by themselves.

As Prophet to the Lord, I now declare:

"The Doors of Hekhal are now open, says the LORD of all. My heavenly temple is open to all who would enter. My glory is being poured out on the earth once again. I am removing all barriers and stumbling stones from impeding access to My presence! Therefore, look up! Your deliverance is very close, and all who desire to carry My glory shall be completely satisfied! So be it according to the Spirit, the water, and the blood!"

Latter Day Saints – Mormon Trumpet Removed –

June 5, 2020

Matthew 28:2 *And behold, a severe earthquake had occurred, for an angel of the Lord descended from heaven and came and rolled away the stone and sat upon it.*

The Holy Spirit gave this verse to Kirk and the words "angel" and "earthquake" stood out. Kirk googled "angel" and "earthquake" and found an article in which there was a 5.7 earthquake in Utah on March 18, 2020. The statue of the angel Moroni that is on top of a spire at the LDS church had been holding a trumpet. During the earthquake, the trumpet fell out of his hand.

The Lord then spoke, "I have removed the trumpet from the angel of the Latter-Day Saints. Their voice shall be silenced. They have said they represent Me, but they are doubleminded in all they do. Watch as I remove their voice because they opposed My Trumpet (Donald J. Trump)! Watch also for My mighty angels to descend to earth! Some see the events on earth as a tug of war between evil and good. I Am releasing angels to show that this is not the case. They come with great power and the earth will shake at their arrival.

There will also be another sign regarding this."

Winds of Change has Begun His Work & Angels Released – June 9, 2020

Psalm 118:6 *"The Lord is for me; I will not fear. What can man do to me?"*

"Do not fear! The Winds of Change has begun his work. You will see it rolling out in this season. Tomorrow is the beginning of real change. Keep your eyes on My Trumpet during this time. The other sources of 'news' will be breathlessly and frantically hiding the truth. Even so, this will prove to be a fruitless effort. Do not fear the threats and intimidation! The lawless ones will feign power and authority using terms such as 'military coup,' 'police resentment,' and 'majority uprising.' But I say to you, Kirk, it's all a facade. My anointed holds the real power because I AM is with him".

"My Holy angels have been released! The earth <u>will</u> shake at their arrival! The anger and rebellion of those who hate Me will soon be turned to either fear or repentance! My angels will be doing their work in the <u>open</u> and for those who have eyes to see, they will be breathless with joy and excitement. I will surely vindicate and lift up those who love Me. The latter rain will be POURED out on all who desire Him. And they shall possess what the nations desire. My light will shine, and none shall be able to deny its power! And I shall be called the Lord in the land! Amen."

Angels Going to Battle & What the Devil does is Irrelevant – June 15, 2020

This morning the Lord is saying, "Look at My angels in battle!" Looking, I see Michael; he is full of faith and completely fearless. He doesn't draw attention to himself by wearing flashy things, but every angel in heaven has heard of his power and faith! His exploits are told far and wide in the kingdom. Michael is right now leading the charge! The angels in heaven are anxious to join him. They expect to have a glorious testimony at the end of this battle. Michael will bring with him the power of the Lord and has been charged with its distribution.

As I look at all of this, it appears as if Michael has the anointing of an Apostle and Gabriel has the anointing of a Prophet. Gabriel is now bringing the words of the Lord, working and fighting alongside Michael. Gabriel is also used to fighting and is a very skilled warrior. Somehow, he seems more refined than Michael and has great faith as well. The Lord says, "Gabriel is creative." And I can see that Gabriel's words are creative in nature. It's a part of his anointing according to the Lord.

The Lord says, "It is beginning. Look to the heavens and the earth because there will be signs as this rolls out. Pay no attention to the antics of the evil one. What he does is irrelevant."

First Contingent of Angels has Arrived - Tulsa Earthquake - June 21, 2020

A magnitude 4.2 (later upgraded to a 4.5, which is 4+5=9, which means judgment) happened last night at approximately 10:30 p.m. This is 80 miles from where Trump's kick-off rally for his second term had just taken place in Tulsa, OK.

The Lord says, "Kirk, the first contingent of My angels has arrived! This is the beginning, a rather small contingent who will help My anointed. The earthquake too was rather small; however, it is a sign. A sign that points to the much larger change, <u>much</u> larger shaking."

This is the start of what the angels have been waiting for! There is much excitement among the angels.

Prophetic Word 2020-2040 – June 23, 2020

Jeremiah 6:16-17 (NASB)

"Thus says the LORD, "Stand by the ways and see and ask for the ancient paths, where the good way is, and walk in it; And you will find rest for your souls. But they said, 'We will not walk in it.' And I set watchmen over you, saying, "Listen to the sound of the Trumpet!" But they said, 'We will not listen.'"

"Kirk, My watchmen have declared another 4 years for My Trumpet! Yes, 4 more years, but I say it will be 10!

2020 shall be a year of celebration for My people. And prosperity and goodness shall take the place of riots and protests.

2024 Are you (My people) tired of winning yet? Another Trumpet shall rise up, and his boldness and wisdom shall be spoken of far and wide. My anointing shall rest on him, just as if a torch had been passed to him.

In 2027 the people will forget that it is possible to lose. He shall win another term. However, the foolishness and ingratitude of the people will cause him to leave his work unfinished.

2034 will be a time of remembrance and My people will again desire Me! I shall have compassion on them and provide a very righteous Margaret Thatcher who will unite the nations of the world! (Not a one world government, but true unity.) She shall be an Apostle of the highest order and a true and faithful leader. The world at this time will be witness to the end time revival! And the billion-youth harvest will be in full swing.

2040 The sheep nations are fully in lock step with the United States and Israel. The goat nations appear as North Korea appears to the world in 2020."

(Note: See word entitled "2021, Year of the Great Reset – January 1, 2021" for more information.)

Obedience Unto Salvation – June 25, 2020

*F*or He has said somewhere concerning the seventh day: *"AND GOD RESTED ON THE SEVENTH DAY FROM ALL HIS WORKS;" and again in this passage, "THEY SHALL NOT ENTER MY REST." Therefore, since it remains for some to enter it, and those who formerly had the good news preached to them failed to enter because of disobedience, He again fixes a certain day, "Today," saying through David after so long a time just as has been said before, "TODAY IF YOU HEAR HIS VOICE, DO NOT HARDEN YOUR HEARTS." (Hebrews 4:4-7 NASB)*

"Kirk, in these last of days, I want to show you what obedience unto salvation is. Some people teach that obedience to a book, yes, a holy book, leads to salvation. Indeed, if this holy book is followed as intended, it does lead one to actually hear the Savior's voice. And many do hear His voice because the Word of God is very near! They hear! Only to go astray in their hearts once again. They fall prey to the doctrine of demons and the seeds of the Word are picked up by the birds of the air and produce no fruit in the hearer. The holy book they stake their eternal future on exhorts from cover to cover to listen to His voice and obey it! But instead, they create an idol of it and worship letters on a page. They mouth the words therein, sing songs of praise and look so good. But their hearts are far from Me, and their lives are lived according to their own desires. I hold out My hands all day long! I knock on the door desiring entry! Come My people! Come to Me! The answer of a good heart and ears to hear is all it takes! TODAY IS THE DAY OF SALVATION! AMEN."

When the Dust Clears a Second Time – Haitian Prophecy – June 28, 2020

Today Father is speaking about Haiti.

"Kirk, Today I hear the blood of the Haitian fathers calling out to ME! I see the fathers, those who have walked and those who are walking in righteousness! Though many believe that because of their past, that I have forgotten them, I have not! A new season is beginning and when the dust clears a second time, The Winds of Change will also blow there. I have many who do not bow down to idols there and are ready to stand up and fight the wickedness in high places. The corruption will be exposed in Haiti, says the Lord of Hosts! Where there exists deep darkness, the light shines brighter. I will NOT be denied My victory in Haiti!

Therefore you – My righteous ones, do not hang your heads in defeat! Do not agree with the 'wisdom' of the world saying, 'It will never get better here.' Stand with Me and I will stand with you! Escape is not victory and the Lord your God does not run from the darkness! When you turn on a light, has the darkness ever remained? I, the Lord of Hosts, say no! The light is always victorious and sees the darkness flee! So, watch for the dust to clear the second time. An astonishing event will happen. The darkness will try to cover it up but will not be able! AMEN!"

*Note – On August 14, 2021, Haiti had a 7.2 earthquake. The Lord said the earthquake was not from Him, but this earthquake is the dust clearing the second time for Haiti. The first time was the earthquake in 2011. There may be more to the dust clearing, as the word came during a time of a dust storm over Haiti that had come from the Sahara Desert, but this is what we've heard so far from the Lord.

Jesus is Our Sabbath Rest – June 30, 2020

Jeremiah 17:21-23 reads,

"Thus says the LORD: 'Take heed to yourselves, and bear no burden on the Sabbath day, nor bring it in by the gates of Jerusalem; nor carry a burden out of your houses on the Sabbath day, nor do any work, but hallow the Sabbath day, as I commanded your fathers. But they did not obey nor incline their ear, but made their neck stiff, that they might not hear nor receive instruction.'"

The Lord is saying that His servant in these verses was actually prophesying of Jesus. He says Jesus is the LORD of the Sabbath. Yes, and He is our Sabbath. The Sabbath prophesies of Him (Jesus)! Our rest is in Him. We cease works in Him. We do not bear the load of the law in Him.

Father says, "JESUS IS YOUR SABBATH! Do not bring a load into your houses. Do not carry any load through the gates of the city nor do ANY work to try to find favor with ME! Do not be like this people who did not listen or incline their ears, but instead stiffened their necks in order not to listen or take correction. Do not allow anyone to put their yoke on you or bind you to work which is not from Me.

Jesus is the Head of My Church, and His yoke is easy, and His burden is light. I no longer require 'works of service!' Instead, as it is written, 'If you love Me (Jesus), you will do what I have been doing.' Amen."

A Vision of the Holy City – July 5, 2020

The Lord says, "I'm preparing a City."

Kirk sees a vision... I see myself in a very sandy place, a desert. I have in my hand a level and some sort of rod. I am on the perimeter of something. I look up and see a myriad of what I suppose to be angels flying in the heavens. Then I go back to work.

There are others working too. The perimeter we are establishing is immense. I wonder what exactly it is. Then I hear: "I Am establishing the Holy City here."

Again, I wonder, how will there be enough people to fill it? I hear: "Look up again!" So, I look up. One of the beings which I had supposed to be angels comes closer. I saw that it was one of the saints. A cloud of witnesses was watching and waiting. After seeing their number, I started wondering if this place would be big enough!

The Lord's voice came again: "Do your work well prophet! Your Apostle, and yes, the saints wait and watch. The world, the nations are wondering what you will do. All are in anticipation, but I Am not in wonderment. I have trained up Apostle and Prophet and I Am standing in faith with you."

I then turned and went back to work with the tools and those who worked with me.

As I work with my Apostle, I notice that a shadow is trying to creep in. At first, I don't understand. My angel says: "It's a demon. They have no idea what's going on, because they live in an atmosphere of lies and deception. They have no capacity to know the truth from a lie, but they are curious anyway."

I watch the shadow as it crosses the perimeter, going underneath things, behind, and tries its best to stay hidden. As it crosses, suddenly a loud shriek and a small puff of smoke where it had been. Again, my angel speaks: "There are no shadows or places to hide behind the veil. Everything is laid open and no evil can exist there."

Explanation:

The Lord says that the tools in someone's hand are indicative of that person's work. As Prophet, Kirk has a level and a rod (more like a staff). He receives the Word of God, and it keeps things level and is the measure by which all things are measured/judged. The rod or staff has to do with leadership and discipling. The level has to do with discernment to see where the word is being abused. He's building the true church. Many people don't understand who the church is, what it is, or who Jesus is. The Lord is done with the watered down, lame excuse for the church.

He's raising up the real church, true believers who truly follow Him.

As Apostle, Tiffany is holding a book and an iron scepter. The iron scepter is judgment and the execution of the judgment rendered. It's indicative of a ruler who rules, like overseeing, as well as rendering judgment. The book is indicative of revelation that apostles receive. Then the LORD gave Tiffany a vision regarding the book she holds:

I see cement steps. There's a concrete door. I push open the door. It feels cool, and it's dark. There's light in the center where Jesus is. I walk toward the Light. It's warmer and of course brighter by Him. He hands me a book. A book of mysteries, of revelation. I wonder if it's the Bible and I'm reminded of a vision Kirk had years ago where I was surrounded by scrolls of revelation. Jesus says, "Your Prophet will tell you mysteries that you will understand as revelation and write in a book. You will rely on My Wisdom, on Me, not your own wisdom."

The apostles and prophets who the Lord is raising up will work together to help to build the city of God, the true church, the one built on the revelation of Jesus Christ, and Him alone.

Vision of the Winds of Change in Middle Heaven –

July 10, 2020

I (Kirk) see the Winds of Change in "Middle Heaven." The demonic try to come and attack him, but he is able to generate a "wind," which actually blows them apart. The power of the Spirit of God is upon him! Nothing can withstand the Wind of the Spirit that goes out from the Winds of Change angel!

The Lord says, "Kirk, keep your eyes on Me! Yes, it will get even more crazy on earth! Nothing is beyond My control, however, and the Winds of Change has just begun his work. Watch for a sign in the heavens and another from My Trumpet! These signs are the beginning of the end for the demonic in high places. Then will come confusion as their deception is unmasked among those who have been their followers, and a window of time will open for them to repent. Be ready for this window to open with love, forgiveness, and acceptance! Avoid condescension and finger pointing. Avoid and reserve it for those whom I will show you. Finally, STAND TALL in your Lord! It will be a testimony you will not tire of telling! Amen."

Trump Card Prophecy - July 31, 2020

I (Kirk) see the Lord's Trumpet playing the trump card. When this trump card is played, the game is over. No card outranks the trump card, so there is no discussion or argument regarding who has won. The holder of the trump card, played at the perfect time, means game over! In this "game," the winner takes all. There is no division of the spoils and NO discussion of or about terms in any way.

I also see the "Scales of Justice," and the scales are tipped totally one way. I look closer and see that there are all kinds of heavy-looking metal things on the losing side of the scales. All this makes me wonder what could possibly win against all of that. I look over to the other side (the right side of the scale). On it is just a card. Printed on the card is the flag of the United States. As I look, I hear, "Stars and Barrs." [Stars refers to Donald Trump, who was a star before becoming president. Barrs refers to Attorney General Barr, who is tasked with bringing indictments against those criminals in the political class.] A veil is taken away, and I see the finger of God, which was invisible prior, on top of the card.

Then the voice of the Lord says, "Justice is Mine alone. My justice is true and fair, My justice and Mine alone. Justice apart from Me is no justice at all. Nothing can tip the scales away from Me. I Am Justice! Do NOT be deceived. Social change, the laws of men, lawyers, and those in the higher positions of the governments of men only hold the places which I Am allowing them to hold. Keep looking at Me and listen for the Word of Truth."

The same day Kirk received this vision, I (Tiffany) saw a cloud shaped like a gavel in the sky. I asked the LORD what it meant, and the LORD said, "The season of Justice has begun." I looked away from the cloud and then looked back and it was completely gone!

Do Not be Deceived About the End Times –

August 7, 2020

B oth Matthew 24 and Luke 17 speak of the last days and liken them to the days of Noah and the days of Lot. Both speak of an event (Noah got in the boat, and Lot left town), and after the event a judgment came. Both Noah and Lot were obedient to what God had told them to do.

A clear distinction is drawn between "they" or "them" and Noah and Lot. Jesus is clearly saying that there will be those who are being obedient and hearing instructions from God and also because of their hearing will know the times and seasons. And there will be "they" and "them" who do not hear His voice and do not understand, and "they" will be taken away. So, there will be a sign or event that everyone will be able to see (like lightning or something like that) and then the day of the Lord will begin.

Father is saying that we don't have to study each word and come up with some theory about how this might work. Jesus has clearly told us how it will work. He is asking why this is not clear to us? The main thing the Father is concerned with in these verses is deception. He says, "Read these verses (Matthew 24 and Luke 17) as a child would. Simply believe! Listen to My voice! Do not be deceived!"

The Second Shot Heard Round the World Prophecy –

September 5, 2020

Today the "news" is full of pictures of Black Lives Matter "protesters" beating people up, burning businesses, burning cars, harassing restaurant patrons, and simply being completely lawless and thinking they project power.

"Thus says the Lord, 'Cursed is the man who trusts in mankind and makes flesh his strength, and whose heart turns away from the LORD. For he will be like a bush in the desert and will not see when prosperity comes, but will live in stoney wastes in the wilderness, a land of salt without inhabitant. Blessed is the man who trusts in the LORD and whose trust is in the LORD. For he will be like a tree planted by the water, that extends its roots by a stream and will not fear when the heat comes; but its leaves will be green and it will not be anxious in a year of drought nor cease to bear fruit." (Jeremiah 17:5-8)

The LORD is saying: "Take your eyes off the mask, off the violence. Don't consider the implications (what if this happens or that?). Do not engage with the lawless ones because that is exactly their plan. They have no power, and their wisdom is foolishness to Me. They are in a prison without strength, with a hope that will never come. These people are cursed, declares the LORD!

Blessed are those whose hands are clean and whose heart is pure! They trust in Me! And I will do it!

The LORD declares that these riots and demonstrations shall come to a sudden end, and when the Trump card is played, it will be at great cost to My enemies, says the LORD! A dramatic action which no one but My Prophets see coming shall take place. The troublemakers shall be put in their place, and those who would support them shall be put on notice (and dare not oppose this action).

My Trumpet shall fire the second 'shot heard round the world,' and gladness and boldness shall erupt in his homeland! Amen."

7 Years and 7 Years – September 19, 2020

The LORD says from 2020-2027 will be 7 years of plenty and then from 2027-2034 there will be 7 years of drought (ingratitude and not remembering the LORD). In 2034 the Lord will have mercy and compassion on us by sending us a very righteous Margaret Thatcher.

What do we store up in years of plenty? We store up oil, like the wise virgins. People will come to those of us with the oil of the Holy Spirit. When the people forget Him, the oil of the LORD is missing. We need to remember Him and thank Him for what He's done. When Israel went astray, it was because they forgot what He had done, were ungrateful, and started to grumble and complain. Repentance would then bring back His compassion. We are to seek first His Kingdom and His Righteousness, and all these things shall be added to us.

Waking Up into Spring Dream – September 26, 2020

I (Tiffany) dreamed this morning that Trump was standing watching a TV where there were famous people (actors & singers) in a circle. Dolly Parton was the only one I recognized. I think they were holding hands. They were singing, "Daddy King, You've always been our LORD."

Trump turns to us and says something about it.

I wake up and hear the LORD say, "They're waking up into Spring."

They will wake up to the LORD and to Trump as His anointed. Praise God!

The Lord is Putting His Finger on the Scales of Justice – November 16, 2020

The Lord says, "It truly looks bleak for My anointed, doesn't it? But I say that <u>today</u>, things will begin to change! Today is the day that I will put My finger on the Scales of Justice, and a shift will begin to be seen. The Trump card has not been played yet, but when it is played, all will stand to their feet and be left speechless!"

Trump Train Vision – Part 1 – Theater – November 27, 2020

"Behold the proud, his soul is not upright in him; but the just shall live by his faith." (Habakkuk 2:4)

"For in it the righteousness of God is revealed from faith to faith; as it is written, 'The just shall live by faith.'" (Romans 1:17)

"But that no one is justified by the law in the sight of God is evident, for 'the just shall live by faith.'" (Galatians 3:11)

"Now the just shall live by faith; but if anyone draws back, my soul has no pleasure in him." (Hebrews 10:38)

The Spirit of the Lord says, "Don't waste this opportunity! Have faith in God. Do not shrink back as those who have <u>no</u> faith! Has God said that His anointed shall not be president? Has He said the corrupt political class will never be brought to justice? Has He said the mask is now the rule? <u>Where</u> is your faith? Rise up <u>you</u> who hear ME! Have faith!"

A vision then ensues:

The curtains spread open at a theatre. In the middle of the stage is what looks like a judge's bench. It is not at floor level. It is considerably higher and more ornate. It also appears that the one behind this "bench" is standing. There doesn't seem to be a gavel, either. The one behind the "bench" is Donald J. Trump. Although he has no gavel, he nevertheless is directing what is going on. He points to a person, and they go – or maybe approach him to speak. I see Nancy Pelosi is one of the people he is directing. The curtains close again. I'm watching for something to happen. Some time passes.

The curtains begin to open again. A train is coming toward me off the stage and slightly to my left. It's an old-fashioned steam locomotive that looks massive and heavy – lots of smoke and steam. As it passes, I read on the side of the engine, "TRUMP TRAIN." It seems to me that as the train approached, it was slowing down, but now, as it passes me, the powerful engine is again at full power, propelling the behemoth forward, and it's gaining speed.

I start to notice the cars behind the engine. There are a lot of them! They appear to have bars on the windows. As I stare intently, I see people in these cars. They are well-dressed in expensive clothes. The look on their faces appears either rebellious and proud, or some look dejected and totally defeated. Some of the faces look familiar – politicians or judges; others are strangers. Behind the train there are thousands or maybe more – people in an untold number running and cheering with flags and posters, ecstatic people! The curtain closes again. And again, I wait and stare at the curtain, wondering what will come next.

It finally opens once again. As it does, I see a globe, a huge globe, with all the continents and countries and their borders, which are very clear and distinct. The globe slowly spins on the North and South axis. Soon I see North America come into view. I can clearly make out the United States of America! As I look at her smiling, I see what appears to be something like a bomb that is exploding in the very center of the USA. There doesn't seem to be the expected destruction, however. Instead, there are what look like ripples from a stone tossed into still water going out. However, the ripples do not propagate smoothly. There are fits and starts, as well as slower and faster movement across the entire globe. I'm wondering, what is going on?

Suddenly, I am able to look closer as if I had binoculars and focused in for a clear view. Ahead of the "wave," I see people looking with great interest in the direction from which the wave is coming. After the wave passes, they erupt into uncontrolled joy and celebration! Again, the curtain closes. I wait, but nothing seems to be happening.

Positioning in December 2020 – December 7, 2020

"December 7, 2020, is a day of positioning," says the Lord. "A day to put the pieces in order, set and bait the traps for some, and position others to ascend to which I, the Lord, have destined them. Only the astute will notice what is in motion."

"By December 12, a pattern will be seen. Those with eyes to see and ears to hear will begin to be (possibly overtly and publicly) excited because of what is transpiring."

The LORD laughs, "Yes, by December 14, there will be a sort of chaos. (Like rats leaving a sinking ship) The enemy will realize his predicament, and an emboldened and beat down President will lay down the Trump Card in this season."

Trump Emboldened and Filled with the Holy Spirit – December 12, 2020

The Lord says to watch for President Trump to become emboldened and his countenance to rise, even as the Red Sea experience would suggest that this change is foolishness.

"My Trumpet will encounter Me in this season. He will be shown that in the strength of men, even very good men, well-meaning men, that this battle is lost. He will 'see' that as the time approaches when there is no place to go, I, the Lord, will make a way. The Left and Babylon will be drawn into the sea of red and destroyed. My anointed will see that the 'Trump Card' was never his to play, but that the Lord has always held it. He will fall to his knees at this time, and I will fill him with My Spirit, says the Lord! Then the world will marvel at My Trumpet because they have never seen Righteousness, Boldness, Honor, and a Right Spirit on a world leader before."

Trump Train – Part 2 – Love & Justice –

December 13, 2020

I (Kirk) was again told to sit in the theater. So, I closed my eyes, and there I was. The place was empty and darkly lit. The curtain was closed in front of me. As it opens, I start to see a clandestine meeting. All of a sudden, the attendees of the meeting scatter as the police show up. Those leaving look full of fear and make a determined escape. I see city streets that are clean and orderly. People are walking and driving places. Everyone looks over their shoulder as they go. There is order, like it's too orderly, and fear is rampant. So, I turn to the Lord as I watch the scene in front of me. I ask, why am I seeing this? He answers, "This is the world of the conservative and the religious. Love has been replaced with the Letter, and the rule of law has replaced My Spirit." The curtain closes. I stare, considering what I have just seen.

Again, the curtain opens slowly. I see scenes of war-torn countries. The people are beaten and sad. I see the United States after the Revolutionary War and after the Civil War. I see the jubilation on the winning side and the sadness on the losing side. I see the soldiers on the winning side and also the losing army. I also see the cost of war in the number of the dead. The young and the old are changed because of war. Then I am surprised to see an outstretched hand! The winners of the wars are actually helping and repairing the losing side of these wars! All of them. Then I realize that all of these conflicts had something in common – the United States of America! But I don't understand why I am seeing all of this.

The Lord says: "Kirk, the current war of 2020 must end as all the others with the outstretched hand and reparations. If things done in the name of Justice are allowed to go too far, the first scene of Law without Love will take hold. Justice must be meted out, but it cannot be allowed to consume the nation. Love must accompany Justice."

2021

2021 Year of the Great Reset – January 1, 2021

Father says everyone is being put through the fire right now.

"The enemy is doing everything he can to turn My faithful ones away from Me because he knows what's coming (the gig is up). So, he is frantic to trip up all of those that he can. The lies upon lies upon lies are beginning to unravel. The government, big tech, the media, etc. shall be brought into the light. This will be a process, however. It will be similar to when you (Kirk) or Tiffany are deceived and then humble yourselves and receive deliverance from the lies. There will be a cascade effect when this gets started. In the beginning, there will be a hardness of heart and pride. Then as it goes on, a readiness and far less resistance to repentance and truth.

2021 shall be the year of the Great Reset. In 2020, the things necessary for the reset were unlocked, and a season of justice was started. Your enemy had planned on a 'Great Reset' but so did I! People will find the 'New' President Trump to be different than they had imagined at first, for their eyes will be opened to see him as honorable and honest. With the deep state under his feet, he will be very different indeed!"

Note: The Lord prophesied on June 23, 2020: "2024, Are you (My people) tired of winning yet? Another Trumpet shall rise up, and his boldness and wisdom shall be spoken of far and wide. My anointing shall rest on him, just as if a torch had been passed to him."

We thought this meant another Trump, like one of President Trump's sons, but the Lord is indicating that this new Trump is President Trump, but he is different than he was the first time around. He is an administrator of justice and is filled with the Spirit of God – a new man!

Are You Tired of Winning Yet, My People? –

January 3, 2021

The Lord had me (Kirk) look up "unlock." It means (Merriam Webster) – to become unfastened or freed from restraints.

Then He said: "My justice will free My people from their restraints. My Prophets will be freed from their restraints and will freely speak. And I will surely speak to them whenever I am about to do a thing! The false prophets of religion will have some explaining to do! They will not survive the freedom and My Spirit being poured out. And faith shall increase! I will roll out the promises which I have spoken to My faithful ones. As this happens, it shall be as a thunderclap and as lightning flashes across the sky! Each one (answered promise) will put another exclamation mark behind My Name!!! I will NOT hold back! Are you tired of winning yet, My people?"

Something in Georgia to be Noticed – January 5, 2021

The Lord says that He is going to do something in Georgia today that the whole world will sit up and notice.

Psalm 34 Instructions to the Church – January 10, 2021

The Lord is showing us that right now, as of today, it appears the USA will become a socialist state. The tech giants have cut off our president from communicating with us. Twitter, Facebook, and even Parler are affected. Speaker of the House Pelosi is calling for the impeachment of President Trump, and he only has 10 more days to serve. Big Media is pumping out lies 24-7 about the supposed break-in at the capital. Trump's cabinet members are quitting on him. Yes, we can see the dust rising from the army in hot pursuit and the water of the Red Sea in front of us. Praise God!

- I will bless the Lord at all times!
- My soul will make its boast in the Lord!
- O magnify the Lord with me!
- I sought the LORD, and He answered me!
- He delivered me of all my fears!
- Our faces will **never** be ashamed!
- The poor man cries, and the LORD hears him and saves him from his troubles
- The angel of the LORD encamps around those who fear Him! And He rescues them, too!

- The Lord is good; taste and see!
- Blessed is he who takes refuge in Him!
- Fear the LORD, you His saints!
- For those who fear Him, there is no want!
- Come and listen; I will teach you the fear of the LORD!
- Keep your tongue from evil and lips from deceit!
- The eyes of the LORD are toward the righteous, and He hears their cry!
- The fear of the LORD is against evildoers
- The righteous cry, and the LORD hears them!
- The LORD delivers the righteous out of their troubles!
- The LORD is near the brokenhearted and saves those who are crushed in spirit!
- Many are the afflictions of the righteous, but the LORD delivers him out of them all!
- Evil shall slay the wicked!
- Those that hate the righteous shall be condemned!
- The LORD redeems the souls of His servants!
- NONE of those who take refuge in Him will be condemned!
  (Psalm 34 NASB)

The Lord says,

"To the **Apostle** – stand! When you have done all to stand, then, STAND!

To the **Prophet** – No hedging! Speak My words. No more. No <u>less</u>!

To the **Evangelist** – Get excited! Listen to the Prophets and fearlessly evangelize!

To the **Pastor** – Guard the sheep! Do <u>Not</u> allow the message from those who are weak, are hedging, those who are falling away!

59

To the **Teacher** – the Gospel. Ignore the circumstances altogether!

To the **Faithful** – Look up! Your redemption draws nigh! Listen to My voice!"

The Faithful Given the Keys to the Kingdom of God –

January 14, 2021

The Lord says: "To My faithful ones I give the keys to the Kingdom of God. Yes, to those who get up each day and strengthen the weak, those who in moments of doubt simply look to Me for faith and comfort. And also, to those who refuse to quarrel and point fingers of blame at their brothers and sisters. For these, My Father's interests are greater and more important than life itself. These are the ones that I long for! These actually know what it means to have troubles in this world, and yet to KNOW that I have overcome the world! These have been given the keys because sons always have access to My Father.

So then, be encouraged you who are sons! My Father never disappoints! These are trying times! My Father knows that all men are being tested. But remember that He is the One who administers the test. He also scores the test, and He also gives the faith to pass the test! So then, faith is all that is needed to pass, and you will pass if you do <u>not</u> quit!

Do not allow your enemy to steal your faith then! Shut off the news. Stop looking for the pathway using your intellect. Get away from the naysayers! Keep your eyes on Me. Believe what I say. Listen to ME! So be it."

Is the Trump Thing Taking Too Long? —

January 21, 2021

Yesterday, Joe Biden was inaugurated in a fake inauguration. Afterward, the Lord spoke to Kirk.

"Turn to Genesis 16 and read it." It is the account of Sarai, Hagar, and Ishmael. After reading Genesis 16, the Lord posed a question to me: "Has this thing with Trump been taking too long, Prophet?"

I answered: "Lord, I have been disappointed several times, and yes, it does seem to be taking a long time."

The Lord: "Prophet, where is your faith? Can you not watch and pray for such a short time?"

Kirk: "Lord, I can. I guess that I am looking for things to happen according to my wishes or desires."

The Lord: "Prophet, your faith is strong. You are not wondering 'if' but desiring a different 'when.' Therefore, look at My Son. It appeared to some that all was lost when He said, 'It is finished' too. Watch for the 3rd day, for another resurrection. Do not be dismayed! I have not changed My mind on anything I have said to My Prophets. You, therefore, must not change your mind either."

Prophets Will Breathe a Sigh of Relief –

January 25, 2021

*G*ive the king Your judgments, O God, and Your righteousness to the king's son. May he judge Your people with righteousness and Your afflicted with justice. Let the mountains bring peace to the people, and the hills, in righteousness. May he vindicate the afflicted of the people, save the children of the needy and crush the oppressor. (Psalm 72:1-4 NASB)

"Kirk, change the word 'king' to 'president' for this word. The meaning is very clear indeed. This is a prayer. This is what the people of the world, My people cry out for. Therefore, My righteous ones will not be disappointed. My Prophets will breathe a great sigh of relief, and their faith and those who have stood with them shall be rewarded, says the Lord."

Ground Will Shake in D.C. – January 27, 2021

My (Kirk's) angel appeared to me and said, "Get ready because something big is about to happen."

I could see the angels flapping their wings, restless with anticipation. When the event the angel was referring to happens, a huge number of angels will be released to come to the earth. They will shake the ground in Washington, D.C. with their arrival.

How Prophetic Words are Given – Assembly Line –

January 28, 2021

In a vision Kirk saw an assembly line. In this case it was used to ship things that had been ordered. There was a track with wheels that allowed the worker to push along a box, putting in the box things that had been ordered. The filled boxes were numbered and in order so that when they were received, they could be opened in sequence.

The LORD is saying that this is the way prophetic messages are sent from Him. They are sent in order and in a sequence. The items in the box look to be totally random, but the Lord doesn't do anything by chance or randomly. So, when a box is emptied, the removed items may look to be totally unassociated. However, when put together, they form the complete order (word). Prophets hear things in different ways (visions, dreams, words, impressions, etc.) and when put together, they form a message from God.

Obviously, this isn't the only way Father sends messages through the Prophets when He is about to do a thing! He is saying that one can be certain that a thing is established when the company of prophets are all hearing the same thing. Don't lose heart therefore!

Righteous Will Reap a Harvest – Recompense Swift & Severe – February 5, 2021

The Lord is saying that His recompense will be swift and severe! Those who have sown in honesty and righteousness shall reap a harvest. So, too, will those who have entered into a treacherous scheme of evil. He is saying that we are near a crossroads, where violence and vengeance could erupt, but righteousness must prevail. The traitor must be dealt with according to the law, but the defectors must be welcomed and indeed loved and led according to the Spirit of God into all Truth.

"My people have been stolen from, restricted, and berated, and My recompense to them will be more glorious than the world has ever seen. Yes, the riches of the dark world will come to them! But I say that the whole world will not marvel at that. No! It will marvel at the generosity and thankfulness that will be exhibited. My people who are called by My Name do not live to simply enrich themselves! Those who live in darkness do that. My people give as I have also given.

Sure, there will be celebration! And yes, it will be to excess! Amen, says the Lord! But they have My heart, and as such, they will lead the entire planet into a time of plenty. Remember the 7 years and the 7 years!

Those who embody the 'American Dream,' such as the wealthy do right now, they will become few. Those who work hard and are diligent in their chosen profession will be looked up to! Those such as My Trumpet shall be looked up to! Their wealth will not be their claim to fame, but instead, **their commitment to Me**, **their work ethic**,

and their generosity is their calling card. This calling card shall be passed from nation to nation.

Gold and silver shall be commonplace!

Food production shall increase as I bless the work of the farmers' hands.

The evil that held back and restrained shall be replaced with honesty and goodwill.

Socialism shall be viewed as the scourge on humanity that it really is! The people of the world will rise up against it, and they shall be successful.

My church – no not that one – MY church! It shall rise up, and the network of Apostles and Prophets shall be normalized.

A great purge of the filth in entertainment, the internet, and in government shall happen and anything less will not be accepted.

Schools shall be for learning!

Banks for saving!

Entertainment shall be fun again!

Work will become honorable!

Business shall be for the mutual benefit of the owner and the customer!

My churches shall be filled with My Spirit!

Amen."

Sands of Time – Holy Spirit Signet Ring –

February 9, 2021

The Lord told me (Kirk) to go up to the sands of time again. So, I did. I entered an area that was dimly lit, except the center of attention, which is the Sands of Time. There were prophets standing all around the Sands of Time. I knew who they were; although, I had not seen many of them before (the greatest prophets of all time). I was told by the Lord to walk toward the Sands of Time. I began to walk, but wondered how I would get through all of those who were around the Sands. Then the Lord said, "Son, hold your head up."

So, I lifted my eyes to look into the eyes of all the prophets there. As I walked, they stood back and cleared a path for me to approach the Sands. These who had suffered, been martyred, done the greatest miracles and those who had the faith to move mountains – they allowed me to go before them to the Sands of Time!

I was told once again to put my hands into the Sand. As I did, I again felt a box. I lifted it out and brushed it off. It appeared to be a simple box of wood, dark because of age, and it had a simple latch that would lift to open it. After looking at the box, I looked around me. The others were anxiously looking at me. I heard, "Open the box."

So, I undid the latch and opened the top. Inside there was nothing but a gold ring. I reached in and turned the ring over in my hands and studied it. It was very simple – a signet ring. On the signet was a dove. A man came forward and took the ring from me. He said, "Hold out your right hand."

So, I did. I looked up at Him as I held out my hand – He had no face. He took my right hand and held it. With His other hand He slipped the ring onto my right hand. I did not know what the ring signified, but by the look on the others' faces, it is very significant. I was told to ask my Apostle, Tiffany, what this meant.

The Lord says, "The ring is My signature. He (Kirk) bears My mark, My approval, My signature. He represents Me where others have failed to do so. He has passed yet another test. It's My seal of approval and as I approve things, he approves them. As he approves things, I approve them. We work as one for he has been found worthy to represent Me.

With the signet ring of approval, prophets sign or seal a thing. As they do, they are putting My approval and blessing on a word, decree, or declaration. Therefore, when an Apostle of the Lord brings a word with the Spirit's signature on it from a Prophet, the power of God is released."

Then Holy Spirit revealed that the prophets who bowed to the Haman spirit (those who turned back on the word of the Lord) rejected their place to receive the ring and in fact have given it up to those who have stood, just as what was Haman's was taken and given to Mordecai. (See the book of Esther for clarity on Haman and Mordecai.) But Kirk (and other prophets who have stood still believing the word of the Lord regarding Trump, etc.) have been given the ring of the Spirit. Kirk and these other prophets now walk in the authority of the Holy Spirit. (More explanation given in the video on Rumble & YouTube.)

The Lord is Dealing with the World System –

February 20, 2021

The Lord says, "These are the last days. I'm about ready to do a new thing. In times past I have dealt with people, but I will now deal with the world system. Those who are part of this system will also be dealt with. But there has risen up a system on the earth which the political class and those who desire influence have embraced. It is completely evil. I will not tolerate it any longer!

They believe they can hold My Trumpet back from being President again! But they have no power, and their feeble minds only devise foolish plans. Who do they think they are dealing with anyway?

My Prophets and Apostles are standing, says the Lord! I will not disappoint them, and their reward on earth and in heaven shall be great! Everyone who hears My voice and stands shall not be disappointed. But woe to those who only stand when it's convenient for them. Crowns will be given and crowns taken away. The last shall be first and the first last."

Eagles About to Take Flight – February 26, 2021

"Tiffany, the hour of My justice has begun. This is the time when I will judge the wickedness in the earth. This is not the end, but it is the beginning of the end. The revelation of My Son is badly needed. My Son's Apostles have been prepared. Even the young eaglets are being filled with revelation of Jesus Christ. They too will fly."

I ask, "Will the USA worship Jesus after You save her?

"They will worship My Son. The name of Jesus will be boldly declared. Those who have stood will not have it another way. They will speak Jesus' name and so will the world, for they will know that God has visited them and only I Am could save them from this darkness."

Regarding the apostles depicted as eagles, the Holy Spirit is showing us Matthew 24:28, which reads, *"For wherever the carcass is, there the eagles will be gathered together."* And also Luke 17:37, where it is written: *"And they answered and said to Him, 'Where, Lord?' So He said to them, 'Wherever the body is, there the eagles will be gathered together.'"* And lastly, Job 39:27-30.

The Lord says, "Does the eagle mount up at your command, And make its nest on high? On the rock it dwells and resides, On the crag of the rock and the stronghold. From there it spies out the prey; Its eyes observe from afar. Its young ones suck up blood; And where the slain are, there it is."

The Holy Spirit says the eagles are the apostles. Wherever the body of the Lord is, there the eagles will be before Christ's return. The Lord is getting ready to send them out. The prophets who are standing right now are making the way for that. Also, the eagles have come to bring deliverance, and they utterly destroy and consume the enemy as they make the way for the Lord, hence they will be where the carcasses are, and their "young ones suck up blood."

Ephesians 3 and 4 make it clear that the foundation of the church is built upon the apostles and prophets with Christ Jesus Himself as the Chief Cornerstone. The apostles and prophets, with the help of the evangelists, pastors, and teachers are charged with building up the body until we all reach the unity of the faith and of the knowledge of the Son of God, to a perfect man, to the measure of the stature of the fullness of Christ. This last revival will not end, as its foundation will be secure.

The Lord continues: "Tiffany, My eagles are about to take flight. The apostles. They are carried on the winds of the Spirit. The USA is the land of the Eagle for she is apostolic in nature. She leads, is strong, nurtures, and loves. She is a brave warrior and does not fail in battle, for her God is with her. Some say the USA is in a battle, but I say the battle is already won. I have told your Prophet how it is and how it will be. From the Land of the Free and the Home of the Brave I Am preparing many eagles to fly, and they will join others from other nations."

I respond, "Father, what do You mean 'about to' take flight?"

The Lord: "The time has come. The great upheaval that turns everything on its head will also loose My eagles who have been waiting. The Prophets are ready and prepared. Their time is now as they have declared My words and then stood, watching for the rain to come. The apostles have been in the background, waiting. They will be seen as they fly forward."

Rejoice at Judgments & Blessings Even in Lean Years –

March 2, 2021

The sons of Eli the priest, Hophni and Phinehas, were particularly evil. In 1 Samuel 2:25b, it says, *"But they would not listen to the voice of their father (Eli), for the Lord desired to put them to death."* Then in 1 Samuel 4:11, it is recorded that during a battle with the Philistines, they both died.

Father is saying that this word from Him may be hard for some people to take. He says that everything about Him (God) is good. His blessings, His love, mercy, and yes, His patience are all good! But in His love, He also makes judgments, metes out His recompense, and stands for all of those who are His! In His wrath, He pours out judgment on the wicked. All of His sons and daughters are expected to rejoice at this, even if it's a bloodbath, because we know that it has happened because of His love and goodness!

"Therefore," declares the Lord, "heed the lesson of Eli's sons, Hophni and Phinehas."

And just as they did not see fit to acknowledge God any longer, God gave them over to a depraved mind, to do things which are not proper, being filled with all unrighteousness, wickedness, greed, evil, full of envy, murder, strife, deceit, malice; they are gossips, slanderers, haters of God, insolent, arrogant, boastful, inventers of evil, disobedient to parents, without understanding, untrustworthy, unloving, unmerciful; and although they know the ordinance of God, that those who practice such

71

things are worthy of death, they not only do the same, but also give hearty approval to those who practice them. (Romans 1:28-32 NASB)

The Lord says, "They have made their choice, and I have given them over to it! They shall have the death they have chosen.

My hands are full of blessings. Yes, I will pour out and allow the latter rain to fall on all of those who are Mine! All the riches of darkness shall be gathered in the light, and even in the lean years when men have forgotten what it is like to lose, yes, even in those times, the hungry will be fed and clothed, and when they turn once again to Me and remember the days of their fathers, I will again pour out My blessings on the earth! And once again, My Trumpet will be spoken of, and people will say: 'Are you tired of winning yet?'"

Trump Put in His Rightful Place and will Bear the Sword of Justice – March 6, 2021

The Lord says, "First will come the earthquake. This will serve as notice (a sign) for those who believe to open their eyes. This shaking will be the third and last sign. It marks the beginning of My manifest involvement." (The other two signs were one from the Trumpet – a letter he wrote – and another in the heavens – all the snow around the nation.)

"The world will again recognize Who they are dealing with! My angels will work in the open, and My enemies will openly be at war with each other. Things will change suddenly, and people will realize that they have been given a chance to win.

After these things, My Trumpet will again make his appearance. He will appear as a savior and a deliverer openly. The people will 'put' him in his rightful place. After these things happen, My Trumpet will <u>bear</u> My sword of justice, and those cowards and traitors who haven't already been stripped of all they have, including life itself, will then meet their own justice. My Trumpet's anger will be apparent. He will deal justly and mercilessly with those who have come against the United States, the Constitution, the President, and the Laws of the Land. All of this will not take years, but instead months.

During this purge, My Trumpet shall preside over a new monetary system as well. Those who have invested so heavily in your (the U.S. & the World's) destruction will pay dearly, and after a time, their people will rise up and prepare the world for a new leader of the U.S. who will usher in a time of peace and working together, as separate countries of the world explore what is mutually beneficial."

Note: Fulfillment of the earthquake sign came on August 14, 2021 as described below.

On August 10, 2021, one of the clocks in my house read "8-14-21." I understood from the Holy Spirit that He was saying something significant would happen on 8-14-21.

On August 14, 2021, Haiti had a 7.2 earthquake. The Lord said the earthquake was not from Him, but that this is the earthquake we've been waiting for as a sign.

I asked why would the earthquake happen in Haiti when that has nothing to do with Trump's return, etc.? He said,

"Where do you think all the children are coming from in human trafficking?"

He doesn't mean every child of course, but a great many come from Haiti and other impoverished nations that the globalist elitists have purposely kept in poverty. Trump's return and the demise of the world system has to do with this. It's all related. Many leaders of nations and organizations will be exposed and brought to justice.

Additionally, this earthquake is the dust clearing the second time for Haiti. The first time was the earthquake in 2011. There may be more to the dust clearing prophecy, but this is at least a part of it.

Vision of Time Machine – March 9, 2021

I (Kirk) went in a vision back to the time machine I had been in previously. I went to September 3, 2022.

I was in a town in Michigan. I went to a grocery store and looked for signs of COVID because I didn't see anyone wearing a mask. The only things I saw related to COVID were a stray sign saying that you must wear a mask and light spots on the floor where social distancing signs had been.

Then I went to New York City. It looked like there were about half of the people that once lived there.

Like Nebuchadnezzar, Biden will Always Carry the Moniker of Lunacy – March 16, 2021

Today, the Lord simply said, "Nebuchadnezzar." I (Kirk) read a history of him, and then was instructed to read in the book of Daniel about King Nebuchadnezzar. It is said that nine tenths of the ancient bricks found in the area of Babylon are inscribed with his inscription. He is said to have been the greatest ruler Babylon has ever had.

The Lord is saying that the story of Nebuchadnezzar is meant to be a warning to those who aspire to be "king of kings" (Daniel 2:37) as he was, and who also do not "recognize that the Most High is ruler over the realm of mankind and bestows it on whomever He wishes" (Daniel 4:32).

"This is a lesson for those who declare themselves to be something which they are not. I, the Lord, declare that suddenly I will answer the cries of a people who are called by My Name. I will not delay any longer!"

The Lord spoke to Daniel in a vision of a great tree, and He speaks to His prophets again. He says that the Scriptures record as a testimony the lunacy of King Nebuchadnezzar. The Lord declares that the name of Biden and the name Nebuchadnezzar will always carry with them the moniker of lunacy.

"Do these people really think the 'Most High' will sit by idly and watch them steal from Me? I AM has clearly portrayed who I, the Lord, have chosen. My Trumpet has been 10 times more productive, more honest, and more forthright, than any president to date. Therefore, they may not read the Scriptures or even know Me at all, but My Hand has been clearly shown to them! No one who knows Me could have any doubt who has My right hand upon them. This should be readily apparent even to the blind, says the Lord. Therefore, the sheep and the goats have clearly been divided. Yes, those of the world clearly give themselves away, as do those who are of the light!

Those who worship their religion, the world, and yes, the devil himself are the same in My eyes, says the Lord. They shall receive what they fear most. My faithful ones, the ones I love, shall receive everything they desire! They only desire Jesus all the time and they shall not be disappointed. Do you really think I will not also pour out blessing upon blessing on them? The blessings that have been held back are about to burst forth; the dam is breaking because of the depth of the blessings behind it! Look around you! Do you know anyone who loves Me who isn't waiting for something? Your wait is almost over. Finish well then. The testing, the trials are almost over! Have faith!

My name is the Lord of Hosts. My army never loses. We never even have thoughts of that! I AM Good. You are in good hands!"

The Goodness of God – March 18, 2021

Matthew 16 speaks of signs and heavenly knowledge ... but "they couldn't understand." Matthew 24:38-39 says that "they" didn't understand revelatory wisdom until it was too late" (flood came and took them all away). In Romans 6 we find revelatory knowledge... everyone who is "in Christ" knows that participation in sin is a choice.

Sin is not our master. Righteousness is our bent. Those to whom this is not known are tossed here and there and righteousness is something to be <u>worked for.</u>

In Romans 16:17-20, notice how those of us who are His react to "those who cause dissensions and hindrances contrary to the teaching which you learned...". Do we call out loudly "false prophet" or "false teacher"? No! We turn away from them.

The Lord is saying that His goodness will be evident in those who are in Christ. They are not <u>offended</u> because they are in Him and have abandoned pride. They actually know Him and are not <u>intimidated</u> by the religious. <u>Arguing</u> small points is below them because they have His understanding. <u>Accusations</u> are deflected easily by the sword of the Spirit of Christ. <u>Heavenly knowledge</u> and <u>wisdom</u> deny earthy knowledge and wisdom their glory. "But it is My GOODNESS that brings in the sinner!"

The King of Glory says: "I AM about to express My goodness on the earth! Because of all these things, My People, ignore what you see in the natural, and close your ears to everything that runs contrary to My words and My Kingdom. I AM going to release on the earth My goodness! You have been deceived long enough! The good that I have desired for you has been stolen from you and hidden from you, My People! You have been anticipating relief from debt. Relief from your constant striving for provision. Relief for that is on the way says the Lord. But I say that this provision is the <u>least</u> of the goodness which I have reserved for you!

Look, you have a renewed mind! The mind of Christ! This is a creative mind that creates for the <u>good</u> – not for fighting, enrichment, or evil! I AM <u>releasing</u> creativity and goodness which dreamers have only dreamed of! Inventions for travel, fuel, healing, social encounters... dream big My people! The great harvest will not be one of struggle and pain, nor of poverty and striving either. It is My goodness that will go before you, and gladness will be so attractive that people will be drawn like a moth to light. Dump that striving. Get rid of your fear for the future. My Joy is breaking forth and shall be more contagious than the most virulent sickness! Look UP! Amen!"

Now it Springs Up! – March 22, 2021

"REJOICE, I'm doing a new thing. NOW it SPRINGS up. Can you not perceive it? Love for Me is deepening in My saints and prophets and apostles as they wait. Patience in suffering conforms one more into the image of My Son. This remnant will be strong, fearless, and filled with faith, for they have been found faithful. Spring is the time of new beginnings. The angels are excited. The saints in Heaven and Earth are excited. Hallelujah to the Lamb! Great is the LORD and worthy of GLORY! All praise and honor belong to Him! Great are YOU LORD and worthy of praise! Amen!"

Faith Sees Beyond the Temporal & is Obedient to the End – March 23, 2021

Considering Joshua 6, the conquest of Jericho, the Lord asks, "What was it that caused the walls of Jericho to fall? The priests? The trumpets? The ark? Shouting? I tell you, NO. It was not the warriors of Israel, or the people, or what they did. It was one man's faith and obedience. Joshua followed at My command, and it happened as I told him it would. He did not understand how or why it would work, but by faith he commanded things to be done according to what he had heard Me say. I have not changed, says the Lord. Faith and obedience will always bring about the thing which I have promised."

God waited 7 days after Noah entered the ark and the door was shut to bring rain. God waited until the Egyptians had overtaken the Israelites and Moses by the sea before He delivered them. The first 6 trips around Jericho did nothing. The walls stood. Father is saying that faith "sees" beyond the temporal, beyond the logic, and denies the natural course of things its way. **Faith is obedient to the end.** Faith sees the promise, the victory, the goodness of God.

He says, "Do not give up now My People. I am not done yet! My prophets have shown you the future! They speak My words; they do not lie!"

It's Time to Leave Shittim Prophecy – April 14, 2021

The Lord takes the Israelites across the Jordan in Joshua Chapters 3-5.

And the LORD said to Joshua, "This day I will begin to exalt you in the sight of all Israel, that they may know that, as I was with Moses, so I will be with you. You shall command the priests who bear the ark of the covenant, saying, 'When you have come to the edge of the water of the Jordan, you shall stand in the Jordan.'" (Joshua 3:7-8)

So Joshua said to the children of Israel, "Come here, and hear the words of the LORD your God." And Joshua said, "By this you shall know that the living God is among you, and that He will without fail drive out from before you the Canaanites and the Hittites and the Hivites and the Perizzites and the Girgahshites and the Amorites and the Jebusites: Behold, the ark of the covenant of the Lord of all the earth is crossing over before you into the Jordan... And it shall come to pass, as soon as the soles of the feet of the priests who bear the ark of the LORD, the Lord of all the earth, shall rest in the waters of the Jordan, that the waters of the Jordan shall be cut off, the waters that come down from upstream, and they shall stand as a heap." (Joshua 3:9-19,13

Then Joshua called the twelve men whom he had appointed from the children of Israel, one man from every tribe; and Joshua said to them: "Cross over before the ark of the LORD your God into the midst of the Jordan, and each one of you take up a stone on his shoulder, according to the number of the tribes of the children of Israel, that this may be a sign among you when your children ask in time to come, saying 'What do these stones mean to you?' Then you shall answer them that the waters of the Jordan were cut off before the ark of the covenant of the LORD; when it crossed over the Jordan, the waters of the Jordan were cut off. And these stones shall be a memorial to the children of Israel forever." (Joshua 4: 4-7)

So the priests who bore the ark stood in the midst of the Jordan until everything was finished that the LORD had commanded Joshua to speak to the people, according to all that Moses had commanded Joshua; and the people hurried and crossed over. Then it came to pass, when all the people had completely crossed over, that the ark of the LORD and the priests crossed over in the presence of the people. And the men of Reuben, the men of Gad, and half the tribe of Manasseh crossed over armed before the children of Israel, as Moses had spoken to them. About forty thousand prepared for war crossed over before the LORD for battle, to the plains of Jericho. On that day the LORD exalted Joshua in the sight of all Israel; and they feared him, as they had feared Moses, all the days of his life. (Joshua 4:10-14)

So it was, when all the kings of the Amorites who were on the west side of the Jordan, and all the kings of the Canaanites who were by the sea, heard that the LORD had dried up the waters of the Jordan from before the children of Israel until we had crossed over, that their heart melted; and there was no spirit in them any longer because of the children of Israel. (Joshua 5:1)

The LORD then had Joshua circumcise all the sons of Israel because those who had originally come out of Egypt had been circumcised but died in the desert because of their unbelief leading to disobedience. So, these new males were circumcised.

And it came to pass, when Joshua was by Jericho, that he lifted his eyes and looked, and behold, a Man stood opposite him with His sword drawn in His hand. And Joshua went to Him and said to Him, "Are You for us or for our adversaries?" So He said, "No, but as Commander of the army of the LORD I have now come." And Johsua fell on his face to the earth and worshiped, and said to Him, "What does my Lord say to His servant?" Then the Commander of the LORD's army said to Joshua, "Take your sandal off your foot, for the place where you stand is holy." And Joshua did so. (Joshua 5:13-15)

Then the manna ceased on the day after they had eaten the produce of the land; and the children of Israel no longer had manna, but they ate the food of the land of Canaan that year. (Joshua 5:12)

The Lord says the history of Israel crossing from Shittim to Gilgal is a picture of what shall occur in our time. Donald J. Trump is Joshua in this prophecy. The prophets are the priests who have put their feet in the water. Just as Joshua sent the military across first, so shall President Trump send the military across first. The people on the other side will be wetting themselves in fear, and their spirits will leave them. Those on the side of the enemy will fear Donald J. Trump. The people, however, will follow him. Those who have stood in faith will pick up the stones and make a memorial. The stones will be something we'll remember this by – our journey from Shittim to Gilgal.

The people will know when they cross over that God will also defeat all their enemies – all the giants in the land (He who began a good work in you will carry it to completion...). God will finish what He started. It's not in these chapters, but it's also true that the people will be carrying all their possessions, just as the Israelites left Egypt with all of their possessions, as well as the possessions of the Egyptians. We're not losing on this deal. This is no longer about crossing the Red Sea into the desert. This is about crossing the Jordan River into the Promised Land!

However, after we pass over, it is not a time to feel exalted. Instead, it's a time to be circumcised in our hearts. It's time for Jesus to be lifted up. Those of us of the Spirit of Christ with faith have consecrated ourselves to this, but most of the people still need help. They need to be circumcised in their hearts.

As we have believed the words of the LORD and as He crosses us over the Jordan into the Promised Land, we have joined battle with His angelic army, and we are fighting with Him for victory. His Commander has come to lead the way and He has no thoughts of losing. We are for the LORD, and He has come.

It's time to start eating the food of the Promised Land! We don't know the timing, but it's soon. This is a prophetic word, so it is a word showing us what will come to pass.

The Lord says that when Donald J. Trump sends the military ahead, it will be a sign of projected power – a show of strength. All those in the land will be dispossessed before us.

Lastly, as soon as the Prophets cross over and their feet hit dry ground, the time of the Apostles has come.

Prophecy Regarding the Church According to Jesus' Example – April 17, 2021

"Therefore bear fruits worthy of repentance… And even now the ax is laid to the root of the trees. Therefore every tree which does not bear good fruit is cut down and

thrown into the fire. I indeed baptize you with water unto repentance, but He who is coming after me is mightier than I, whose sandals I am not worthy to carry. He will baptize you with the Holy Spirit and fire. His winnowing fan is in His hand, and He will thoroughly clean out His threshing floor, and gather His wheat into the barn; but He will burn up the chaff with unquenchable fire." (Matthew 3:8, 10-12)

The addition of the New Testament to the book doesn't change God's view of the Bible. You still don't find salvation in Scripture. Jesus said, *"You search the Scriptures, for in them you think you have eternal life; and these are they which testify of Me. But you are not willing to come to Me that you may have life."* (John 5:39-40) Therefore, salvation is found only in Jesus. So, the bearing fruits worthy of repentance … that's in Him.

You cannot say you are saved and have no fruit worthy of repentance. Man can baptize you with water, but if you want the baptism of the Holy Spirit and fire that Jesus gives, there must be repentance.

Wouldn't repentant people desire the Holy Spirit? Isn't that agreeing with God? Even NOW the ax is laid to the root of the trees. Even NOW the winnowing fan is in the hand of the LORD! Now is the time! Repent and receive the Kingdom of Heaven.

"Who is this 'church' that looks nothing like Me, says the LORD? What is this religion that makes a mockery of Jesus Christ by claiming His name and bearing no fruit? Do I bear no fruit? I tell you, NO! I always bear fruit. A repentant heart is one found in Me, one that agrees with Me.

The time of the Church Age has begun, the real Church Age, the real Church – the one that glorifies Me, the one that lifts up only Me! This is the age of the Apostles. This is where the Apostles and Prophets will once again work together as one to bring the Kingdom of Heaven to earth. This is the age where My body will bring glory to Me, the Head. I Am cleaning out My threshing floor. None shall escape. Repent and be saved!

You who believe that you do not NEED the baptism of the Holy Spirit, was John the Baptist wrong then? Did the disciples not NEED the baptism of the Holy Spirit that Jesus told them to wait for? Jesus has the winnowing fan in His hand. You must decide.

Kirk and Tiffany, you have been teaching about the fivefold ministry. Rightly so. But I say that My church without spot or wrinkle will be the one after My words and My example – not another way. Not by wisdom of men, not by theology and doctrine or programs. It will be the one that follows My Spirit, says the LORD."

The Time of the Apostles – April 23, 2021

God is preparing for the time of the Apostles. The time of the Prophets is coming to an end. Not that He will not use the Prophets! He most certainly will. The Prophets who have stood, meaning those who have only stood on His words, no more, no less – yes, those Prophets who didn't change their minds when the things that they had prophesied looked impossible, these, He will certainly use! However, the time of the Apostles is coming!

His Prophets will take a back seat during this season, and they will be expected to come to the aid of the Apostles, yes, to serve them and literally lift them up before the people. The Prophets will then in turn be lifted up by the Apostles because the Apostles whom Jesus have chosen know how to lead and also that true leadership in the Kingdom is servanthood. The Apostles will be lifting up the rest of the fivefold ministers as well, who will then in turn lift up the true church.

So, the Lord is saying, "Apostles, you need a Prophet! Yes, each one of you! Prophets, you need an Apostle. Yes, everyone one of you! This is the Jesus way of doing things! He has given the Church gifts. Did you really think you could do it another way?"

Also, the Lord is saying that most of the ministers in the fivefold are currently unknown! He is doing a new thing – do you not perceive it? These new ministers in the fivefold mostly know who they are and are waiting for the dam to break so that they can be poured out and cover the land. The Lord is looking for disciples of Jesus Christ of Nazareth. Yes, signs and wonders – the greater things Jesus said that believers would do! He wants to once again *shake* the ground during prayer meetings! He wants to set prisoners free because someone prayed in power! He is ready to be poured out in the Latter Rain in POWER!

Where is Joe Biden & the Real Deep State Turns on the "Middle" People – May 1, 2021

The Lord is saying that "they will fake Biden's death in time to come" (pretending he just died), but he has been dead for a while already. It will not be a long time coming. Kamala will not become president (not that Biden was really president anyway). She thought going into this, that she was pretty street smart, but now realizes she is in way over her head. She realizes that she is in deep trouble. She is looking for the exit right now and finding that it may not be possible. They'll be trying to make Kamala president, but she'll be reluctant and not want to take the job, knowing the consequences. But she won't be president.

The panic has not set in for everyone in this "administration" yet. The Democrats, the RINOs, even the Obamas are thinking that they will find a way out. They are all being played by the real "deep state," however. The super rich are now planning their own escape strategy. Trying to figure out how to keep their fortunes is paramount. They will sacrifice anything or anyone for this cause and never even think twice about it. Nations, peoples, their own "leaders" whom they have put in place, their own organizations – nothing means anything to them – except that they use these as tools.

The Lord says that when the "middle" people realize what is happening, it will be the most dangerous time. They will realize that no one has their back, like they thought. Then they will be like cornered animals. They'll turn on each other, throwing each other and the economy under the bus. Whatever they have control of, they will use. However, the tide is turning, and they won't have much control by then, so it's really too late. By the time the real deep state shows that they have turned on these "middle" people, their options will have almost run out. They won't have much ability to do anything, except make a scene. This doesn't mean it will not be dangerous, however, as these "middle" people will still be in their positions of "authority" as they try to hurt people. But it's really only dangerous if you listen to them... obey them.

For people who are "enlightened," and have done much research and they think they have it figured out – these people must ultimately doubt Trump's ascent back to the presidency because this is the Lord's deal and He's not going to share His glory with those who have "figured it out." You can't know what's going to happen by man's knowledge. Look at all the battles won supernaturally in Scripture. Those people did not have it figured out then, and they are not going to this time either. That's why the prophets who are no longer standing, are no longer standing – because they went with man's knowledge and not the Word of the Lord.

The handwriting is on the wall. In Scripture, the handwriting on the wall spoke of the demise of a king. This time it's the demise of the Cabal. The Winds of Change is blowing, and everything hidden will be exposed. The Spirit of Truth is moving at this time. The lies will be uncovered, and everything will be turned on its head. It's like we have been slaves and never knew it. But we're going to be set free. We will know then what true freedom is like.

Amen.

Dream – Government Increases Pressure Regarding Jab – May 5, 2021

I (Tiffany) dreamed my dad took me and my kids through the town where we used to live when I was young. We stopped at a restaurant there. There was a woman working there who I recognized from years ago, but she looked a lot older. She knew who I was, and she was very adept at her job. She asked me if I wanted a prophylactic, but I said, no, I wanted a cappuccino. Then my dad was gone, and I was in a hotel with my children, who were much younger.

Interpretation from the Holy Spirit:

The Lord says that my dad in this dream represents an authority figure. The authority figure wants me to go back to the old life. The restaurant waitress is asking if I want a prophylactic, which prevents one from getting sick, like a vaccine.

This dream is not really about me but is speaking to people in general. The government is trying to tell people that if they get the vaccine, things will go back to how they were – like when the kids were young and it was fun, etc. It's not true. You can't go back.

The Lord is saying there's going to be more pressure. People want to go back to the way things were in the good old days and they see getting the vaccine as their way back to how things used to be. They desire to take the vaccine for this purpose, even though they know it's detrimental to their health. We cannot fall for it and must warn others not to as well. They can't go back.

Sands of Time – Joseph Son of Jacob – Enduring Faith – Promises in Promises – May 6, 2021

As I (Kirk) was praying, I was told to go to the Sands of Time again. So, I did. I was again in the room with all the Prophets. The faceless Man came to me. He didn't say anything, but I knew I was to follow Him. I also knew I was going to meet Joseph, son of Jacob. The faceless Man led me through those gathered there. When He stopped, we were standing in front of Joseph. The faceless Man then turned to me and said, "Kirk, ask him your question."

So, I faced Joseph and asked him if it was difficult to have faith in the visions (dreams) for all that time? He said that he thought he was going to die a number of times. "My situation looked impossible. I didn't understand how things were ever going to work out. I did despair, even of life itself, but I did not give up. Now the Father has said that I have great faith, and that is true because He does not lie." Then he said, "Real faith isn't some grandiose thing. It is not giving up, and it is waiting for the promised things."

Then the faceless Man led me to an empty area. Nobody but the two of us were there. It was exceedingly bright there – white pure light. It seemed like that's all there was – light. We walked on it and breathed it and moved through it. The faceless Man's robe glowed in the light, even brighter than the ambient light. I was almost blinded. The faceless Man came close and waved His hand over me. As He did, my mind was filled with the name "Jesus" and then I could again see.

Then the faceless Man opened my eyes to see the future, my future. I could see all the visions and words given to me coming to reality. I saw the difficulty in waiting. I saw others struggling, waiting, and hoping too. I saw NONE of them giving up! I also saw that there were promises inside the promises, things that we were hoping for that were in addition to the main subject. We all were like children opening presents, wondering what we might discover next.

I noticed that Joseph faced challenges his whole life, and we would too. However, the desert, the lack, the injustice, and persecution all happened prior to his ascent to ruler in Egypt. Our challenges will be different in the future as well. I was kind of lost, or completely taken, looking at all those things when the voice of the faceless Man interrupted and invited me to come with Him to another place.

Winds of Change Angel Agitated – May 16, 2021

I was in the spirit and saw the Winds of Change Angel.

He appears angry or agitated as he begins to generate the wind of the Spirit of God. I understand that he feels that there have been delays and that there were things that should have happened that have not. He is dealing with resistance in the spirit realm. Resistance to the Truth, resistance to his wind, which is blowing the lid off from things which have been hidden. Evil, which is desperate to express itself, is resisting his "wind." I also sense that he has a fresh anointing of power, fresh resolve, and yet impatience of a Godly origin. I see the other angels too. They also look as if they could use a refreshing. They also are looking at the Winds of Change Angel, like hoping for a real change. I also see that fear in the enemy camp has increased. The lies about how they would win in some way are being revealed as lies, but they know they must fight on, or else.

Again, the Winds of Change Angel comes into view. He rises from the earth into mid heaven. This is a very bold thing for him to do because he is in plain view of the enemy ranks, but he rises up fearlessly. He increases the wind of the Spirit of God. Some of the enemy seem to become loose, unable to hang on. They are swept away, screaming and cursing. The wind increases more and more, and the enemy loses about a third of their ranks! The angels of the Lord are greatly encouraged! They battle with an added ferocity now, and a sense of victory is in the air as they advance. The earth is on the verge of experiencing a deliverance on a scale that has never been seen before!

I also see that mankind is mostly oblivious to what is going on, but as the tide of the battle turns toward the favor of the Lord of Hosts, some do see it and wake up. Eventually, everyone will be forced to see the truth, and the lies will lose their power. A new day is dawning, but most do not perceive it for now. I see that the Lord will not let this go on for much longer. The revelation of the things that He desired to be revealed is almost complete. Amen.

Winds of Change and the Facade Falling –

May 23, 2021

I (Kirk) see the Winds of Change angel looking over the earth. He is a picture of strength, rather stoic, but also satisfied at the results of his work. He isn't done, but the task ahead will be accomplished without the resistance that was apparent before.

I also see the archangel, Michael. He too seems to have a fresh resolve. He is rallying the heavenly hosts for a battle.

All of the angels seem to know that there will soon be a great victory. They look like they can hardly wait to get started, but the angels are very disciplined. They desire to follow well and do not second guess and berate their leaders like the enemy hordes do. From what I've seen of the enemy, they do whatever they do out of fear, only serving themselves really. They follow their commanders' orders only to avoid punishment or to gain advantage for themselves and are basically forced to fight.

Michael is preparing for an enormous battle. The angels look up to him. He is a very dedicated and loyal warrior. He has great faith, or trust, in the Lord. The battle will begin very soon, and it will not be a protracted engagement. It will be over rather quickly.

On the world stage this battle and the route of the demonic will also produce fear. It will become very visible as the noose tightens on those whose deeds have been evil. Their pride and bravado will turn to panic. Erratic thoughts and actions will result. Watch as the facade begins to fall this week (May 23, 2021). And look, as everyone will, at the free fall and collapse of the world system!

"Stand, therefore, My faithful ones! It will not be long now, says the Lord of Hosts!" Amen.

Jesus Intervening in the Affairs of Men – May 25, 2021

(Kirk) see two figures approaching, coming straight out of the sun. As they approach, I can see that both are on horseback. They seem to know that they are between me and the sun, and they keep the sun at their back as they approach. I'm wondering who these two are. A voice in my mind says, "They are Michael and Gabriel, the archangels of God." They stop in middle heaven and look over the earth as it slowly turns beneath them. They seem to be talking about something. One points this way and the other points that way. This goes on for some time. Then the sun seems to grow dim.

As I look, I notice clouds passing between the two archangels and the sun. As I continue to gaze upwards toward the sun, I see that the clouds are actually angels. So many that I cannot count them. In my mind I'm thinking, "What could possibly require this many angels?" I hear the Lord's voice.

"I have decided to intervene in the affairs of men. A sovereign intervention. The evil one has been given leeway until now. My faithful ones have been faithful, and I have heard their cries for mercy and for justice. The cup of iniquity is filled. The time has come for My hand to intervene. Evil is rooted deeply on the earth. The world system is such that if not for this intervention, even My faithful ones could possibly be deceived. Therefore, I will root out the deception. I will expose the evil ones, and My people will be set free from this world system. I will clearly show Myself and My desire for those who will believe! There will be those who still will not believe, however, but they shall be few and feeble," says the Lord.

"Therefore, get ready for the Latter Rain and blessings in this life on earth beyond what you can imagine! I Am The LORD, and I do not lie! Amen"

Craftsman Style House Church – Open and Clean – May 27, 2021

Today as I (Kirk) close my eyes to pray, I see a small house of the "Craftsman" style. I go closer to look at it. It has openings for windows, but there are simply openings, no actual windows. It also has an opening for a door, but no door is installed. Looking in, I see that it is completely empty – no furniture, wall hangings, decorations, nothing. It is, however, clean, very, very clean. There's no dust or dirt of any kind. Strange. Asking the Lord why I am seeing this...

After a while He says, "This is My church."

I'm not understanding what He means. It's empty. As I puzzle about this, the Lord says, "I expect the doors to always be open. I want whoever wants Me to be able to enter unobstructed. I also want the windows to allow those on the outside to see inside. I want everyone to know that there is nothing secretive or exclusive going on inside of My Church. I also want My Church to be clean! There are no decisions or deals being made that exclude anyone who might be interested. The wind of My Spirit is able to blow through, and My truth is there without obstruction.

My fivefold ministers are the craftsmen who build My house. These 'Craftsmen' follow My Spirit exclusively and are very bold and open about this! They do not pander but are dedicated to Me alone, says the Lord. They do not bow the knee to the people, to the 'church,' to anything or anybody, but Me. It has been said that anyone who kneels before Me will be able to stand before any man. This is true. The new wine, My wine, My Spirit, can be poured into these small 'churches' and My watchmen and Apostles are to be 'over' My churches, even as the evangelists, pastors, and teachers do their work there. They are all servants of Mine. I have chosen them, and, in My Kingdom, I Am is King and chooses as He will. So be it, says the Lord."

Clouds of Angels – I AM Will Win Completely –

June 1, 2021

Today looking in the spirit, I (Kirk) see the "clouds" of angels. They are spread out in the heavens, neatly and in an orderly pattern. I don't see the archangels this time, but I sense their nearness. I also see angels which are doing battle already on the earth. These seem to be doing quite well. They seem encouraged and seem to me to be taking ground. I'm looking at all this, amazed at the numbers of angels in the heavens, pondering and still wondering why so many? As I'm thinking about this, the Lord reminds me of His desire to intervene.

Then He speaks into my mind, "Kirk, when I decide to do a thing, I do it in such a way as to not allow even a miniscule hint of victory for My adversary. I Am The LORD of Hosts. Who would even think that they could come against Me and take ground, even in the smallest measurement known? The Great I Am will win completely and then the nations will surely see that I Am is Lord."

I said, "When Lord?"

He answered, "By now you know that this is the time, and this is the season. This is for you to know. It is for Me to set things in motion and to stop things according to the wisdom of the Father. He alone sets the day and the hour, and He (Father) also reveals what He will to His prophets."

I'm asking if He wants me to know anything else...

The Lord says people need to know that faith is required during this time. "Do not be of those who shrink back! I have given My Prophets a voice and a platform. Let the people know that they should listen to My voice, whether I speak directly to them, or if I decide to speak through My Prophets."

The Lord Sending Legions and Legions of Angels & His Recompense – June 5, 2021

The Lord says, "I Am going to open your eyes to see things that nobody has been shown, and to see things that will be as I Am rolls out His justice. So then, open your eyes and look across the sea, and open your eyes to look across the oceans."

So, I look. I see the waters in a rage and the waves thereof roaring! There are also signs on the land. Yes, earthquakes in the usual places, but also in the unusual!

The Lord reminds me of Isaiah 37:36 where one angel killed 185,000 Assyrians in one night. When the people woke up in the morning, there were dead bodies everywhere. Then He says, "I Am sending legions of angels, yes, legions upon legions of angels this time.

I Am going to generate a reset, and it will make those things which I have done for My people Israel look like child's play, says the Lord of Hosts. A rescue mission, YES! But more than that, this action will pay a recompense. Yes, the recompense of the Lord will be meted out! My beloved ones shall receive their justice! I have heard their cries from heaven, and they shall receive their compensation, says the Lord!

Those who stand against Me shall also receive what they are due, along with those who will not stand. They have proudly flaunted their adulteries and worked against everything that is good. Their sneers and mockery have been duly noted by the courts of heaven. They will receive what they fear most, says the Lord.

Therefore, look up, you who tremble at My name! Your redemption is very near! Amen."

Craftsman Style Vison 2 – How the Church Operates – June 10, 2021

This morning, I (Kirk) am seeing the craftsman style house again. It's the same one I was seeing on May 27, 2021. As before, I approach the house. This time I hear voices from within. As I approach, I hear the voice of the Lord saying, "This is My pastor speaking."

Then I hear the pastor speaking of recent events of the church as well as things coming up. He speaks as a servant of those gathered with the authority that comes from the Lord. As he finishes his part, he invites an evangelist to take the lead. She comes to the forefront and invites those gathered to a time of praise. Afterwards, she gives a short word from the Lord and invites those who do not know the Lord to accept Jesus as their Lord! After this, the pastor again raises his voice in inviting anyone with a praise or a word to raise their voice and bring their encouragement. Also, those who need healing or other kinds of needs are invited to receive prayer for those things.

I notice that those attending this church seem to all be friends. There are no "outsiders" or anyone who looks marginalized or alone. I'm wondering if these people have been here for a long time and are like "old friends"?

The Lord's voice comes again, "Kirk, about half of these people are new followers of Me. The reason you're wondering is because in My church there is no fear. No one is <u>worried </u>how they will get this or that done or if the new addition will be paid for, etc. There is no addition! The pastor isn't concerned that someone will 'take over' his place or he won't get his way because this is My church. In My church, there isn't a problem with 'unity' for those who are in Christ or issues with doctrine and theology because all of My fivefold ministers are only concerned with following My Spirit. They know Me and will not follow another," says the Lord.

As their time together ends at the church, a teacher gets the floor and invites anyone who wants to go deeper in the Lord to meet with him.

Amen.

A Great Deception and an End Time Jubilee – Part 1 –

June 13, 2021

The Lord is speaking about a great deception. First, the Lord showed me how great the deception is already. So many people (Christians), pastors, whole churches, almost all the churches, closed because of a virus. A virus, which as it turned out, was nothing compared to what we were told about its severity. Then there were so many who were duped into taking something experimental and untested for a sickness which was over 99% survivable, the effects of which have yet to play out. Others were deceived into wearing face diapers which, as we now know, were useless to stop the sickness which they were worn for, and in fact contribute to poor health. But some were not fooled. There is always a remnant. After seeing all of this, I was left wondering how in the world we as a people could possibly escape a "great deception."

Then the Lord says, "Behold, I Am is warning you against this great deception! You have been conditioned to fear! But I say, do not fear at all! I Am King in My Kingdom. My faithful have no reason to fear at all. Look to Me! Am I ringing My hands worrying about anything? I say NO! I sit on My throne. Nothing has or will escape My notice. I still hold all power and knowledge and wisdom, and I say: do not fear!

Behold, I Am holding the winnowing fork in My hand, and I Am separating the wheat from the chaff. I Am also separating the wheat from the tares! There will be no tares on My threshing floor says the Lord! The coming deception will clearly separate the wheat from the chaff!

Only My wheat will be left, and the chaff will be blown away to another place, gathered, and burned, says the Lord. Likewise, My people shall be gathered together in an end times jubilee, but the end is not yet.

Rejoice, therefore, My people! I Am for you and not against you. I will bless you and I will remove from their place those who hate you! Look up! Your redemption is near! Amen."

A Stench and God's Anger Burns Hot – June 17, 2021

"A STENCH! A rotten stench comes up from the earth, says the Lord of Hosts! It stinks of rotten flesh, and the cries of My faithful ones constantly draw My attention to it. My anger is greatly aroused and those whose intents and ways are always and only evil will reap what they have sown! I Am the LORD. I will repay! Yes! Those who thought they could keep secret, and yes, they even thought I couldn't see what they were doing!

This system, the world system, the system of darkness, the system of kill, steal, and destroy, yes – that system!

My anger burns HOT! Those who have ignited it shall feel what real power is! I shall bring upon them what they fear most, and those who have climbed the ladder of darkness shall find that they have climbed up into the deepest pit of hell.

Fear NOT My faithful ones! Everything that the darkness has aimed at you, intending to destroy you, behold, I will turn it into a great blessing! The riches hidden in darkness, yes everything that has been stolen and stored up, great abundance in every good thing shall be doled out. I shall take great pleasure in your astonishment, My people!

Even those of you who are aware of what is going on shall be aghast at the depth of the evil people that will be removed, and even more amazed at the riches hidden in darkness. You have no idea about the extent of your slavery, and you have no idea what freedom really is! But you will! Again, do not be deceived and driven to fear! Do not fear! And again, look up! Your deliverance is very near! Amen."

A Great Deception – as a Feather Blown in the Wind –

Part 2– June 24, 2021

"The great deception comes. It comes as a feather blown in the wind, not as a hammer that strikes a blow. Behold, it ramps up slowly, but in its wake is wailing and cursing because this new sickness is a true pandemic – a sickness enhanced by man, and even as man again tries to intervene and mitigate the effect, he is deceived again and only makes it worse, and the toll climbs higher because of his intervention.

The inherent evil in all of this, from the start to the finish shall NOT have its desired effect, however. It (all the evil playing itself out) shall actually have the opposite effect as I Am turns it for the good of those who love Him. This does not mean that these faithful ones will not taste the sting of war, however! My faithful ones shall experience sorrow, even though their experience in the end will be a great triumph of good overcoming evil. Do not go into fear, therefore! Those who allow fear to come in will make decisions based on that fear and these (decisions) will be devastating. Keep your eyes on Me, says the Lord. I will not lead you into destruction, but into peace and love and hope! Amen."

*Note: The planned fake pandemic of COVID came like a hammer, suddenly. We suddenly shut down, etc. This coming deception, the LORD says, will be a real pandemic, but will come gradually, like a feather floating down. The COVID was a sickness enhanced by man as well, but the intervention of man made it worse – the injection. There will be sorrow, but the end is a great triumph of good over evil and we must keep that within our sights. We MUST be led by the Holy Spirit and nothing else, especially fear! We've been warned several times. We also believe this is something we can pray against so that it doesn't happen. Therefore, we have prayed accordingly.

The Lord is Doing a NEW Thing – July 1, 2021

7-1-21

7 = God

1 = New Beginnings

2 = Relationships

1 = New Beginnings

Isaiah 43:19 NASB *"Behold, I Am going to do something new. NOW it WILL spring up; will you not be aware of it? I will even make a roadway in the wilderness, rivers in the desert."*

"Yes, Prophet! Listen up! I Am doing a new thing! The Lord of Hosts, yes, I even I, Adoni. I Am visiting a new thing upon the earth! It will be a NEW THING for which there is no precedent and <u>nothing</u> like it has been done before. Looking at the past while trying to envision the future is worthless. Have I not said a new thing?

My anger has been aroused and My patience has waxed thin for those who only think of and do evil. And yet I Am making a road in the wilderness and <u>yes</u>, a river in the desert. My faithful ones I will not desert, and those who have My Spirit I will not leave, for I Am jealous for My Spirit, and I love those who have been faithful.

This is a rescue mission, says the Lord! In My great Mercy, Love, and Patience, I Am going to intervene in the affairs of men once more. But the end is not yet.

I Am releasing My Holy Apostles after this time, and they shall only bow the knee to My Son, and only follow Him. My Apostles and Prophets shall build a church! This church shall be the one without spot or wrinkle and it shall be glorious in the depth of its faith in Him and in the revelation of the Christ! My Shekinah Glory shall once again be found on earth! I shall settle on a people, and their light shall shine into the darkness, and those outside of this light shall be drawn to it just as a moth is drawn to light. The stench shall be put out of My nostrils, says the Lord, and My people shall experience prosperity and favor, and they shall praise My Name. Amen."

Trump Administers Justice – July 2, 2021

The Lord led me (Kirk) to read 1 Kings 3 in which Solomon asks for a discerning heart in a dream. The Lord grants him this and much more that he didn't ask for. Then the two women come with the live baby which he threatens to cut in half with a sword. The mother is determined to keep the child alive, etc. Then the verse that the Lord wants to speak about... 1 Kings 3:28 NASB *"When all Israel heard of the judgment which the king had handed down, they feared the king, for they saw that the wisdom of God was in him to administer justice."*

The Lord says, "The Trumpet, My anointed one, truly walks in righteousness. Look at him! He has withstood years of withering accusation, outright lies, fabricated evidence, and constant court battles for him and those around him! Yet, he is so confident in his innocence before the Law that he boldly trumpets out all of the things he has been accused of! Then he says he will beat all of the upcoming accusations and court battles as well. He has no fear! I, even I, have chosen him and he will not fail, says the Lord. He is My instrument, and I Am with him.

I Am training My Trumpet in the administration of judgment! The Lord has said of Solomon that no one was ever like him and no one like him shall arise after him. And this is true! However, My Trumpet will be a just judge, and he will require justice in the land once more! The breadth, depth, and reach of this justice will be beyond what most of the earth's population has even dreamt of!

As it begins, there will be a great celebration. But for the good of the nations, I the Lord, shall sour the hearts of even those who most desire justice (justice would go too far...). Yes, blood will be spilt, and real justice meted out, and the world shall remember this forever! Never again shall evil rise up to the level now being experienced.

And as all Israel feared King Solomon, so shall the United States and also the world fear My Trumpet, says the Lord. I, the LORD, shall be lifted up, and in turn, I shall prosper all of those who are in the light, from one corner of the earth to the other. Amen."

Cascade Beginning in August 2021 – July 9, 2021

"The Prophets have said, 'The 4th of July! The 4th of July!' In the natural, nothing appears to have happened, but to those who see in the Spirit, a shift has surely happened. There will be signs in the natural in July too, but watch for the promised things to come in a cascade beginning in August.

This will be a dangerous time. The liar will be fully engaged in doing his work. Many will believe him. A full court press will be put on people to take poison to protect them from another pestilence. (See A Great Deception word parts one and two.) This pattern will be repeated for as long as people can be fooled. After that, and even in conjunction with it, fear will be ginned up, using whatever the liar believes will work to seduce people into obedience to him.

Therefore, have I not warned you, My people? Do not consider the lies at all. Look to Me! Listen to My voice! Turn off the 'news.' Do not listen to the usurpers in government. Can they do anything besides kill, steal, and destroy? Rise up in your holy anger! Prophesy truth! Intercede for truth! Speak truth! Or do you want to fall for their lies? No! I say, No, says the Lord! My faithful ones are Mine! No one can pluck them from My hand. They hear My voice and will <u>not</u> follow another!

I have said, 'Do not fear' many times already. Pay attention. These are dark days, and there is panic which is growing to a fever pitch in the enemy camp. But I, even I Am not impressed, and My faithful ones should not be impressed either. I, the LORD, am still on My throne, and this rise of evil and this time of evil is something I will not even rise from it for. I have released heaven's armies to do My bidding in this case, and they cannot lose.

I Am giving you, My faithful ones, permission to plan the party and the celebration which you will have after this time of resetting, says the Lord. Start to think about the oppression that will be gone, the riches of darkness flowing to the light, all of My little ones who will be spared, all of the liars and usurpers removed from their places.

Most importantly My people, think about the Spirit, My Spirit, poured out in the latter rain! The gospel comes with power, yes, Power! He (My Spirit) will be carried by anyone who desires Him. He has been grieved for a time, but He too will be FULL of JOY after this time. And He will pour out His water over the whole earth. And there *will* be rejoicing and celebration because of Him! Amen."

Bringing Down the World System – July 11, 2021

(Read Isaiah 14:1-27.)

"As I have brought Lucifer low, so shall I bring down this world system and all who do evil in it. My righteous ones shall shine like the sun in all its brilliance.

Just as those conquered in Isaiah's prophecy clung to Israel, so shall those left seek out the faithful. I will elevate My faithful ones and pour out My glory for I Am a just and merciful God.

I will deal with those workers of iniquity and answer the cries of My children. It has begun, as you have been told. Let freedom ring!

When My eyes see My faithful ones, I cannot help but rejoice and pour out My love and blessing on them. They have stood fast in trying times and truly I delight in them. My peace shall reign in their hearts, for they listen for My words and believe them. Their eyes continually look to Me, and their ears continually listen for My voice. They love My Spirit. They love My Son, and all of Heaven rejoices with Me for My children.

I Am bringing My sons and daughters from afar once again, but not to make a physical nation, but a spiritual Jerusalem. Praise the LORD all you hosts! Praise His Holy Name! Great is the LORD and worthy of glory! Great is the LORD and worthy of praise!

Therefore, do not let your hearts be troubled. I cannot be beat. Amen."

God is Good – July 20, 2021

I (Kirk) see the Lord looking at His people. He is so in love with them! As He looks, minutes, hours, days, weeks, and months pass. Yes, even years pass before Him as He is looking. He sees His people go about their daily tasks or doing the work of their profession or job. He sees their interaction with other believers and also the world in which they live. Their words come up to His ears, the concerns for their future and for their loved ones. The ones He love also pray and listen to His voice. After a while I notice a look of concern come onto His face. Not anger or anything like that, but a concern that comes from love. I'm wondering what is on His mind, why such concern? When I cannot stand the curiosity anymore, I just blurt out, "Lord, what's wrong?"

He turns toward me and says, "Kirk, Prophet, speak to the people and say ... I, the Lord, have seen that over the years, yes over the decades and centuries, your enemy has been working on a system of rule that works from the shadows, one that supersedes governments and countries. And the goal of this system is not to simply kill, steal, and destroy people, although that is true also. This system's goal is to embarrass Me and make Me look bad. Yes, to mock Me and paint Me as bad, untrustworthy, and to paint My Son in the same light. So yes, your enemy despises, hates, and loves to make you and every human on the planet suffer, ultimately forever. But as much vitriol as he has for you, he HATES Me much more!

Therefore, the 'world' system which has been set in place is there to harass Me and of course the ones I love. I see the people of the world, and even those who are mine, have to one degree or another 'bought in' to this system. When I send a Prophet to the people to warn them of what is to come, to tell them to avoid the coming evil which might befall them, they believe it and regard the Prophet highly! Conversely, when I send a Prophet a message of the good which I have planned for My people, they call him a fake prophet! They believe the world can only become worse than it is currently. They speak to one another about the future in a lament! Yes, Even My obedient ones have taken an attitude of being defeated! They say within themselves that it will never get better! Each one who does this is prophesying their own doom. I, the Lord, say, 'Look up for your redemption draws near!' and they look down at the ground...

This should not be My people! Am I too weak to change things? Is My goodness <u>not</u> good enough? Is <u>not</u> My justice just? Answer Me you who can only 'see' a bleak future! I Am requiring an answer! I Am requiring a change of attitude and belief! I, even I, have never failed! I will not be seen as a failure either!

Fear has to be 'put out' of your lives, out of your belief system. I Am the Lord. Faith must be 'put on' every morning and carried during the day. I will NEVER leave you or forsake you! I will hold you up by My strong right hand! Rise up in your most holy faith! I long to pour out My grace (empowerment) to help you! I love each one of you. Amen."

The Lord Expects Respect for His Fivefold Ministers, Especially Apostles – July 27, 2021

The Lord said, "Many are called, but few are chosen." Then He said, "respect." Matthew 22:14 is where the "many are called few are chosen" verse is found.

Matthew 22:1-14 NASB

Jesus spoke to them again in parables, saying, "The kingdom of heaven may be compared to a king who gave a wedding feast for his son. And he sent out his slaves to call those who had been invited to the wedding feast, and they were unwilling to come. Again he sent out other slaves saying, "Tell those who have been invited, 'Behold, I have prepared my dinner; my oxen and my fattened livestock are all butchered and everything is ready; come to the wedding feast.'" But they paid no attention and went their way, one to his own farm, another to his business, and the rest seized his slaves and mistreated them and killed them. But the king was enraged, and he sent his armies and destroyed those murderers and set their city on fire. Then he said to his slaves, "The wedding is ready, but those who were invited were not worthy. Go therefore to the highways, and as many as you find there, invite to the wedding feast." Those slaves went out into the streets and gathered together all they found, both evil and good; and the wedding hall was filled with dinner guests. But when the king came in to look over the dinner guests, he saw a man there who was not dressed in wedding clothes, and he said to him, "Friend, how did you come in here without wedding clothes?" And the man was speechless. Then the king said to the servants, "Bind him hand and foot, and throw him into the outer darkness; in that place there will be weeping and gnashing of teeth." For many are called, but few are chosen.

Father is saying about this parable, that the king expected to be respected by those who were called. He also expected that respect to extend to his son and also to those who were sent. This expectation was not met, and the offenders were destroyed. And again, the slaves went out and invited everyone, and they came. The king evidently offered wedding clothes to those off the street who came, but he found one man not wearing them. When asked why, the man had no answer and was bound and thrown into outer darkness. We don't know exactly why this man was not dressed properly, but it must be that he did not respect the king highly either.

The Lord has chosen his fivefold ministers to go out and invite everyone to the King's wedding feast for His Son. During the time of the Apostles, He will once again be expecting His servants to receive respect. The Son has personally chosen His fivefold ministers. The time of the Prophets will wind down and the Apostles will rise up. At this time, the Holy Spirit of God will be poured out once again in the latter rain. Power, the very power of God, will be on display and the shekinah glory will once again be "settling in" on earth.

During the first outpouring on Pentecost, Annanias and Sapphira found that they needed to have more respect than to lie to Peter and the Holy Spirit. Acts 5:11 says great fear fell over the whole church and all who heard those things. The Apostles during the Time of the Apostles will once again be placed in <u>VERY</u> high esteem because the Holy Spirit will again demand a respect for Himself and those who are chosen by Christ Himself. The power being poured out at this time will demand respect for the <u>King</u>! Destruction will be the alternative.

The whole fivefold will command respect, but the Apostles and Prophets will be standing in His glory, a covering for the other 3 (Evangelists, Pastors, and Teachers), and a lightning rod for the disrespect, but the power flowing from them shall overcome the world. Amen.

Event Horizon – July 30, 2021

The Lord said something about an "event horizon." The definition reads: (aerospacengineering.net)

"An event horizon is the threshold around a black hole where the escape velocity surpasses the speed of light. According to Einstein's theory of special relativity, nothing can travel faster through space than the speed of light. This means a black hole's event horizon is essentially the point beyond which nothing can return."

So, it is the Point of No Return.

The Lord says, "Prophet, speak to the people and say: The Event Horizon of the earth has been reached. The Father has decided to intervene. Now, today, there will be no going back. The events on earth demand intervention because of love. From today He will intervene as He has said He would. This IS a sovereign intervention, but according to His design, and His way. The Holy Spirit of God is still the Paraclete, or Helper. He works with, or through, men, and continues to do so. This intervention will increase in intensity all over the globe.

It may appear chaotic, but it is not. The father of lies will use everything at his disposal to create fear and violence. Do not be deceived by these gyrations. It will be very easy to go into fear, depression, and feel that there is no hope! That is exactly Satan's plan! Don't fall for it.

It has been said: 'Get the popcorn and sit by and watch to see what happens.' But I, the LORD, say, 'Watch and pray. Follow My Spirit. Go where He says to go. Do what He says to do!' I'm calling My faithful ones to battle! Yes, I Am a Warrior, says the Lord! Come join Me in battle, join the battle and prepare to revel in the spoils! Do NOT fear, but only trust, have faith. It is Me. I Am leading this intervention, and I will have My victory, says the Lord.

Much of the earth's peoples are used to being represented by someone else. In their church, government, schools, virtually every institution has a few leaders who represent everyone else. The ones who are represented stay away then. They pay their representatives, and other than that, they have very little interest in what is going on. A reset is needed, and it is coming, says the Lord. This laziness on the part of My People will come to an end and My Spirit will lead them in paths of righteousness and wisdom! They will no longer 'settle' for less than I desire of them. Amen."

Courts of Heaven Vision – Jesus is the Gospel –

August 5, 2021

A vision. The Lord said: "Come up here!" So, I asked, "Where Lord?" He said, "Come to the Courts of Heaven." So, I went there.

I (Kirk) appeared at the back of a very large room. In the middle of the room there was an aisle and on both sides. There was seating which started at floor level, and then each row was higher than the one in front of it. The aisle was wide and had huge angels standing in full armor on either side. In the front of the room were steps that went up to a raised area where a large, ornate chair was. The angels lined the aisle up to the raised area as well. There were also some seats on either side of this raised area, but they were few in number.

In the back of the room near me, people began to come in. It seemed like a waiting area. A man (the Holy Spirit) came near me. He asked, "Son, what do you notice about the Courts of Heaven?"

I looked around and turned back to Him and said, "It looks like the people here in this area are those who are still alive on earth."

He said, "Yes. The accuser is always accusing. And sometimes the Father is so proud of one of His saints that He allows them to go on trial, just because He loves them so much. The accuser will put on a show, accusing the saint of every sin. Yes, each word which was uttered will be examined and the accuser will point to the saint and declare him guilty! The saint will be asked for his defense, and he will simply answer by looking at Jesus and uttering that name of above all names – Jesus. The whole place and all of heaven will erupt in a thunderous praise to Him – Jesus! At the same time, the saint will be pronounced holy and blameless, and all three persons of God smile with joy!"

I asked why I was there. Am I going to be put on trial? The faceless Man turned to me and said, "No, not at this time. You are here because the Lord wants His people to know what makes them Holy and acceptable and what does not. Jesus is the Way. There is no other way, just Jesus. Jesus is also the Truth. The Bible contains truth, but Jesus is the Truth. Jesus is the Life. There is no life without Jesus. The alternative is death. This is the Gospel then. Jesus."

His words had so much POWER! I blinked and was back, praying. Amen!

World System Collapsing from Both Ends –

August 12, 2021

I (Kirk) see a great earthquake. Mountains and islands are moved from their places. I hear the Lord: "These are the movers and shakers in the world system. Their houses shall be shaken. Yes, the very foundations of their houses will be moved from their places, and they shall be no more. The very bedrock of their safety shall become their tomb of habitation which they shall not return from.

And there shall be a vacuum in the structure of their rule which many will attempt to fill, but I, the LORD, have decided that this vacuum should not be filled. Therefore, the world system will be collapsing from both ends. Yes, the powers and the rulers and the spiritual forces will be fighting each other, eating their own, and fear shall be rampant because of the shaking. Fear will increase greatly on the earth at this time because of those who have believed in the current system, and this fire will be fed more fuel as the horrors of this system are exposed.

These will feel as if there is no hope, but where the darkness increases, the light shines brighter! As anyone who has been looking knows, I have shown you the future and the hope in the coming days! Yes! You have a future and a hope! Look up, therefore! I will cover you with My wings. I Am a Redeemer, and I love you with an unquenchable love! Keep your eyes on Me. I will not disappoint. And as you do, your joy will not cease. Yes, and it will only increase. I Am the LORD your God! Amen!"

No Fear in the Wisdom of God – August 12, 2021

Who among you is wise and understanding? Let him show by his good behavior his deeds in the gentleness of wisdom. But if you have bitter jealousy and selfish ambition in your heart, do not be arrogant and so lie against the truth. This wisdom is not that which comes down from above, but is earthly, natural, demonic. For where jealousy and selfish ambition exist, there is disorder and every evil thing. But the wisdom from above is first pure, then peaceable, gentle, reasonable, full of mercy and good fruits, unwavering, without hypocrisy. And the seed whose fruit is righteousness is sown in peace by those who make peace. (James 3:13-18 NASB)

The Lord wants you to recognize His wisdom, His understanding. In this Scripture from James, He wants us to point out that all the so-called "wisdom" which is earthly, natural, demonic, is focused on self. It is described by the words "jealousy, selfish ambition, arrogance, earthly, and natural." Can you see that He is saying that this "wisdom" regarding self is exceedingly rampant in the world right now?

What a man thinks in his heart is of the greatest importance because the heart is what the Lord is interested in! If we only think of self-preservation, our own ambitions, our rights, our own protection, who we <u>feel</u> like we are, we have opened ourselves up to be led by fear! Disorder! And every evil thing!

God is love. When our heart is focused on Him, then the wisdom that flows from us is pure, peaceable, gentle, reasonable, merciful, unwavering, without hypocrisy, and produces good fruit. Looking at our world then today, August 12, 2021, what do we, or should we pay attention to? The chaos? The jab? The violence and threats directed towards those who refuse the vax? Government corruption? The cabal maybe? Will we lose our job or maybe our life?

The Lord says, "No! Rest in Me. I Am good. I do not fear, and you shouldn't either. Draw near to Me and I will draw near to you! Listen to My voice. Come on, I desire to know you! I love you! I want you to have unending joy, My people! Reject the chaos, the disorder, and all the evil. Give your fear over to Me! In My presence is perfect peace and joy! Come to Me; I will give you rest! Amen."

He has Given us Grace in these Times –

August 19, 2021

Paul writing to Timothy -

You therefore, my son, be strong in the grace that is in Christ Jesus. The things which you have heard from me in the presence of many witnesses, entrust these to faithful men who will be able to teach others also. Suffer hardship with me, as a good soldier of Christ Jesus. No soldier in active service entangles himself in the affairs of everyday life, so that he may please the one who enlisted him as a soldier. Also, if anyone competes as an athlete, he does not win the prize unless he competes according to the rules. The hard-working farmer ought to be the first to receive his share of the crops. Consider what I say, for the Lord will give you understanding in everything. ... It is a trustworthy statement: For if we died with Him, we will also live with Him; If we endure, we will also reign with

Him; If we deny Him, He also will deny us; If we are faithless, He remains faithful, for He cannot deny Himself. (2 Timothy 2:1-7, 11-13 NASB)

The Lord says: "Prophet, tell the people: I have said, 'Do not fear' and also, 'Look up, for your redemption draws near.' I have also said, 'Keep your eyes on Me' and also, 'Keep the faith.' They have been told to follow My Spirit, and this is right, but I also want to show them what this looks like.

Be strong in My grace. Have you been given the grace to prophesy? To heal? To intercede? To lead? Whatever you have received from Me has come by My grace. I owe you nothing. But My love for you has no end, and I long to empower you with My grace!

You will suffer hardship. You are in the world, but not of it, soldiers bringing heaven to earth in My name. I have won the war, but there are still battles to be fought. So, remember Who has enlisted you! Do not raise the natural world in which you live above its proper place. Whatever you are called to do as work there to make a living, remember that you are still a soldier in the Lord's army. Do not become excessively entangled in the worldly system.

An athlete trains for an event, learns the rules, and does his best to win the event. So too, you are placed in a specific place and under specific circumstances. Strong or weak, rich or poor, you are where you are because the Lord has put you there, and He has given you His grace to empower you in that particular place. Look to Him. Ask Him what you are supposed to do. Your mission is critical to those around you! The Lord is holding a great prize for you!

Just like a farmer who works hard should be the first to receive his share of the crops, do you believe that I (the Lord) will withhold the prize which you have labored so hard for? Follow My Spirit, (the rules must be followed [and the rule is to follow the Holy Spirit]) and receive all that I have reserved just for you! Come on! Live with Me and reign with Me. I love you. You cannot lose with Me! In fact, the only way you could possibly lose is to quit. Amen."

The Lord's Timing – Decide to Believe the Spirit – August 24, 2021

*N*ow having been questioned by the Pharisees as to when the kingdom of God was coming, He (Jesus) answered them and said, "The kingdom of God is not coming with signs to be observed; nor will they say, 'Look, here it is!' or 'There it is!' For behold, the kingdom of God is in your midst." (Luke 17:20-21 NASB)

I (Kirk) was told to write this Scripture down. Then I leaned back and asked what He wanted to say about these verses.

I find myself in a chair in the dark, outside. As I sit there, I see stars in the sky, and it slowly becomes light. In the twilight I see cacti in differing varieties and other desert vegetation, rocks, sand, and mountains in the distance. Then as soon as it gets to be fully daylight, it begins to get darker as the sun sets again. As I watch the full darkness come, it begins to get light out. Soon, the days and nights last only a few minutes. Then they accelerate even more. In a few seconds several days go by, then weeks and months and years pass by in seconds. I see vegetation grow up and die off in seconds as if 100 years just passed by. Mountains grow up and wear down. The desert turns to a fertile valley...

Then I am taken up above the earth. Now I can see the whole earth as it rotates below me. After a while, I realize that the Lord is now with me. He desires to show me something, so He points down at the earth and I see all of history happening. He seems to be showing me all of history as easily as one might open a book and show another person the contents.

Then the LORD Jesus turns to me and starts to explain. He says: "The Father has set times and seasons for all things. He is sovereign, and there is no other. Yet in His love and mercy, He has desired to partner with men. He wants to partner through His Spirit who will lead you into all truth. On this day, He desires to show you how to understand the times you live in and yes, the end times also. He wants you to see the Scriptures that declare and predict the appearance of Jesus. He is simply asking – did the scholars know when He would appear? Or where? Or in what manner He would appear? I say, No!

And yet in the year 2021, the scholars again think they can figure it all out. With great pride they point out how the Prophets are all wrong because what they say doesn't somehow line up with what they have figured out, or the signs that they have decided mean something. You must decide what to believe: words on a page, or My Spirit whose words will line up with the Scriptures. Amen."

The Trump Train – Part 3 – Leaving the Station –

August 27, 2021

(Kirk's vision)

In the spirit, I'm in an auditorium, I'm sitting about in the middle of the seating, in a "fold down seat" type chair. No one else is in attendance. As I look around, the lights begin to dim. When it's almost dark, I see the curtains begin to open.

Like in another vision, I see a huge old train engine, a steam engine. As I look, I see what look like mechanics busily working around the engine. Some are working on the outside, like doing something to the wheels or drivetrain or something. Others are working inside where the engineer would be.

There are only a couple of additional cars that look like they are attached to the engine. The one nearest the engine looks like it's being filled with coal.

A well-dressed man appears and walks around the engine and cars, looking inside and out and appears to be checking the work which is being performed. By his dress, I'm guessing he is from the military. As he does his inspection, he briefly chats with the mechanics working on the train.

As he nears the window where the engineer would be, a man leans out of the window and yells over the noise there to the military man, "Hey! When must this engine leave the maintenance depot?"

The military man looks up at him and yells back, "September 7!" The man nods to him and continues his work, seemingly unconcerned about the schedule.

The curtains close, and I stare at the closed curtain, thinking about the train. Then the curtains open again. In front of me is a very large white screen, and as I watch, a movie starts. It's all short clips of news from around the world — mostly violent, senseless engagements between police or military and plain-clothed people in the streets of cities. As I watch, these skirmishes get more and more violent. These are not small. There are perhaps millions of people involved.

Then, I also see leaders who look to be in total panic. They hold meetings that look official and low-key, but I can tell they are in total panic! They, too, watch the people as they wake up and decide to lash out at them in any way possible. Many are killed as the militaries are called in to keep order.

Fertile Valley Vision – Testing of the Saints –

August 31, 2021

The Lord tells me (Kirk) to prepare for a vision. When I close my eyes, I see a fertile valley full of all manner of plant life growing in profusion. It is very fertile indeed. The Lord says, "This is how I see the earth."

So as soon as He says this, my mind goes to Afghanistan, Australia, and other places where trouble for the saints has flared up. He directs my thoughts to go back to the fertile valley and says, "So when has Christianity flourished in the world? During times of peace and plenty or when there was persecution and division?"

I answered that I believed that Christianity had flourished more during persecution and division.

"You have seen correctly, Prophet."

But I still didn't get what He was saying, so I asked, "Lord, what are You trying to show me then?"

"Prophet, of what use is someone who claims to be a follower of Jesus but is never challenged? Does this person have faith or not?"

I answered that I didn't know. He answered and said, "Both faith and love have to be tested to find their strength."

He continued, "Anyone can claim to have great faith or love, but some will quickly lose heart and turn away, while the ones I love will become even stronger in faith and love."

He added: "Having great faith and love from reading words on a page is very difficult, but in a relationship, love comes naturally and then faith. Anyone who knows Me loves Me, and to him more faith is given. Therefore, make every effort to develop a relationship with Me, says the Lord! Listen to My voice because without two-way communication, is there really a relationship?"

After a few minutes of reflecting on what the Spirit was saying, the fertile valley comes back into view. As I look, His voice comes again. "During this season I am cultivating relationships like never before in all of the earth's history. The ones I love hear My voice and they know Me. I Am calling some more into My flock, but time for them is running short. Pray that they will come to Me and truly love Me. Prophet, make sure the people know that they are being tested, and the only way to fail this test is to give up and turn away. Don't give up! Amen."

Vision of a Garbage Dump – September 7, 2021

Today I (Kirk) see a garbage dump. It's very big. As far as I can see there are heaps of refuse, and there is an acrid smell in the air that I can also taste. Maybe it's burning plastic or something. I turn and look nearby at a place where a sound had come from. I see what looks like a rat, vermin, hiding in the garbage, scrambling about looking for food or water, maybe. A terrible place for sure.

Then I feel a hand rest on my shoulder. The Lord is standing next to me. As I turn to look at Him, I see that His face looks deeply saddened. He appears to look into the distance and begins to speak to me: "This is what people on the earth have chosen instead of Me and My way. This is their life on earth. Dirt and filth and a constant searching for something but never finding it. An emptiness in every step they take, an excitement that comes from doing the bidding of the evil one and then the letdown of failing once more to find happiness. An endless search for meaning in a pile of garbage. The evil one lies to them, telling them that doing his bidding is fun, and that he will raise them up to be powerful, and that they are smarter and stronger than the foolish ones who follow Me."

Then He turns toward me. "Son, tell the people that as this reset happens that they must have compassion on those who were deceived and now desire to come to Me. There will be a temptation to retaliate, to mock, but I say that love will always win! Yes, crimes must be paid for, and justice will come to those who deserve it. Justice has to be meted out. My justice is always done in love.

There will also be those who are unable to come to Me because of pride or stubbornness, or they have simply 'bought in' to the deceiver to the point that they simply believe in the ways of evil. These must be prevented from gaining influence and cannot again be allowed to gain power over the people. They must be 'outed' and kept in check.

Being a complacent Christian will no longer be a virtue. The old way of the 'church' must be left behind and discarded. My Spirit will be fully apparent and empower anyone who will be willing to carry Him. Simply following His leading is all that's required. Amen."

Times and Seasons – September 10, 2021

The Lord says that the minutes, hours, days, and years are for men. The times, seasons, epochs, and eons are the Lord's.

"Therefore, I have made time for men, but My kingdom stands forever and is not dependent on time. My Prophets look into the things of the kingdom. They see things that I have set in motion. I tell them when I am about to do a thing. They 'translate' what they see and hear from My Kingdom and bring it to men. This 'translation' is difficult for them because of the transition from the eternal to the temporal. Also, I, the Lord God, reserve timing and the knowledge of it for Myself sometimes. Mark 13:32 reads, *'But of that day or hour no one knows, not even the angels in heaven, nor the Son, but the Father alone.'* Therefore, every generation looks into the 'end times' and believes the events, days, and prophecies line up during their time.

Do you really believe that I, the Lord, have shown you what is to come so that you can hoard food, buy gold, or maybe hide somewhere during this time? I say NO! I AM has already provided for your physical welfare in My Son. I have shown you these things, the times and the seasons, so that you don't lose heart, so that you are filled with the oil of the Spirit of God, and especially so that you will have the grace to complete the work of My church. Salt preserves My saints and seasons the unseasoned ones! Therefore, be salt and light in all seasons! Do not fear. I hold you, the earth, and time in My hand. What can you really say you need beside Me? Amen."

Vision of the Ships – Part 1 – September 19, 2021

I see a great ship on the water, a vast body of water. The ship is in a turn toward its port (left) side and the one steering it is the character Joe Biden. This ship is the USA. On the horizon in front of the ship it says, "Liberalism, Totalitarianism, Socialism, Marxism, Communism, Satanism." The crew seems to be doing everything they can to cause this ship to go faster, to turn harder, and to accelerate toward this horizon. As I watch, I can't understand why they desire to go to their own destruction.

Then the Lord speaks. He says, "They are all deceived. They totally believe they are doing the right thing. They cannot even entertain the idea that they are heading to their own destruction."

He continues, "The evil one has been turning this ship toward his goal for centuries, but it did not start out this way. When this ship first set sail, it was heading toward righteousness, holiness, freedom, and true Christianity. But it has slowly been turned the other way. The evil one has been patient, even allowing some turns back toward the good, but then again slowly turning... but now he sees that time is not in his favor, and things must be sped up. And I, the LORD, have increased the headwind working against the ship's progress. My Trumpet has made a great turn against the progress of the evil one, which is why all the stops have been pulled out. The ship itself is suffering damage due to the rough handling and the pushing of it, which is beyond its ability. Even the one at the helm is being pushed beyond his now limited ability.

This ship is one of many vessels. (Each vessel is a country/nation.) All are experiencing the same thing but are at different stages in the turn toward evil. During the slow turn, people put up with a few crazy lefties, but now, seeing this lurch to the left has opened eyes, and it will not be tolerated. The people will be ready when I, the LORD, send a boarding party onto the lead ship. When this happens and My Trumpet plays the Trump Card, it will send the other ships into chaos and fear. They will all experience their own turn back to the right! Amen."

The Lord is showing me that the boarding party has launched their plan to take over this ship (the USA). Things are in place and the assets are ready now. The order has not been given yet, but it is coming soon. Also, it has taken centuries for things to get where they are. The Lord will change things in a moment. It's time to be happy, to look up, to declare His faithfulness!

The boarding party that is to take over control of the ship will not use the regular laws and courts of the states and country. The laws used will be like those used during wartime. The boarding party is Trump & the military. ("Maritime" may be the term for the laws.)

Vision of Jesus with His Armies – September26, 2021

The Lord Jesus said, "Come up here" and as He said it, I (Kirk) was walking with Him in a field of ankle high grass. I was barefoot and wearing a white robe. I could feel the grass as it sometimes went between my toes. I could also smell a smell like what it smells like in springtime, very fresh and refreshing. As Jesus and I walked, He came close to me. I looked up at Him. He looked a lot like the picture that the little girl had painted of Him, very comforting and pleasant. He reached out His left hand as if He wanted to take my hand in His. So, I lifted my right hand and put it in His. As He closed His hand on mine, suddenly everything changed. There were flashes of light and peels of what sounded like thunder. A great wind washed over us. I didn't know what was going on, and yet felt no fear. I was just looking around in amazement.

When I turned my gaze toward Jesus once again, He was huge in size and looked to be made of light. His hair was now white, and His skin tone was lighter too. When He looked down at me, His eyes were a blazing fire with endless depth. His tongue was like a double-edged sword just as it was described in the Scriptures. When He spoke it was like thunder, and what was spoken came in the form of every language of men and of angels and carried infinite meaning, knowledge, and wisdom. I understood that what the Word of God had spoken could be studied for eternity and the full meaning would still not be known.

All this and yet the grip on my hand never changed and as He looked my way, I only felt love. I knew too that the only reason I was standing was because He was holding me up. I felt so small and yet the King was holding my hand! Then I "heard" (not audible) "the King of Kings and the Lord of Lords." I saw movement and looked around again. I saw all of heaven's armies all around us. Angels, huge angels on horseback in full armor riding, looking straight forward, fearless. And I've never seen such an orderly and confident group ever. They didn't look to the left or right and the horses didn't even look like they needed any input from their riders.

I again was feeling rather miniscule and yet I, yes I, was holding the hand of the LORD! I started wondering why. Why was I there? What was I in the presence of the LORD of Heaven and earth and in the middle of Heaven's Armies for?

Suddenly, everything and everyone stopped. Everyone stood still. There was a great silence. I was standing there in awe! How did they all know when to stop exactly? Why did we stop?

Jesus turns toward me, kind of turns still holding my hand, and stands in front of me. The thunder again comes from His mouth. He says, "Son, this is all for you. Tell the people I love them so much, and that they should *not* fear. Don't give up! I see the suffering and I have received the martyrs. Again, do not fear! Those who would save their lives shall lose them, but those who lose their lives for My sake shall live eternally with Me. Vengeance is Mine! I will repay! Justice is not far off as some believe, but it is very near, and is already being carried out. Death and destruction will come, but for those who have stood with Me, they will reap a harvest that few could even dream of. Therefore, stand strong! Do not fear! Rise up and fight! I, the LORD of Hosts am with you!"

Note: The little girl Kirk is referring to who painted Jesus is **Akiane Kramarik.**

Vision of the Ships – Part 2 – October 7, 2021

I see the ships again. Yes, the great ship which is the USA, and the others, great and small. I'm looking at them from some distance. I see that they are still heading toward the horizon on which it is written: Liberalism, Marxism, Communism, Socialism, and Satanism. As I watch, though, I can see that their progress is not the same. Some are still on course and proceeding rapidly toward their own destruction.

For others though, the headwind of the Lord is having a greater effect! These are slowing and the other ships are going around them and passing them. There seems to be some confusion among the captains of the ships because of this. Their skill and leadership, or the lack thereof, is causing friction among those who are followers and crew on the ships. Even some of the true believers (in this evil) are, or have, entertained some doubt, although they can hardly speak of it because of the fear they live under.

I blink, closing my eyes for a second. When I open them, I see spirits – demonic spirits – big and small. Some are seemingly powerful and over all the ships. Some are only controlling one person. Some of the people are completely possessed and others simply bow to the influence of the demons. The spirit of fear seems to be the motivation of all of these under the influence of this evil. All seem concerned only about themselves and trying to gain an advantage for themselves that they think will relieve some of the stress due to fear. I'm amazed at the number and power of the demonic, all based on lies.

Suddenly, the Lord is standing next to me. As we look, He says to me: "Can you see why this is a rescue mission now?" I answer yes, I do. Speaking again, He says: "People have allowed evil to dominate all of the high places in the world. Call it the 7 mountains if you want (Media, Arts & Entertainment, Government, Family, Religion, Economy, and Education.) All of these have been slowly taken over, and each one enhances and supports the other.

This rescue mission is a sovereign move of God, but My Church has not been relieved of its responsibility, power, or authority. My decision to partner with My people has not been rescinded, and in fact says the LORD, I Am pouring out the Latter Rain of the Spirit at this time! Get in the fray My People! Rise up! You still have authority over your enemy! He is under your feet! Join in this battle and pray! Follow My Spirit! Do not shrink back, do not hide, do no fear at all says the LORD of Hosts! Eternal rewards await those who will not bend to the wishes of the enemy, and who will stand in the power of My Spirit says the LORD."

I blink again and I see the ships in complete disarray. The boarding of the USA ship has begun. The USA ship turns to the starboard (right side) and sends the others into chaos.

Even those who have passed the USA ship look back in terror. They know that their end is now certain. They cannot escape the wave which will circle the whole earth. A wave of prosecution for treason, and the terror of that which they feared most will now come upon them. No escape. No escape! And the peoples of the earth REJOICE! Amen.

Vision of the Ships – Part 3 – October 11, 2021

I see the ships again! I see the USA ship nearly turned around. Some of the others are following it. And yes, chaos appears to be the word of the day. But now there is something else in the mix. The headwind of the Lord is howling hard now. The ocean is no longer just rolling swells but is being whipped up into very large waves. Progress toward the horizon of Liberalism, Marxism, Communism, Socialism, and Satanism has been slowed to a snail's pace. The fear of the captains and crew is also raging.

Even as this happens, the fear of the people is much less. Some are facing the loss of their businesses, some are simply put out of work, many, many people are turning to the Lord simply because they have nowhere else to turn. As these people completely lose confidence in a failed system of corrupt politicians, they are awakened from their slumber and realize that they must stand against the old system of bondage and theft.

The young people of the world who have grown up, or are growing up, look around them and realize how the system of kill, steal, destroy has been used against them at every point. Even though the ships are separate vessels, this pattern of waking up begins and as it continues, it cannot be contained by the evil one anymore! His "great reset" has become the Lord's "GREAT RESET" and "GREAT AWAKENING." The bad actors are exposed and the people's desire for justice leaves no room for remorse at their executions. But the Lord has also kindled His love, and as people see the saints and their ability to render justice in all of its severity and yet love, they are amazed and desire this love also.

The outpouring of the Holy Spirit has also come! On every ship people are in need of hope. The saints on each ship are ready to give it! Thousands of "little Christs" turn into millions, turn into... yes, a reformation, yes a reset, yes, yes, yes! This reset extends to the powerless, boring system of religion as well. It is not based on the wisdom of men, but on the power of the Spirit of God. The feckless system of rules, laws, and principles will not be able to hold a candle to the wind of the Holy Spirit of God. Amen.

The Lord Settling the USA and Other Lands –

October 19, 2021

The Lord speaking to me (Kirk) this morning is saying: "Those who oppose Me or oppose what I Am doing will NOT fare well. This will be and is true wherever and whatever I Am doing. When I Am settling a land for Myself or giving a land over to My people, those resisting have not and will not fare well. Such is the case in North America. I brought My people there. I directed them to settle and make the land theirs, just as I have done in the past with My people Israel.

Now, the spiritual forces of evil have come against Me in the Nation which I have brought to life under My Name. Yes, and they now seek to make a mockery of Me, says the Lord God. But I, even I, says the LORD, have always known the end from the beginning! I made a mockery of Satan by defeating him. Yes, My Son came as a Man and ripped his authority from him! A mockery will again be made! But it will not be of Me says the Great I Am!

The United States will again be settled, and I will do it, says the Lord. Man will once more make a mockery of My enemies! Even now My Prophets are at their stations. My watchmen are not fooled by the trickery and lies of their enemies! Right now they are bringing down the strongholds of darkness and raising a standard against them. The cities of government in the East have fallen, and just as the settlers moved from the East to the West, so shall the spiritual forces of heaven move! The spirits over the 7 mountains will be taken down on this move to the West. The ax is right now being laid to the root of the tree!

My watchmen are right now calling out those whom I the Lord have kept hidden! These newly minted Apostles, Prophets, Evangelists, Pastors, and Teachers will bow to Me alone! I have raised them up, and I will keep them!

I, the Lord, will settle things first with Israel and the United States because one of them was called by Me and the other called on Me! After that time, those who opposed Me shall meet Me, and they shall not fare well. All of these shall fall, and the fall will be great. All of the people who love Me and call on Me shall be blessed, however. And this blessing shall be greater than the fall of the wicked. Amen."

Jesus with the Winnowing Fork – October 26, 2021

I see the Lord Jesus with a winnowing fork in His hands. He stands in the grain on His threshing floor. I stand next to His threshing floor looking at Him. He turns to me and says: "Prophet, tell the people that I have been at work and have almost finished threshing this crop of wheat. Tell them, therefore, that they should not hesitate, but decide today whom they will serve. The current churning and blowing of the winds will soon be in the past, and those who have stood the test will be clearly seen.

The wind has swept away the chaff. Yes, My wheat has been stripped of its protection. Everything which has kept it hidden is or will be removed. For My wheat will look to Me alone for its welfare and not any earthly protection anymore. Prophet, tell them that this sifting and winnowing is a violent process, but afterward comes the gathering into the barn. Peace shall again reign and prosperity and generosity shall be the norm. I, the Lord, will be put back on the throne of the people's hearts. Amen."

Trump Administration Takes the Stage Dream –

October 27, 2021

This morning, I (Tiffany) had a dream in which I was standing with others in a room watching a white house briefing on a TV that was hanging on one wall. It was the normal Looney Tunes briefing from the fake administration. Then, a man came up to the microphone and spoke. He said something like, "We are for the Trump Administration and will do everything according to that administration starting today."

The bad guys were initially oblivious because they didn't realize what he was saying. Those of us watching weren't sure we heard correctly. I turned to Kirk and said, "Did I just hear that right?" And he said, "Yes!"

We were so happy! The people were like, what's going on? We were hopeful and not sure. I went outside, and someone said we shouldn't go out, and I said, "I'm going out!" I was excited.

When I went outside, I saw the man who had been speaking on TV was changing the outside of another man's garbage truck. He put the man's photo on the truck instead of the logo that had been there. It seemed that the garbage truck driver was very humbled by what was going on and didn't know what to say.

Interpretation from the Holy Spirit:

Kirk heard and saw...

That's how it will go. Not a shot will be fired. It will be such a bold move, people on the left will be completely clueless. The military surrounds them, walks in, and takes over, except for the meeting room where the left leaders are meeting. Those leaders have nowhere to go. They are completely caught, surrounded. This guy very boldly comes in and says what he says, and they're aghast, waiting for someone to arrest him, but it doesn't happen. They're completely caught off-guard.

Fear says, "Don't go out there," but I say, "I'm going!" What I see outside is that Trump will elevate the American workers, so they're proud of what they do again. Right now, they're being assaulted with injections, masks, distancing, and all kinds of baloney. They won't be assaulted anymore. They'll be lifted up as workers. We'll be proud to be American once again. And what the Lord said previously is true: those who are His will be known for their work ethic, commitment to Him, and generosity!

Halloween Will be a Dud – October 29, 2021

The Lord of all says: Halloween will be a dud in the spiritual realm this year, as well as in the natural realm. I have instructed My prophets and those apostles who have a prophet to take down the powers and authorities in the demonic realm. They are doing what they have been instructed to do, and some of the high places of evil have already fallen.

Note: Halloween was a definite dud where we could observe it. There was not the participation on the normal levels, and we didn't even find one smashed pumpkin in the streets or anywhere else afterwards!

Look Up! – October 30, 2021

"Kirk, I have begun something that is unprecedented on the earth. My Holy Prophets have been speaking of this event which they have seen in the future. It will live up to everything they are saying and seeing! Although, few of them can see the scale of the work which I, the Lord, will do and have already started.

Prophet, from here on, show the people this event, not from a local, regional, or even from the view of a particular country. Israel, yes; United States, yes, but I say this move will be exceedingly more than even the Prophets are seeing right now! Open your eyes, My People! I want to show you what My heart is set on! Where My love is being poured out! Stop that small thinking that you have been taught. Look at ME! I AM the great I AM! Lift up your eyes! I said Lift Up Your Eyes! What has being downcast ever gotten you? NOTHING! says the Lord of all.

All of you have been chosen to live in this time, a time others have only dreamed of. But I have chosen YOU! Therefore, build yourself up in your faith. Use the authority I have given you. Heal the sick. Raise the dead. I AM the Lord and I have said that you will do greater things than I did on the earth. Yes! Bring GLORY to the Father. That is My desire for you, all of you, everyone! My Spirit will be poured out. Will He find those who are willing and, yes, ready to carry Him?

Look in the Scriptures and see what those who followed My voice have done. And these, during a time when only a few carried My Spirit. These exploits are merely a down payment on what is to come. When I say My Spirit will be poured out in POWER, what do you think I mean? LOOK UP! Amen."

Discern the Time of the Lord's Visitation –

November 6, 2021 & April 3, 2019

Word Given to us April 3, 2019 ...

As He (Jesus) approached Jerusalem and saw the city, He wept over it and said, "If you, even you, had only known on this day what would bring you peace – but now it is hidden from your eyes. The days will come on you when your enemies will build an embankment against you and encircle you on every side. They will dash you to the ground, you and the children within your walls. They will not leave one stone on another, because you did not recognize the time of God's coming on you." (Luke 19:41 TNIV)

The Lord is saying that we need to "see" what would bring us peace. If we are not open to looking and simply move on, it will be hidden from our eyes. He doesn't leave the opportunity for change open forever. The Jews in Jerusalem were called white-washed tombs – looking clean on the outside but filled with filth on the inside. Religion covers up its faults, and the religious live their lives as a facade of goodness, holiness, and redemption in Christ. We must examine ourselves by the Holy Spirit and eject the strongholds that we have allowed to remain in us. We cannot "settle." This work must be accomplished! It cannot be said of us that "we did not recognize the time of God coming on us!" Or if we do settle, truly it will be said of us that our fate is the same as the Holy City, with not one stone left upon another.

Now, we can see that Jerusalem was blinded by religion and pride. This need not be so for us. We have the ability

140

in the Spirit of Christ to humble ourselves before the One who knows us completely, confess our mistakes, wrong-headed beliefs, pride, and be completely FREE! In fact, this is not a choice. It <u>must</u> happen. Remember to love in this process! Be considerate, defer to the Holy One!

Word Given November 6, 2021 ...

The Lord is speaking to His Church today and He is referencing the word given on April 3, 2019 (above). He is saying that the time is now to recognize the time of His visitation, to "see" the work He has been doing, to come alongside Him and work with Him. No more will He tolerate the religious and the facade of following. He is looking for those who follow in Spirit and Truth. He created the heavens and the earth in 6 days and rested on the 7th, and He is expecting us to follow His lead. "Working" for Him one day a week and living for yourself 6 days will no longer work.

This isn't to say He's advocating a religious duty of taking a day off a week, but He's showing how absurd it is to think we can "work" once a week for Him. As the Scripture says, *But Jesus answered them, "My Father is always working and so am I"* [John 5:17 NLT]. And in Hebrews 4:7-10 it is told us that Jesus is our Sabbath rest and we enter in by believing Him, His words, and works.

... again He designates a certain day, saying in David, "Today," after such a long time, as it has been said: "Today, if you will hear His voice, Do not harden your hearts." For if Joshua had given them rest, then He would not afterward have spoken of another day. There remains therefore a rest for the people of God. For he who has entered His rest has himself also ceased from his works as God did from His.

141

Therefore, as we enter into the works of Christ, we cease from striving with our own works.

His church will be in His image and likeness, or it will not be His church. His church will differentiate itself by moving in power because He cannot be separated from his power. Where His presence is, His glory will be. Where His glory is, power will be present. Even now those who are part of His church know who they are. These are the ones who are dissatisfied with the institutional church.

"They desire more, and I will provide the more they desire, says the Lord! Power! Yes, Power! As My Spirit is poured out during this time and the time of the Apostles and the House Churches come, Power will force people to decide whether they are for Me or against Me says the Lord! Amen."

The End Times Harvest – Billion Youth – Part One – November 12, 2021

"A billion youth? Yes, a billion, and more than that! Prophet, tell the people of the world to lift up their eyes. Yes, look up and see! You who have eyes to see, look forward in time. Look beyond the current news, beyond the fit of rage your enemy is throwing, beyond your needs for today and wants of tomorrow. Look beyond the temporal.

Can you see the Winds of Change Angel blowing up a great wave? Yes, he is blowing the lid off from all the lies, corruption, and incompetence. But look! Even the church is being implicated in the deception of what is called 'today'! Can you see the wave forming now? Can you see My Church getting behind this wave? Do you see newly minted Apostles, Prophets, Evangelists, Pastors, and Teachers getting ready to take their places in the coming time of the wave? Yes, look with Me! Past the short time of crisis and to the End Times Harvest that is coming! A billion youth? Yes! And more than that!

You older ones! Yes, you who are called as Joshua's, get ready to get behind this wave! Finance it, raise up the younger ones. Help it. Just don't get in the way as it starts because if you do, you will be bowled over by the wave!

These youth who are forming the wave have seen it all. They have seen the governments lie, cheat, and steal. They have seen the church that claims to have power but doesn't. They have seen the super-rich lord it over the people. They have witnessed the emptiness of immorality, drugs, and the pursuit of 'happiness' in the world. They seek the Truth, and they shall find Him, says the Lord of all. And when they do, they shall be given the faith of God, not simply faith in God, but the faith of God! The faith of God does not know the words 'if' or 'maybe.' It only sees what it believes as DONE. Therefore, these youth shall be fearless. If one falls, the others will simply raise him up! These will be unstoppable! Amen, says the Lord of all."

The End Times Harvest – Billion Youth – Part Two – November 18, 2021

"I'm coming back for a pure bride. This remnant that shall come out of this severe testing, they are the ones to train the billion plus youth to follow Me. They will be making disciples of Me. The difference between real disciples and disciples in name only will be astounding. My remnant will not be fooled. They will know who is truly following Me and who is not. This end times harvest will be the greatest in every way – scope, number, intensity, and purity. That is who I'm coming back for."

"Why do the people plot in vain and the kings of the earth take their stand against the Lord and against His anointed?" (Psalm 2:1-2) It is a vain thing to fight against the Lord. The enemy's attacks are useless. The Lord shall have His way. He never loses and never even has thoughts of it.

Fill the earth and subdue it is still the command of the LORD – meaning, make disciples and bring the Kingdom of Heaven into all the mountains of influence in the world. The authority is ours in Christ Jesus. Take down the strongholds and lift up the Name of Jesus! Our God is for us. We cannot fail! Let His love compel you! Amen.

All Joy Instead of Fear – November 16, 2021

The Lord is showing me (Kirk) that fear is rampant on the earth right now despite all the warnings that He has given regarding it.

I see things coming that will cause more fear on the earth. In the short term there will be violence, shortages, and change. There will be things that you have held onto as truth that are not. There will also be people, leaders great and small, near you, and also those far removed from you, whom you have believed in that have deceived you.

Believers, yes you who are Spirit-filled, you who know the Truth, you will ALSO come to know that things are not as you have believed! You have taken in things from your education, your culture, yes there are lies hidden right under your nose! The Lord is showing me that our enemy has been spreading deception for a very long time, and some of it will be difficult for us to receive, and fear could take hold.

Saints, we cannot allow that to happen! Fear is the primary method our enemy uses to control. We may fear going outside without a mask on our face. We may fear a sickness excessively so that fear makes unwise and foolish decisions seem prudent. We may be masking fear in our lives by believing that it is wisdom or that protecting ourselves is simply the smart thing to do.

Fear also manifests itself in our life of serving Jesus Christ. Fear of praying for healing because we might look foolish if the person isn't healed. Or fear of giving a word of knowledge or a word of wisdom because maybe it won't be a "hit." Anxiety about money or food or whatever so that we hoard things for ourselves. Even fear about listening to the Lord's voice. I mean, what if He asks us to do something we don't want to do? Fear about lifting our hands in praise. Fear of what others might think of us for not getting the jab, etc.

The Lord is saying, get rid of this fear! Resist the devil and he will flee from you. Look at the Son of God. He is our example! He did not base His decisions on fear, but instead followed the Holy Spirit, doing what He saw the Father doing, or speaking what the Father was speaking. The Scriptures say that *God has not given us a spirit of fear, but of power, love, and a sound mind*.

So, being that this spirit is not from God, why would we entertain thoughts of fear or make choices based on fear? We are seated in the heavenlies with Jesus with everything under our feet, including fear! We have authority to kick fear to the curb! Let's do it! There is never a shortage of things to be in fear about. In the coming days, the very foundations of our lives are going to be shaken. Prepare now, and practice looking only at the Way, the Truth, and the Life (Jesus)! Faith in Him will make the coming changes a walk in the park, all joy for those who are "in Christ." Amen.

Everything Changing and White House Imposters Leaving – November 23, 2021

"We're nearing the end of the imposters in the White House," says the LORD. "You will see more of the trickle of justice coming out. The cabal will even throw some of their own under the bus to entertain and distract now. This will buy them the time they need to plan their next move. But their demise has begun, and the cascade effect has started already.

At first, it was barely perceptible. Now, it is being seen openly by those who have eyes to see. Soon, the entire planet will be witness to the 'greatest show on earth' as the covering is blown off by the Winds of Change Angel. I have said that the ax has been laid to the root of the tree, but now I'm asking those who have eyes to see to again open them up and look. Again, discard your worldview and your training in your culture, your education, etc., for a time. Come to Me and truly see. Come to Me and hear!

The industries, banking systems, manufacturing systems, distribution systems, education, entertainment, and virtually everything you have gotten used to or depended upon are about to change. Your very life, the way you think of others, the way you see other races and ethnicities, other nations and countries, is about to change. Your view of health and healthcare, processed food, cosmetics, and even exercise will all change. Now is the time to open your heart to embrace change, says the Lord! Those who will not embrace change will be marginalized, or worse, left behind during this time.

My church will undergo the most radical change of its entire history, and it shall be the most glorious time for those who are ready. Their hearts shall sing the praises of the Lord! But for the religious, this shall be a time of either repentance and coming to the Lord, or a time of stubbornness and hardening of the heart. Fear shall then be their companion.

My people! Again, I say, do NOT fear! For I, even I, the Lord of all, Am behind these changes. Come and cross over to the Promised Land with Me. I love you so much, and I will not lead you astray. Patience! Yes, you will need patience. Look to Me. I have given you a measure of faith. It is enough! Amen."

Recovery Happening During Latter Part of Shaking –

November 30, 2021

Today the Lord is speaking about the recovery that will be happening during the latter part of the shaking and beyond. He is showing us that by this time the people's faith and patience will have worn thin, and fear will be prevalent that the current conditions we're experiencing now will continue and keep getting worse.

"People will be weary of listening to the prophets and entertain distrust. The institutional church will continue its slide to the left (world). Many will be looking for the 'Spirit and Life' that comes from the Spirit of the Living God. The house church will be where He will be found at this time, and the time of the Apostle will come.

The fivefold ministers will also rise up and come out from under the places that I have been keeping them hidden. The Apostles and Prophets will be calling them out in great numbers at this time, and My joy shall be very great, says the Lord!

This then shall be the change regarding My church that I have spoken about. When you see many people going from 'church' to 'church' looking for the solid Rock, you will know this time has begun. Have patience then! Depend on Me! I <u>have</u> given you faith to weather this time of shaking and restlessness that I Am using to separate both the wheat and tares and also My wheat and the chaff, as I have already detailed to you.

At this time, My Spirit will once again be poured out, and those who have stood, those who are believing still, will be

My targets for this outpouring. Those who can be trusted with real power and real authority! They will then, in turn, <u>pour</u> My Spirit out on those who will come to them, but especially the fivefold ministers (will be pouring out the Spirit on those who come).

This is what My Saints of old have looked forward to. It is this move of the GREAT I AM that they desired to be a part of. And it is this move of the Spirit that the angels in heaven have been speaking to each other about in wonderment. Do NOT be discouraged My people. Look, you can start to 'see' the beginning of this time already! Amen."

The Medical System – December 2, 2021

The Lord is speaking to me (Kirk) regarding the medical system on the earth. He is showing me that in the future there will be a much smaller medical/health care industry. The large institutional health care monopolies will be replaced by much smaller and much more personal services. Pharmaceutical companies will go out of business. All of the big medical institutional corporations will be broken up or go out of business. There will be change on a scale that no one who is used to the current system(s) would believe!

The reason for these changes is <u>trust</u>. After the public begins to understand that they have been lied to, made to take poison, and had procedures done to them, <u>not</u> for their benefit and certainly not for the betterment of their health, but purely for the bottom line of these corporations, they will have nothing to do with the current system!

During the time of correction in the healthcare industry, the Holy Spirit will also have been poured out. Healing by the Spirit of God will become essential and trusted. The love, mercy, miracles, and healings will be normalized during this period. People from every walk, creed, color, economic means, and from everywhere in the world will come to depend on the Great Physician. The Lord is saying that this dependence will be out of necessity. There will be a great reduction in the number of doctors, nurses, and all medical staff available to help people.

As this rolls out, there will be an increase in the lifespan of the people of the world. Healthy food choices will not only be available, healthy eating will become normal. Chemicals and additives will be replaced with alternatives that increase health and benefit the people as well as the producer of the product. Laziness will not only be frowned upon but also be very rare. The Lord will give grace to those who love Him! Work will be seen as good and enjoyable for those who have followed the Holy Spirit. He will lead them into the destiny that the Lord had planned for eternity.

The Lord is also showing me that there will be training/ schools that will train people in how to take care of their bodies. Diet, vitamins, minerals, etc. will be the "go to" for health instead of the drugs that are so popular now. We will learn that even some of the most benign drugs that we have used were in fact very bad for us. We will also find out that the healthcare industry has hidden or held back some of the cheapest and best treatments as well. The Lord is blowing the lid off all the deception. The truth will be seen. Amen.

It's Almost Over! – December 9, 2021

"It's almost over, My people! Keep the faith, therefore! With all boldness proclaim the truth to whoever will listen. You are on the winning side. Where is your joy? By now you are certainly seeing your foe falling, day by day, falling. The lies are being exposed by the minute and your foes are now eating their own, yes throwing each other under the bus! Now is the time to rise up and stand. Yes, stand and declare the works of the Lord!

There may be chaos and some attempts to gin up fear once again as the evil is snuffed out, but it will not work. The people have seen this play before and now scoff at the attempts to cow them into foolishness again. Full on panic will be the plight of the liars and charlatans now as they realize that they are nearly out of options.

Are you, My people, ready to take your place in the world and stand for what is right? Yes, you will be required to actually <u>do something</u>! I, the LORD, am on a rescue mission, that is true, but good must take the place of evil. This is no time to shrink back. I take no pleasure in cowards or sluggards! I will play My Trump card very soon. Are you ready? Come and join Me in this great victory! I love you, My people, and I Am providing a great opportunity for you to take back the world system in the name of the Lord. Amen."

Vision of House Churches – Apostles and Nodes –

December 14, 2021

The Lord is showing me what the "church," His church, the Bride of Christ, will be like. I saw that the Bride of Christ will mainly be made up of house churches. There may be a few churches that actually have a building that is set aside as a church building, but these will be very few in number.

The house churches will require a great number of fivefold ministers. They will be very great in number. Apostles and their Prophets will be given a number of these churches which they will preside over, and there will also be some Apostles with their Prophets who will be over other Apostles. This arrangement will be set up in the same fashion as a Network. It will have connections like a web and nodes at the places where the connections come together. For example, an Apostle may have a "node" with his twelve churches, another's "node" will have five churches, etc. There will be an Apostle over the two apostles and their nodes, and on and on.

The Lord will cause each "node" to specialize in a particular facet of the Gospel, like mission work or evangelism, healing, the prophetic, etc. So, if training were needed in one of those areas, a person could simply be sent to the proper Apostle's node to be trained in that area.

The Lord will require that each Apostle is paired with a Prophet and together they will, with the other Apostles and Prophets, pull in the same direction as directed by the Spirit of God. There will be no competition for congregants, power, or resources, because the Spirit of the Lord will lead them and direct them to the Truth.

Also, the different ministers in the fivefold will not be paid positions. They will be "part time" in nature due to the size of the house churches and the number of house churches that could be easily handled in a "part time" way. There will be a few who actually are full time in the Apostle's Apostle position who may be paid, and they will be the servant of all they are over and will be called to this position by Jesus Christ Himself.

How Much Worse Will It Get? – December 16, 2021

How much worse will it get? It seems that people keep asking if things will continue to get worse. Others claim to know that it will keep getting worse on the earth. The Lord has asked me to write a word on this. I was led to read Matthew 24 and 25. Matthew 24:4-14 NASB reads,

"See to it that no one misleads you. For many will come in My name, saying, 'I am the Christ,' and will mislead many. You will be hearing of wars and rumors of wars. See that you are not frightened, for those things must take place, but that is not yet the end. For nation will rise against nation, and kingdom against kingdom, and in various places there will be famines and earthquakes. But all these things are merely the beginning of birth pangs. Then they will deliver you to tribulation, and will kill you, and you will be hated by all nations because of My name. At that time, many will fall away and betray one another and hate one another. Many false prophets will arise and will mislead

many. Because lawlessness is increased, most people's love will grow cold. But the one who endures to the end, he will be saved. The gospel of the Kingdom shall be preached in the whole world as a testimony to the nations, and then the end will come."

And then I heard to read 1 Timothy 3. The first few verses stood out.

But realize this, that in the last days difficult times will come. For men will be lovers of self, lovers of money, boastful, arrogant, revilers, disobedient to parents, ungrateful, unholy, unloving, irreconcilable, malicious gossips, without self-control, brutal, haters of good, treacherous, reckless, conceited, lovers of pleasure rather than lovers of God, holding to a form of godliness, although they have denied its power. Avoid such men as these. (verses 1-5)

So then after reading these verses, I asked what He wanted to say about them. The Lord then asked which of these things is not happening right now? I said that I thought all of the things that I read about were happening right now.

He said: "That's correct. Could you really say to the Coptic Christians, the Chinese Christians, or the Christians living in Pakistan or many other places on the earth that things were going to get much, much worse? Worse than mass beheadings, burning alive, drowning, etc.? Could you say child sacrifice is going to get much, much worse? (There were 40,892,880 abortions this year in the world so far on December 16, 2021 at 6:40 p.m.) Could you say that those who control the world economy, the nations of the world, really the world itself will get much, much worse? Even though they are under Satan himself, and as such endorse any and all kinds of sin, some we have never heard of yet!

There are other things we could talk about, things that are so foolish regarding sex, sports, health, and the welfare system, arts & entertainment. Is there anything, including the so-called church that isn't broken and corrupt?"

The Lord has said that He is on a rescue mission and that things would *never* get this bad again. We believe it! Corruption will be exposed. Evil will be punished because justice is His foundation of His throne! Amen.

Wisdom – Don't Call Prophets False –

December 28, 2021

*D*o you not know that you are a temple of God and that the Spirit of God dwells in you? If any man destroys the temple of God, God will destroy him, for the temple of God is holy and that is what you are. Let no man deceive himself. If any man among you thinks that he is wise in this age, he must become foolish, so that he may become wise. For the wisdom of this world is foolishness before God. For it is written, "He is the ONE who catches the wise in their craftiness" and again "The Lord knows the reasonings of the wise, that they are useless." So then let no one boast in men. For all things belong to you, whether Paul or Apollos or Cephas or the world or life or death or things present or things to come; all things belong to you, and you belong to Christ; and Christ belongs to God.* (1 Corinthians 3:16-23 NASB)

In asking the Lord about these verses, wondering what He would like to say about them, He asks, "What is called holy in these verses?"

I answer, "We are because we are the temple of God."

The Lord responds, "You are correct. Now can you see what the Spirit is saying here? I tell you that the wise of this age truly believe that it is their job, yes that they are doing the work of God, to tear down the temple of God! They study and study the words on a page. They even dare to tell God which version of the Scriptures He is allowed to speak through. They declare themselves to be wise and have no humility nor regard for My servants. I the Lord say, 'Study this you who would be wise!' For what do the Scriptures say? You <u>must</u> become foolish so that you may become wise! Will I not destroy those who destroy My temple?

Therefore, do not deceive yourselves you who desire wisdom. Humble yourselves and come to Me. A spirit of pride has come upon you and hardens your heart to the Truth, and no love is on your lips for those who are the very temple of the Lord. Your cries of 'false prophet' or 'false teacher' are falling on deaf ears because your words have no power. My words are always words of love, even when I speak of destruction, because I AM is love and cannot be something different. I will not let the abuse of those I love go unpunished. Amen."

2022

Winds of Change Uncovering Evil & Coming Judgment

– January 4, 2022

"Do you see what the Winds of Change Angel is uncovering? Is there a conspiracy theory you can think of which has not been uncovered and is now recognized as a conspiracy reality? I need My people to see the facts regarding what happens when men come to think more of themselves than they ought, when money corrupts, and when love has no meaning to those who have been led astray and have completely bought into Satan's plan. These men are the tares. They cannot bow to Me. They know who they now serve and do so willingly and completely. Indeed, these are sold out to the darkness. They will never desire the light. They kill their own with no remorse and have less regard for those who are against them.

This is the 'world system' then. Innocent life, babies, the old, different races, none of these mean anything to them except to use them to express the hate that Satan himself has for Me! They say, 'depopulate!' And I Am will give them what they desire! Their bunkers, provisions, and 'security' are useless, and their names shall soon be forgotten as I snuff out their candles.

Look My People! The endless wars, yes, they were the work of these people in one way or another! The disease and anti-fertility vaccines, again, yes in various ways it was the work of these evil ones. Virtually any way conceivable these have tried to achieve their depopulation agenda! Well, the Winds of Change Angel has more to uncover, and he will, but as those who eagerly desire the Truth, you must open your eyes! And you must learn to stand against this 'world system.'

Have you noticed that My people Israel are and have been warriors? Jeremiah 20:11 (NIV) says, *'But the Lord is with me like a mighty warrior; so my persecutors will stumble and not prevail. They will fail and be thoroughly disgraced; their dishonor will never be forgotten.'*

So, look up! Your redemption is near! Call on your leaders to join in this fight. Donald Trump, listen to the Lord! Or else I will raise up another! I, the LORD, have already won. Join Me in this fight and taste My victory! Amen!"

The Lunatic says Dennis Dream – January 5, 2022

I (Tiffany) dreamed Jill Biden dropped Joe off somewhere by himself. I was there, and so were some other people. He slipped in his speech and said Jill's real name, and I said, "Who?" And then he said it again, and I said, "Who are you? You're not Joe, are you?" "No," he said. Then he said his name was Dennis or something similar to that. He went on to say that "Jill" would be so mad he had told who they were.

When his handlers picked him up, we laughed and said, "Bye, Denny," and Joe was in his jammies and acting like a bumbling idiot. We felt slightly sorry for him, but I felt that perhaps the actor would be or could be saved.

Interpretation from the Holy Spirit:

The dream is real, but not all the details. The bumbler is going to give himself away publicly. The mainstream media will be scrambling to try to fix what he said.

Angels in the War Room Vision – January 11, 2022

The Lord calls to me (Kirk), "Come up here!" I ask where Lord? He answers, "The Courts of Heaven." So, I went. I met Jesus in the main hallway of the court. No one was there, just us. He greeted me and started to walk. I couldn't stand it, and asked if I could hug Him? He said, "Of course!" I told Him that I just loved Him so much, and He said the same thing back to me. Then He said, "Come," and we walked toward the raised area where judgment would take place, by the big ornate chair with the other chairs on either side, etc.

He walked past all of this and went through a doorway into a hall that perhaps four people could walk abreast down (it was that size). We walked what seemed like quite a long way then made a right turn into a large room. The room was REALLY busy! The Lord motioned for me to keep following Him, and so we walked up a narrow stairway. It looked like there were many of those stairways leading to an observation area that you could walk around and observe what was going on below.

The Lord stopped and we looked over the edge of this observation area. He pointed down below us and said that this area was called the "War Room," and the angels received instruction there about what they were to do. As I looked, it looked three-dimensional. I asked what they were currently doing? The Lord said that they were watching current events on the earth, and that they would watch these as they also went into the future.

Then He asked, "Did you ever wonder how the angels placed themselves at just the right spot at just the right time?" I answered that I guess I hadn't thought about that before. Then He said, "Yes, this 'war room' area is for the wars, and mainly for the warring angels."

He again began to walk further down this observation area as I followed. Again, He stopped, and we looked below. The Lord said, "This area is dedicated to the saints on earth. Here the angels learn when and where to interact with My people. They are also instructed as to what form to take. But they also have a certain freedom in those matters. For instance, all of the angels who interact with My saints must know how to handle the will of the saints, how to handle changes in decisions which are made, how much pressure to apply to get one to change his or her mind, etc. In this, the angels are masters and know just what to do, and also follow the slightest nudge from My Spirit."

I then asked, "So how much of the future is available to them?" The Lord said, "All history and all I desire to happen on earth is available to them, but the Father has reserved some things for Himself." Then He continued... "For instance, the day of My return is reserved." Then I was back in my chair praying.

God Has Not Changed His Mind – January 18, 2022

"Kirk, tell the people that the LORD has not changed His mind! I have chosen 45, My Trumpet, to do a task. I have brought him up and enabled him. He is My servant, and I will deal with him. James 4:12 says, *'There is only one Lawgiver and Judge, the One who is able to save and to destroy, but who are you who judge your neighbor?'* (NASB) I have warned him to do the task for which I have also raised him up, and he will do it!

I will not allow the 'world system' to continue, so yes, I AM on a rescue mission. The tares who have risen up in arrogance and deliberately work against Me, knowing that they serve the evil one shall not escape My wrath, neither in this world or the next. Their fate is sealed and their downfall sure!

Neither have I changed My mind regarding My chosen ones, those who stand, who give up family, wealth, ease of living, those who boldly protest in My name, those who encourage and strengthen and feed those who are mine, the Prophets and Apostles who remain standing! I, even I, see you! And your blessing is as sure as the recompense of the evil ones!

I have not changed My mind on the system of 'health care' either! I see the meetings in the plush high rises! I know your motives and that you dispense poison in the name of healthcare! I see the industry of Pharmakia and those who enrich themselves, leaders, scientists, doctors, hospitals. Yes, I see all of you! You will not escape unscathed!

And all of you in politics! Yes, you! You who can do nothing but evil in My sight, your fall will be great, unequaled on the earth. Big and small. From the policeman who obeys evil commands to the military who does the same to the community government up to the presidents of countries! None of you will escape.

Are you one of the wealthy ones? I see you too! Oh, you've made preparations for your survival in case things don't work out? I, the LORD declare here and now, those preparations will fail, and they will enrich My people! So be it, says the Lord of Hosts."

Trump Chosen as World Leader Dream –

January 18, 2022

I (Tiffany) dreamed that some other people (I think all females) and I were in D.C. or possibly Canada for Trump for some reason. We were in his group, and he was there too. He knew we were with him and told someone named "Ellie" to help us find where to put our luggage. I was wearing a patriotic dress. The Canadian woman behind the counter made a comment to the Japanese man who had immigrated to Canada and was also working behind the counter about Japan taking over the world. He said something like, "Bring it on, I'm ready!" He acted like he was joking, but I believe he was serious. I didn't want to check my bags in for the sake of privacy, but I decided to keep my purse and check my three bags in.

Interpretation from the Holy Spirit:

The Lord says that some will want to say they could do it – they could lead the world – they could do it better than Trump (Japan taking over the world comment). But they won't be able to. Trump is the Lord's Chosen. He will be a WORLD leader when he's back in his rightful place. We must be ready for it. When he says something, the whole world will listen. The media won't drown it out this time.

We, the people, are all in for Trump (the patriotic dress) because he's been chosen by the Lord. Some governments will want to resist him, but their people won't let them. Trump can incite civil wars just by speaking, and they know it. He wouldn't hesitate to do it either because he's with the Lord, and he wants to free the world of evil.

Devil Desired Inclusion – January 20, 2022

*T*he Lord God commanded the man, saying, "From any tree of the garden you may eat freely; but from the tree of the Knowledge of Good and Evil, you shall not eat, for in the day that you eat from it you will surely die." (Genesis 2:16-17 NASB)

The Lord is saying, "Any creature that I have ever made, which has a free will, desires to be included. Included in love, included in decision making, included as a part of their particular society or group. I have never made any creature in heaven or on earth, which has a free will, that desires loneliness, to be separated, or not to be included.

Therefore, the deceiver has also been created with this desire, and in Heaven was included in virtually everything. Virtually everything. And because of this desire to be included in everything, this desire became pride, and his pride exceeded every other thing in his mind until it overwhelmed gratitude, love, thankfulness, and nothing would do unless he was equal with Me.

Now Satan has been excluded and desires revenge, and that every other creature in heaven and on earth agree with him and be <u>included</u> with him in his <u>exclusion</u>, both to satisfy his revenge and the desire to be included. He perverts the truth and then entices others into his perversion. In all of this, he uses the desire of every creature who can choose to be included against them. Then he recruits the ones who are deceived to gather more to his lies. And again, to use an inflated vision of self to create the lure to inclusion, to pleasure, to knowledge, to power, and always to embarrass God, and <u>include</u> more and more in this delusion."

Spirit of Life Brings Health – January 25, 2022

"If Christ is in you, though the body is dead because of sin, yet the spirit is alive because of righteousness. But if the Spirit of Him who raised Jesus from the dead dwells in you, He who raised Christ Jesus from the dead will also give life to your mortal bodies through the Spirit who dwells in you. (Romans 8:10-11 NASB)

This is what the Spirit wants to say about these verses. Yes, the body is subject to sin and death. Sickness and every other kind of infirmity affect it. But through all of this, the spirit is kept alive for the righteous!

It is also true that the Spirit of Life brings freedom from sin and death for those who are in Christ Jesus. For when the Spirit of Life dwells in you, He makes divine health available to your mortal body.

"Surely you would not believe that the Spirit of Jesus Christ Himself would neglect to bring healing and health in His wings! Life itself is in My Spirit, says the Lord. He is LIFE and where He is there is life because it cannot be another way. Giving life means defeating death in all of its forms, including sickness, disease, injury, mental issues, and all spiritual issues from our enemy. All it takes to access this is faith. Amen."

The Coming In and the Going Out – February 1, 2022

As I'm taken in the Spirit today, I (Kirk) see people going in and coming out. As I watch over the entire planet, I see this going on. It seems normal to me. People are going to work, shopping, to eat, and for every reason under the sun. As I watch, I see this normality come to a close. Fear grips the earth, and people no longer go about their normal routines. If they venture out, the look of fear is in their eyes. They stay away from others and wear masks.

As I watched, time passed, and again, people began to come out and do normal things in a limited sort of way. Some still wore masks and stayed away. Some didn't. Then, I started to notice anger on the faces of some people. Anger and boldness started to rise up. Then everything came to a standstill, kind of frozen.

As I stared down at the earth, the Lord appeared. I looked at Him, and in my mind, I was puzzling why things had stopped. In a very calm voice, He said, "This is where you are now in history. Now, keep watching. The charade is almost over, but the evil one will not give up easily. My rescue mission is still on, but more of My people needed to be woken up, so My angels are at work even now doing that very thing.

In a very short time, the people will come out without fear. And the Cabal shall be in fear, hiding from the people and justice. Unlike the people's fears, those of the Cabal <u>will</u> come upon them! Yes, the very thing they have feared most, it will come upon them. They will have nowhere to hide. Even the secret places, which they have taken great care to hide, and have been ruthless in doing so, have been, or will be, found out. Then, they will be made to watch as their fortunes are removed from them. And after that comes the justice that is fitting for those who knew what they were doing and getting into, who have left Me and joined with Satan and his servants and cannot, even if they wanted to, come back to Me.

The world will then learn the depth of the depravity it has been under. The history books shall be rewritten, and the truth shall be told to those who desire to learn. But those liars and charlatans who have written all the lies, it shall be that their names shall be removed from every page, every computer, and nobody will even mention their names again out of respect for those who have lost their lives by the hands of these evil ones. Their desire to rule over the earth and their accomplishments erased! No one shall speak of them again. Their names shall be as the scum of the earth that no one wants to think about, says the Lord!

Yes, and the years shall be known (as the prophet [Enlow] declared) Before Trump and After Trump. Amen."

Peaceful Power – Look at Canadian Truckers –

February 12 & 15, 2022

Today the Lord is showing me a peaceful and yet just way of changing the world situation. Like many people, I have come to believe that a massive, violent grassroots uprising would be required to gain justice, and I thought it would happen around the globe.

Today He is showing me something quite different. He says, "Kirk, have you noticed the truckers in Canada?" I answer, "Yes, Lord. What about them?"

He answers, "Peace. Do you see how powerful peace is? My angels have been leading this demonstration of peaceful protest, but don't let its appearance fool you! There is violence! And the violence is more real than any war. Your enemy has suffered VERY GREAT loss and will suffer even more loss! Fear of the government in Canada is virtually gone. Fear about what the military of Canada might do is gone also.

It has also been noticed by most people in Canada that the police are inadequate for the job that they have been asked to do. Even the Cabal has been unable to stir up the usual suspects and cause this to appear violent! And despite attempts to camouflage his running and hiding, the Prime Minister appears to be shaking like a leaf. This has not gone unnoticed by most Canadians, and yes, the whole world. Mr. Trudeau has unwittingly, greatly emboldened the people of the world, and further eroded the power of fear. The carnage in the heavenlies has been very heavy indeed!

Indeed, there is a way out of this! Yes, a peaceful way out! As the enemy is backed into a corner, there will be threats and some violence by the authorities. But the people will know that these desperate attempts to cow people into submission are just powerless and baseless threats coming from feckless and illegitimate leaders of a lost cause. How violent this could get depends on those leaders and the participation of the police and military. But I, the Lord, say that any violence will be worse for those who desire it and carry it out than any nonviolent solution!

Right now, the Cabal is looking to start some kind of distraction, war, or event to take away the attention that is on their failing reset. Escape, jumping ship, disappearing will come next. Close on escape's heels will come justice!

Be bold and do not fear, My people, for I Am is with you and My angels are at work right now! There is a battle raging from one end of the Kingdom to the other, and your enemy, My people, is suffering very great losses. The violence in the heavenlies is unmatched since the dawn of time. Indeed, Satan will never have the resources to wage this scale of warfare again! Look around you! I do not lose! Amen."

Jesus' Righteousness Saves the World –

February 18, 2022

I (Kirk) read Deuteronomy 7, 8, & 9, and then asked the Lord what He wanted me to see in those chapters. He began to show me some of the things that were written there. I saw the way He spoke of His people Israel – that they were not the nation with the most people, but the nation with few people. They were not even necessarily obedient. They complained and did not seem very grateful for the things that the Lord had provided them with. Then in Chapter 9, He told them that they were <u>not</u> to think in their heart that they were taking the land and dispossessing the people of the land because of <u>their</u> righteousness. It was not that at all, but it was the unrighteousness of the indigenous people.

Then the Lord began to speak His thoughts into my mind. I could see as He looked at the peoples of the world, not individual sins, or even the general sin of the nations, it was more like the general obedience or maybe disobedience of the world. Then it was as if He looked over at His Son, Jesus, and I heard the words, "It is finished." I could feel and sense the Father's love for His Son, and the Son's love for the world and every person living there. With the love there was a sadness, and I saw all those who had not made the choice to accept Jesus as their Lord and Savior.

I saw so many who had claimed to be "in Christ" but didn't even know Him. They had taken His name (Christian), but it was in vain. They lived just like the world. There were whole churches, even Mega Churches, where only a remnant actually believed. The leadership of these "churches," only had one concern, and that was the "organization." To grow it, to keep it going, to gain members, what was the money intake this week, build, build, build, keep up appearances at all costs! Serving the Lord by following His Spirit? No – we make decisions based on a board! And of course, the Senior Pastor sits at the head of the board!

As I am considering all this, the voice of the Lord breaks in, "Kirk, I Am judging My Church too! And it will be easier for those of the world to come to Me than it will be for those who have taken My Name deceitfully. It is <u>they</u> who will claim to be <u>righteous</u> and because of their righteousness, the land has been saved! (This is not true.) But as My Spirit is again poured out in the Latter Rain, it will be clear who is truly 'in Christ' and who is not of the Truth."

Then He turns and I see those whose hearts are His and who walk in His grace and favor. He loves these saints so deeply because they have chosen to die to the world, and they only find life in His Son, Jesus Christ. His heart and His desire is for all to find this path to life! These would never claim that it was <u>their</u> righteousness that caused the Lord to find favor with the world, for they have found that true life is found only in Jesus, and if there is righteousness found on the planet, it is only by His work on the cross that has brought it about.

Therefore, people of God, we must choose <u>TODAY.</u> Is it up to us? Can we save humanity from the evil one? Will we become puffed up when the Lord moves upon the land, believing that it was <u>our</u> righteousness that brought it about? Choose TODAY whom you will serve! Amen!

Have Faith for the Greater Things – February 25, 2022

I (Kirk) am speaking to the Lord when He asks me, "Kirk, do you have faith?"

He continues before I reply. "Do you have faith for a vision? For a word from Me? Prophet, do you have faith to prophesy? Well, I, the Lord, say, 'Yes'! You do! But today I Am is calling on you to bring faith for others.

Where is My Church and where are My Disciples? Where are My faithful ones? My eyes go to and fro throughout the earth looking for those who have faith! Do you believe that I Am the God who speaks? Then have <u>faith</u> that you <u>WILL</u> hear Me when you listen for My voice!

Do you believe that I Am the Great Physician? Then in <u>faith</u> step out and lay hands on someone who needs to be healed! I have given gifts by my Spirit. They are available to everyone who has <u>faith</u>! These are the elementary things that those with a <u>measure of faith</u> should be doing!

Yes, today I Am is calling you out, you who profess to have faith. Now is the time to practice this faith that you claim to have! You must first practice and do the elementary things before you can begin to be called into the greater things of the Spirit of God! Come on! Die to yourself and live to Christ! Forget your pride and dignity, and the 'what will my friends think of me' mentality! I Am is calling you higher, calling you into a place where you are doing what Jesus did, and then to the MORE and greater things, to the Glory of God! Die to self. You were never made to live for yourself anyway. Step into real freedom and real faith! Amen."

Actors – March 8, 2022

I (Kirk) have been looking at quite a lot of news lately from all over – my home state of Michigan, the U.S., and the world. Right now, the focus is on Ukraine, of course. My thoughts key in on the "leaders" of the world and their role in the affairs of men. As I was considering these things, the Lord drops into my thoughts "actors." So, at first, I thought of 46 (Biden) because we have been told that he is an actor and not the real person. But I thought I'd continue this in prayer and ask the Lord what He wanted me to know. As I asked, He said that <u>virtually</u> all of those that I had been thinking about were actors. I couldn't imagine that!

He continued ... "Yes, some of those who you suppose to be the elected leaders are really other people. Yes, truly actors! Others are not leaders. They merely act the part but have been compromised through and through. They are acting the part of 'leader,' but they do <u>not</u> lead. They merely follow orders. They would do anything that they were ordered to do – start wars, murder their own people, even go nuclear. They are sold out totally to evil, and they both know it, and actually embrace the evil one, and have decided to follow/obey the devil's minions in their cabal.

Therefore, I, the LORD, Am telling you this, My people, so that you will not mourn the demise of these people who are in leadership and places of power over the nations. I Am also wants you to know that there are those who have <u>not</u> been compromised! There are even those who do My bidding who do not know Me! Therefore, do not give way to fear. I know the end from the beginning. I have NEVER been fooled, never confused, never felt weak. I have <u>never</u> sat wringing My hands in worry, AND I NEVER LOSE!

My <u>Anointed</u> will step forward! The Trump card will be played. And those who deal in fear <u>will</u> become fearful! My justice <u>WILL</u> be served! <u>ALL</u> of this will come into play soon, very soon! So, keep your eyes on My goodness and My promises of the good times to come! Do not bow My People! Do not fear! My Spirit is being poured out on anyone willing to carry Him! Ask for Him. You will not be denied! Amen!"

Snowball Prophecy – March 14 & 15, 2022

The Lord said His Great Reset is like a snowball going down a mountain and it's halfway to the bottom. The last part is where it really picks up speed and mass. We are in this second half.

Now, the Lord is reminding me (Kirk) of the Event Horizon prophecy from June 30, 2021 and the Vision of the Ships from September 19, 2021. When these came, we thought they were "now" words. But the Lord is highlighting them now. He is saying that the snowball is halfway down the mountain; it has picked up some amount of speed and momentum and cannot be stopped now. Yes, you might say that it is beyond the event horizon and cannot be stopped!

He says, "Look at the ships. Can you begin to see the disarray in their formation? Yes, the unity that was apparent in the events the black hats had planned is now falling apart. Some countries forge ahead with the evil agenda, while others are struggling this way and that. Still, others are fully turning to the right. Watch the speed at which this turning IS happening! Momentum 'Big Mo' has changed now, and you will see it. The second half of My Great Reset will happen much faster than the first half. If the first half took 100 years, the second half will take a day. It will be a wild ride, but do not fear! Have I not told you it would be wild? Hold on! The blessings for those who will keep the faith, yes, keep their eyes on Me, shall be even more wild! Amen."

Big Bang Prophecy – March 17, 2022

I hear the Lord say, "Tiffany, the Big Bang is coming. They've propagated a big bang that they know it isn't true, and I'm about to give them a Bang they're not expecting, nor anticipating, in any way. My angels are working in the open and they cannot even see it. Sudden destruction will come upon them and out of the ashes I will create beauty for those who are with Me and who have stood in these most trying times. Gone are the struggles to find Me. My Spirit IS being poured out. He IS here, and things ARE changing. GREAT is the LORD Almighty! Let your prayer be – Welcome, Holy Spirit! You are welcome here – have Your way!

Now, rise up and look with eyes of faith. Cast off criticism and self and look with eyes of faith at every situation and person. What am I saying and doing? Let faith rise up in you! My Son has won! Amen."

It's going to be such a sudden and severe change (big bang), everyone's life will change.

Vision of Lizard in China – March 18, 2022

I (Kirk) saw a giant lizard, or maybe a dragon. It was standing in the South China Sea. Its head was in China and its body was between Vietnam and the Philippines. I saw it thrashing its tail and creating havoc in all the places that the tail could reach. The tail grew very long and affected more and more countries and places on earth. As I watched, I thought, "Who could contain or stop this?"

But after a while, the thrashing seemed to slow, and the lizard/dragon's color began to turn from grey to reddish and then to yellowish. As this happened, the thrashing stopped completely. All of its movements stopped. Then the lizard/ dragon's head seemed to slowly disappear and its whole body was drawn into China, and it disappeared as it was drawn in. After a while, it was no more.

I kept looking at the place where the lizard/dragon had been. Time passed. I kept watching and thought I saw something white in color appearing there. Yes, it was growing in size, but had no form. At first it appeared to be like a teardrop in shape. Then I could make out a bird. A dove! A white dove was covering central China.

Then all of a sudden, the dove spread its wings and completely covered China. It stayed in this position for a time. Then it appeared that the dove's feathers were falling out – that the dove was falling apart! Then I realized that the huge figure of the dove had turned into millions, perhaps billions, of smaller doves. And as I watched, they scattered! All over the globe, to every country and nation! They went everywhere on earth! Then the vision slowly faded from view...

Revelation on the vision...

The lizard is the serpent of old, the devil. He has placed his "head" in China, and from there has been "growing" and expanding his influence. It looks unstoppable. The CCP, which is really the same as socialism, satanism, Marxism, liberalism, totalitarianism, and communism (See vision of the Ships part 1), is where the head is located. But it's all really the same – just called different names.

Just as the vision shows, the dragon will be enraged (turn red), but it's too late, as it's losing power and then turns yellow – sickly – and dies. The grey it started with is because there's no color in hell. It's not life or beauty, but ugly and death and evil. The Great Reset of the LORD doesn't just kill the dragon as it loses influence to the point that it dies, even in China, where the head is, He (the LORD) will bring about the Great Revival there that has already begun, and those who have sown in tears (teardrop shape of the dove) will reap with rejoicing!

The Chinese church WILL have her reward. He's sending in His Great Apostles, Prophets, and Evangelists to help with the equipping and training of the body there and to assist in the revival. The Holy Spirit will be poured out in such GREAT measure that China will never look the same. And they will go out into all the world. Where the enemy wanted to take over, the LORD will take over! Amen.

Artificial Intelligence – April 1, 2022

I (Kirk) asked the Lord about AI after reading a short article about it. I really know almost nothing about it. The idea behind this, as far as I know, however, is to basically create circuitry that can be or is better at making decisions faster than a human brain does. Shortly after that comes the worry that humans will be ruled by these machines. This is what I asked the Lord about.

The Lord replied to my question/observation: "Kirk, there are men who are currently trying to do exactly what you have said. Technology in general has not been used to make men's lives easier, but to enslave them. Time clocks, measures, increased complexity, tracking every movement, cameras – in almost every way possible, and with great distrust of others, these devices have been used to take freedom away rather than to give it."

The Lord says that people are enticed by the promise of ease, quickness, no waiting, and more time away from one's work. To date, these are basically lies. Now we have to take calls and answer messages, video conference, etc. And for others, every step is counted, every movement, and some are even required to bring the physical body's needs and put them under the control of a clock/machine. All of this is done, not to enhance people's lives, but for profit, for efficiency. Social interaction is held to a minimum. Only performing the work before you is tolerated! Now there is a scheme whereby control over people will be accomplished using their money – digital money.

"I Am says this will not stand! The Tower of Babel is again being constructed! The one language is digital. The goal is to ascend to the heavens! To become like GOD! I AM says, NO! I will not allow the Tree of the Knowledge of Good and Evil to cast its fruit! The evil one will again be thwarted! All of these things that have been designed and made for evil shall be walked back and will be used for good! I AM has spoken. Amen."

*W*oe to the shepherds who are destroying and scattering the sheep of My pasture! declares the Lord. Therefore thus says the Lord God of Israel concerning the shepherds who are tending My people: You have scattered My flock and driven them away and have not attended to them; behold, I am about to attend to you for the evil of your deeds, declares the Lord. Then I Myself will gather the remnant of My flock out of the countries where I have driven them and bring them back to their pasture, and they will be fruitful and multiply. I will also raise up shepherds over them and they will tend them; and they will not be afraid any longer, nor be terrified, nor will any be missing, declares the LORD. (Jeremiah 23:1-4 NASB)*

The LORD will once again address the "shepherds," the "pastors," and the "church" administrators.

"Yes, you who claim to be 'called' into the ministry, can you even hear the voice of the Holy Spirit? Did you take the classes, learn from the books (which were written by others who were NOT called) and pay for that diploma so you could be called, 'pastor'? Was your call actually made by the LORD, or did a committee call, and then a board voted maybe? Do you buy your sermons online then? Coordinate with the praise team and production staff? Have they double-checked the smoke machine so you can fake the presence of the Lord? Where then is the LORD? Could anyone tell if He had actually left your 'church'? Maybe your 'church' is a member of one of those denominations who believe that God has changed because now His book is available, so you now have a form of godliness, but deny its power?

I HAVE NOT CHANGED, says the LORD of all! And I AM calling all of the false pastors, elders, deacons, and teachers to repentance today! I have decided to extend My mercy one more time to you! Have you been following Me, or do you follow the devil? Do I fall into fear and call for My church to close its doors? Wear masks? Social distance? Have I said, 'Get the shot for your health'? Do I? I AM is demanding an answer! Today is the day: Repent! Repent! For I, even I Am going to attend to you now because of the evil you have done to My sheep.

But you will say: 'We didn't know,' or, 'We only did what was prudent to do!' I AM says: Your ignorance is no excuse, and your prudence is a mask for fear! Repent! Or prepare to receive what you dread most! Your wisdom is foolishness before Me, and your excuses are smoke in My nostrils! Amen!"

Best of Times / Worst of Times – April 8, 2022

The Lord asks, "Are you the sheep of My pasture or not? Do you not see? This is/will be the best of times for those who are My sheep! Conversely, it will be a time of uncertainty and fear for those who are not Mine. Yes, it will be the worst of times for them because of their lack of faith!

Arise, therefore, My faithful ones! Take your place as the light in a world of darkness! Never fear at all, for I Am is with you. Amen."

A Word for the Nations and the Church –

April 13, 2022

A Word for the **United States**: "Prophet of the Lord, I want the people to know that the Great I AM has not abandoned them, and that there is no Plan B. The words of the prophets shall come to pass. My Trumpet is making his move and there is no other plan. It is My way to snatch victory out of the jaws of defeat! To put My enemies in their place just when they think they have Me! My way is to require faith. Yes, trusting in Me and My ways is a requirement to avoid fear, says the Lord of all. Look at Me, abide in Me, and I in you, and all fear shall dissipate and go!

Watch as the **Russian** leader prevails in **Ukraine**, and the Nazis are defeated. Watch as this IS a victory for good and not evil. Watch as the people of Ukraine benefit, Russia benefits, yes and the entire world benefits from the evil being rooted out there!

Again, take note of what's going on in **China**! That dragon is not being slain from outside forces, but is rotting from within! Yes, the good people of that land are rising up, and they are mighty in Christ Jesus! After a time, no amount of punishment, coercion, or even brute force will keep that dragon alive.

Yes, and watch **Canada** as the Lord is moving there too! Will their leader remain Mr. True, or will he go, asks the Lord of all? He will go! And as the Spirit moves there, and when JT leaves, great fear will run rampant in the remaining leadership as they attempt to gain favor by opening dialogue with the convoy. But this will fail because of the deep distrust of the people!

Take note of **Australia** as well! Will there again be fairness and trust in all the Provinces once again? There will be another try at totalitarianism using technology and strongarm tactics by those who are supposed to keep the peace. This too will fail because of the groundswell of people who will now oppose it. They realize they were duped the first time regarding the jab, masks, distancing, etc. because <u>none</u> of it worked at all.

And watch **Europe**, particularly the **UK**, if any <u>mandates</u> at all are tried there again! Yes, Europe is <u>MORE</u> awake than they have been for a long time! No more just going along to get along!

The Lord is looking for His faithful in every country! This list of countries could be very long indeed! But the remnant, those who are filled with His Spirit, those are the ones He is really interested in. They are His Church! They are the SALT and the LIGHT! These are the ones who will change the world! Amen!"

Rapture – Wheat & Tares Explained – April 15, 2022

*A*nother parable He put forth to them, saying: "The Kingdom of heaven is like a man who sowed good seed in his field; but while men slept, his enemy came and sowed tares among the wheat and went his way. But when the grain had sprouted and produced a crop, then the tares also appeared. So the servants of the owner came and said to him, 'Sir, did you not sow good seed in your field? How then does it have tares?' He said to them, 'An enemy has done this.' The servants said to him, 'Do you want us then *to go and gather them up?' But he said, 'No, lest while you gather up the tares you also uproot the wheat with them. Let both grow together until the harvest, and at the time of harvest I will say to the reapers, 'First gather together the tares and bind them in bundles to burn them, but gather the wheat into my barn.'" (Matthew 13: 24-30)*

Then Jesus sent the multitude away and went into the house. And His disciples came to Him, saying, "Explain to us the parable of the tares of the field." He answered and said to them: "He who sows the good seed is the Son of Man. The field is the world, the good seeds are the sons of the kingdom, but the tares are the sons of the wicked one. The enemy who sowed them is the devil, the harvest is the end of the age, and the reapers are the angels. Therefore as the tares are gathered and burned in the fire, so it will be at the end of this age. The Son of Man will send out His angels, and they will gather out of His kingdom all things that offend, and those who practice lawlessness, and will cast them into the furnace of fire. There will be wailing and gnashing of teeth. Then the righteous will shine forth as the sun in the kingdom of their Father. He who has ears to hear, let him hear!" (Matthew 13:36-43)

This is what the end of the age will look like because God has spoken this parable, and also its interpretation. Pay attention to this then. It is according to Jesus how it <u>will</u> be at the end of the age. This parable and its interpretation form a baseline for what the end of the age will look like.

Take note that Jesus says specifically that the wheat should not be gathered before the tares, and specifically does say that the tares should be gathered by the angels at the end of the age, then the wheat. Other Scriptures regarding "the end of the age" or Jesus' second coming <u>will</u> agree with this. If it is interpreted differently, or a doctrine is formed in opposition to what Jesus <u>clearly</u> taught, it is wrong.

"Pastors" – April 28, 2022

I n this word, the Lord is addressing a specific "pastor" and all "pastors."

The Lord says, "I have called My Ministers into their place in My fivefold ministry. They know without any doubt that they have been called by Me. They walk in authority and power. The Spirit of Christ constantly testifies to their calling. Any challenge to the calling to which I have called them is basically ignored. They know Me, and I testify to their calling, and they feel no need to prove anything.

Their challenge to others is the same as the One who called them. It is this: 'If you don't believe what I say, then at least believe the works that I do.' These works are love itself because I AM Love says the Lord. These works are also impossible for any man to do by himself. Therefore, My ministers minister in the power of the living God, and not in the 'intelligence' or 'wisdom' of men. My calling and My expectation are much higher, yes, MUCH HIGHER than what is possible by mere men!

My Ministers have died, and they are not impressed at all by the things that men prize: money, numbers of followers, size of a church building, men's accolades, etc. But they TREMBLE at the sound of My voice!

Now to those who are imposters! You insolent usurpers who live to debate and argue, who desire to call My true ministers into question! You who call yourself 'pastor,' but your works are the works of men to achieve that which delights men! You who have a piece of paper, but NO power! You who brag about success according to men's standards but have NO works according to the Spirit of Christ! You <u>know</u> who you are. No prophet has ever called you. No apostle has appointed you. And yet you are so insolent and proud of yourself that you believe that you can call for a debate or even have an audience with My ministers?

I say NO! The great I AM says, 'Repent! Repent now!' I AM done with this religious charade, a form of godliness but denying His power. The Spirit without power? How could I allow this to continue? My Spirit with no power? MY SPIRIT WITH NO POWER? Repent or be destroyed!

The end times harvest is beginning, and I will not allow those who give lip service to the power of My Spirit to stand in the way this time. Repent, for the time is at hand, and I will not allow weak cowards to thwart My plans! Amen."

"Pastors" Continued… – April 29, 2022

"Prophet, My fivefold ministers are prized upon the earth for I AM has chosen each one of them. I AM has always had His chosen ministers on the earth, but they are different in these last days. The callings are much higher, and the glory in which they will walk is much higher. Yes, those who will be called into the fivefold in these <u>end times</u> will actually carry that name (End Times Minister).

There are those who actually love Me that have said that I AM has changed, and also that My apostles and prophets have changed – that they no longer carry the same anointing as they did in the Old Covenant or New Testament. This line of thought has come mainly from My Apostle Paul's letters. While he was given authority to give instruction to his churches, to apply these instructions to everyone everywhere is incorrect. The Apostle Paul and those who received these letters already had this understanding and would not need to have this stated. So then, it was common knowledge that God does <u>not</u> change, but that apostles could put in place guidelines for churches to lead them to a place of following the Spirit of Christ. I AM the Lord; I do not change.

Prophet, tell the people that they should expect to see those who are anointed to be in the fivefold ministry according to the example of their Lord, Jesus. Yes, and more than that, for all of My disciples will be endued with power in these last days. For what Jesus has done will be repeated over and over in the last days. Yes, and even what was done at the hands of the Fathers and Prophets of old will be commonplace during the latter rain.

Behold, there will be no place for the powerless cowards and usurpers during this time. For, they will be seen for what they are while they are far off. Amen!"

Vision of the Tree of Life – May 6, 2022

Jesus appears and asks me (Kirk) if there is something I desired? I said that I was hoping for a vision. So, He says, "Yes, come with Me then."

As I walk toward Him, everything changes. I am surrounded by beautiful plant life, walking in low grass, and there are animals all around too. I was concerned by the larger animals – lions, tigers, dogs, bears, and yet they all seemed so calm, and even seemed to get along well together and paid little attention to us. We walked for some time, and not in silence either! But for whatever reason, I don't recall what we talked about.

Jesus is heading right toward a large tree. I didn't have any idea where we were. In the middle of an astonishingly beautiful forest, I guess. As we approach this tree, I notice that there's fruit on it. The fruit looks awesome, bright red in color and rather large, like the size of a grapefruit. It's low hanging and just begs to be picked! Jesus stops before we get there and says, "This is the Tree of the Knowledge of Good and Evil. Don't eat from it." He went on, "Those who eat from this tree will be hungry again, and in fact, will never be satisfied. They will always desire its 'fruit' and chase after it always."

Jesus turned to the right and again started walking. I found myself getting hungry and wanting to eat. Then Jesus turned to me and said, "Just a little farther; hold on for a little longer." So, we kept going. I saw a tree up ahead that He seemed to be heading towards. As we approached this tree, it didn't look as attractive as the Tree of Knowledge. The fruit was smaller and not reachable from the ground. And the tree looked like it would be a bit difficult to climb too! Jesus said, "This is the Tree of Life. If you eat from it, you will never be hungry. Go ahead and eat."

So, with some difficulty, I climbed up until I could reach some of the fruit. It was green and somewhat smaller, like a large apple maybe. I climbed down and took a bite. It was sweet but took a lot of chewing and was hard to swallow at times. As I ate it, I started to feel different, better than I had ever felt! There were no seeds inside, and as I ate, I became pretty full, even though it was rather small when compared to my hunger when I started eating it. I started thinking about just tossing the remaining portion because of the fullness I felt. Right then Jesus said, "You must eat the whole thing for the full effect of the Life which this tree is named for." Amen.

Revelation on the Vision:

To begin with, Kirk follows Jesus. He is seeking Truth, he is seeking the right path, he is seeking whatever it is that God has for him, and that is found by following Jesus. So, Jesus leads him through a beautiful forest. It seems like it could be scary, but it's nice and calm. People who are searching for Truth will find that as they follow the leading of Christ, it can look like it would be scary, but it's really not. All is in order and well with the Lord there.

They come to a tree and for all the world, it looks amazing! The fruit is ripe and big and beautiful. It is easily accessible, but Jesus says don't eat. It won't satisfy. Instead, it leaves one hungering for more and never being satisfied. Why do people eat anyway? They eat to live and to satisfy hunger. The Tree of the Knowledge of Good and Evil looks like it will do that, but it doesn't.

Religion eats from this tree continually but is never satisfied. Ever. Its fruit is easily attainable because they gain it by their own knowledge and understanding. The fruit is enticing because very intelligent people parade their knowledge around and the more you learn, the more degrees you have, the better you look. It looks good to study and to put up guardrails and rules and principles to help you live holy and keep from sinning. All the while, the fruit you're eating never brings life. The endless sermons and serving the institutional church and obeying all the rules of your particular denomination make you feel like you're good because everyone else is doing it too and you think if you do that, then God is happy. It's a lie. It never satisfies and only lulls you into believing you're alive because you keep eating, so you must be alive.

Whereas the Tree of Life looks pale in comparison to the Tree of the Knowledge of Good and Evil. "*For the message of the cross is foolishness to those who are perishing...*" (1 Corinthians 1:18a). The Tree of Life is a stumbling block to Jews and foolishness to the rest of the world (v. 23). And yet, it is the Tree of Life that satisfies.

Jesus is the Way to the Tree of Life. He is the Tree of Life, and He's the Fruit of the Tree of Life. We must eat Him and all of Him! The tree was not easy for Kirk to climb up or down. The fruit was not easy to chew at times and not easy to swallow at times, either. In fact, he was tempted to toss part of the fruit when he felt full. The way of the path of Life is difficult and narrow. It's not walking up to a tree and grabbing some low hanging fruit that goes down easy when you eat it. It's making an effort. It's laying aside what we believe in order to receive what He has to say. *"The kingdom of Heaven suffers violence, and the violent take it by force." (Matthew 11:12)*

It is eating Jesus even when we don't like it. Maybe we don't like what we hear Him telling us to do. Maybe we don't like what He's doing in our lives or the world. It's dying to self so that you can truly live. And in order to have the full effect, you have to eat the whole piece of fruit. Or as we say, you have to partake of the whole Passover lamb and not leave any until morning.

Some people like to settle. They start eating the fruit and decide they've had enough. They tasted the Holy Spirit and that's good enough. They want to maybe feel Him in a worship service or hear "nice" prophetic words, but when it comes to correction from a prophet, or direction from an apostle, or the Holy Spirit tells them they have a stronghold they need to get rid of, then they don't want any more fruit.

Jesus said that His body is true bread and His blood is true drink and if we wanted to live, we need to eat His body and drink His blood. He means He has come in the flesh as a Man, and if we really believe that, we will take EVERYTHING He says and believe it – meaning obey it. We will not pick and choose. He gave His physical body and physical blood for us that we may have life and for that life to have its full effect, we need to eat and drink it all by faith.

So, for example, saying you just want to be saved and that's good enough, you don't need the healing or deliverance or peace He offers means you're not eating His flesh and drinking His blood. You're not eating the whole piece of fruit off the Tree. You're settling.

To say you want people to be "nice" and want the feeling of the Holy Spirit present at your school or your meetings, but you don't want Him to prophesy. You don't want Him to tell you anything difficult to do. You don't want Him to lead you into a desert, etc. means you don't want Him. You're fooling yourself and not only not receiving all that He has for you, but you're rejecting Him when you tell Him "no," especially when you hear Him, know it's Him, and still decide to go your own way.... eating once again from the Tree of the Knowledge of Good and Evil.

But those who love the Lord will do what it takes to follow Him to the Tree of Life, even though they're hungry. They'll do what it takes to climb the tree, grab the fruit, and climb back down. They'll do what it takes to chew the fruit and swallow it, even when it's difficult and they don't want to. They will truly die to self that they may live. They will eat the whole fruit. Amen.

Community – Jesus is the Standard – May 7, 2022

"Did you ever notice that there are various places where there are communities of believers that are very nice? They have low crime, neatly kept communities, and are friendly areas. These encompass whole towns and villages, or even larger areas. These areas are also attractive for unbelievers, and because of the attractiveness, growth in these areas is rapid. People from all over move in, not to become part of the community of believers, but to take advantage of what they have done.

These have no intention of conforming to the standards and beliefs of the community, and in fact, begin a process of change. Change away from the good that they moved into the area for! If this community regards everyone the same: their ideas, their beliefs, and their opinions, then its demise is assured.

Take note of My disciples, the Twelve. I called all of them. They conformed to My likeness. They performed miracles, healings, and signs! When I said that there was one among them who would betray Me, they looked at each other in disbelief because they couldn't imagine that there was one there who would do that! But the point here is that I did call him out, and he was not allowed to change the others! Judas had the same opportunity to believe, but Satan had entered his heart, and he did not reject him."

So, with this in mind, we cannot stop the "others" from moving into our communities, but we must <u>not</u> allow them to set the standards where we, the disciples of Christ, train other disciples! And why would we? Profit? Acceptance? Comfort? NO! WE ARE TO BE DISCIPLES OF JESUS! This must remain first and foremost. Amen.

Note: Jesus is using Judas as an example of allowing evil in and not rejecting it. The evil couldn't be allowed to infiltrate the community of disciples. So, Jesus called Judas out and didn't allow him to continue.

The Jews Ask for Signs & the Greeks Search for Wisdom – May 13, 2022

*F*or the message of the cross is foolishness to those who are perishing, but to us who are being saved it is the power of God. For it is written: "I will destroy the wisdom of the wise, And bring to nothing the understanding of the prudent." Where is the wise? Where is the scribe? Where is the disputer of this age? Has not God made foolish the wisdom of this world? For since, in the wisdom of God, the world through wisdom did not know God, it pleased God *through the foolishness of the message preached to save those who believe. For Jews request a sign, and Greeks seek after wisdom; but we preach Christ crucified, to the Jews a stumbling block and to the Greeks foolishness, but to those who are called, both Jews and Greeks, Christ the power of God and the wisdom of God. Because the foolishness of God is wiser than men, and the weakness of God is stronger than men.*

For you see your calling, brethren, that not many wise according to the flesh, not many mighty, not many noble, are called. But God has chosen the foolish things of the world to put to shame the wise, and God has chosen the weak things of the world to put to shame the things which are mighty; and the base things of the world and the things which are despised God has chosen, and the things which are not, to bring to nothing the things that are, that no flesh should glory in His presence. But of Him you are in Christ Jesus, who became for us wisdom from God – and righteousness and sanctification and redemption – that, as it is written, "He who glories, let him glory in the LORD." (1 Corinthians 1:18-31)

The Lord says: "Will the 'Jews' ever see enough signs so that they might come to faith? I walked among them in My time. I took their bait and healed those who had been invited to the synagogue simply to set Me up. Did they then believe? No. I performed signs and wonders daily, doing things that had never been done before. Did they then believe? No. Therefore, no amount of signs will convince or bring to faith the 'Jews' of your time either!

So then, what about the 'Greeks'? Will their search for wisdom ever end? I, even I, have given them true wisdom, but they did not believe. The 'Greeks'' feeble minds look for reason, knowledge, and a foundation of legalism. They debate and form judgments; they reason that this plus that equals a firm foundation. But no real foundation ever really appears. For one generation finds this 'firm foundation' and then the next tears it down. Real wisdom is never reached.

It should be obvious to the wise, and to the religious by now that the Tree of the Knowledge of Good and Evil is a lure, or a bait, that nothing good can come from. It truly is a black hole that sucks people in and there is no end to it, no real truth, no wisdom. And all the signs that point to its 'value' are false! But the religious, and those who seek after wisdom always think that THEY will be the ones who will find the treasure at the end of the rainbow. Foolishness, all foolishness, says the Lord!

First Corinthians 1:30 (NASB) says, *But by His doing you are in Christ Jesus, who became to us wisdom from God, and righteousness and sanctification, and redemption, so that as it is written, 'LET HIM WHO BOASTS, BOAST IN THE LORD.'*

True wisdom is found nowhere else, and this wisdom is the foundation set forth by Jesus as its cornerstone, and His Apostles and Prophets as the foundation which needs no signs but is found by faith. Amen."

Have Faith! – May 13, 2022

"As I have said: It is My way to snatch victory from the jaws of defeat!

Prophet, tell My people to trust Me! I'm not wringing My hands in worry. Therefore, you should not be wringing yours either! I see what happened in the election in France. I see the inflation. I have My finger on the pulse of this conflict in Ukraine. I see the Cabal at work manufacturing all of the crises. Are these things beginning to have an effect on you? Are you seeing fear ramping up in the world? Do those who have the black lives signs wonder within themselves yet?

Therefore, yes, I AM on a rescue mission. Have <u>Faith</u> because I AM never late, and My timing is ALWAYS perfect, says the Lord! Be of good cheer! Sing praises to the Lord! I have raised each one of you up for a time such as this! Your faith will not falter. Just as My Trumpet will also rise up in faith, and in fact, he is already!

Don't buy into the things of this world, but store up for yourselves true riches! Have faith! Speak faith! Hear only faith! Hold on to the end. It is not far off. Speak to one another about My justice, My generosity, My recompense to the faithful, the REALLY GREAT reset! The day My People will dance in the street, the day those who are against Me will be put to shame! Yes, My People! It is time to get EXCITED! AMEN!"

Truth Abounds More – May 19, 2022

The Lord says, "Have you noticed that when those who have done wrong are accused, if they don't look to Me for help, will respond in half-truths and outright lies? And yet, the Truth always wins because Truth is from Love, and Love never fails.

The lies have increased, rather than decreased. Fear lies. Those who have done wickedly are in fear because the Truth is getting out; it is being revealed. None know this more than My faithful ones, the ones who have stood and kept standing. Yes, prophets and more than that – those who listen to prophets and those who don't know enough to listen but seek Truth and want to know. I help them too. Their understanding is intellectual, but even so, their hearts are being prepped for the seeds of life to be planted.

The lies are abounding, but the Truth is abounding much more. Though the Winds of Change Angel is opposed, he doesn't give up, nor lose. When I want a change, I will bring it about. Therefore, the Winds of Change has been blowing, and will continue to do so until My Great Reset is fully accomplished."

A Word of Encouragement – May 26, 2022

"Look up My people! Look up! Don't give into discouragement now! What are you looking at that causes you to hang your head? Is there some shaking going on? Well, it's just your enemy trying to gin up some fear. Turn from it and look to Me.

Your enemy makes his plans and strategies against you and Me, but I knew about them ten thousand years ago! He works in the dark in deep caves, hidden and secure, and keeps deep secrets which are only known by the most evil and the 'highest' level of the damned! But I already know all of these things and I also know the 'most secret' things that they haven't even thought of yet! In all of eternity, and for all time, Satan has never done anything that I didn't know about before he did it.

Satan now believes he can outwit Me using souped up machines, computers, and artificial intelligence, but I'll simply come along and pull out the plug. This tower of babble will also come to nothing! I do not make plans to counter My enemies! I Am the Lord! I know the end from the beginning. I only have a Plan A because no other plans are needed. <u>EVERYTHING</u> will turn out according to My desire. There is no other choice.

Trust in Me, then. Is there another choice? I Am the Lord of all, the Name above all names that can be named, and I hold everything that I have created together by the Word of My power. There is no one and nothing higher than Me. I don't have a rival, or even a challenge or challenger. Nothing can compare to Me. I have asked, 'Will I find faith on the earth when I return?' And yet anyone can say, 'Yes, I have faith!' But I, the Lord, say that both love and faith need testing to find their worth!

Those who believe that they will simply 'fly away' when the trouble starts should 'see' by now that this isn't the case. Persecution and tribulation are <u>promised</u> to those that believe! Why is this unclear? Can they not see that there is already tribulation on the earth? Therefore, <u>turn</u> and be My Church! Come out from your hiding and turn and help your brothers and sisters in Christ! Can you not see the martyrs, the persecuted, and the poor in My House? Hiding out and waiting is <u>not</u> a strategy that comes from Me.

Finally, My People! I have given many, many 'words' to the Prophets regarding what I Am doing, the prosperity that is coming, My Trumpet, the fate of the Luciferians, the rampant deception, the Winds of Change Angel, the uncovering and the fall of the evil which is governing the earth, yes, and much more. I do not do this kind of revelation for minor events! If keeping the faith was easy, no encouragement would be needed. I Am being very clear in telling you to keep your eyes on Me. Do not fear. Stay encouraged. Gather with others who are like-minded and have their eyes on Me, not with those who will only repeat the bad news of the day! Look up! It's almost over! Amen."

Give the Angels Something to Work With – Faith! –

May 28, 2022

"Prophet, tell the people, My people, not to eat filth, not to believe lies, and not to engage with the world. Do not feign Christianity with the religious. For it IS they who put My Son on the cross. They are in bed with the antichrist spirit. Yet they appear as an angel of light. These idolize a book which they, themselves, do not follow, or understand.

My people! Do not watch or listen to the lies that are called news! This is gossip, lies, and propaganda, and it is all produced and planned to deceive and to achieve a certain outcome! <u>Fear</u>!

So, when My Prophets are prophesying plenty, blessing, and <u>MY</u> great reset, then declare it from the rooftops. Don't believe what you see or what is reported by the news (such as famine, lack, suffering, etc.). Stand as one! Declare My truth! Give My angels something to work with (FAITH). My people! Stand and fight! Come on! Anyone can say they are with Me, but the truth will be <u>SEEN</u> in those who really believe! Or do you think that the great I

Am will credit faith to those who only feign faith but never stand for anything, especially ME!

Speak the truth, declare the truth, stand with My Prophets. My words are truth! Are you repeating the news of the day? Will there be food shortages? Will fuel cost $10 a gallon? What about world war? Will the Trumpet ever do anything? I AM says, 'STOP it!' As you do this, you aid the enemy in ginning up more fear! Speak the words of faith. Why would you do otherwise?

Lift up your heads you gates of brass; you bars of iron yield, and let the King of Glory pass! The cross is in the field! (The Lord brings to mind a song I once heard.)

Yes, this is still a rescue mission, and this mission cannot be stopped. Every knee <u>will</u> bow to the King of Glory. None shall escape His recompense, whether good or bad! Amen."

The Coming Justice – May 31, 2022

*H*ear, my son, your father's instruction
*And do not forsake your mother's teaching;
Indeed, they are a graceful wreath to your head
And ornaments about your neck.
My son, if sinners entice you,
Do not consent.
If they say, "Come with us,
Let us lie in wait for blood,
Let us ambush the innocent without cause;
Let us swallow them alive like Sheol,
Even whole, as those who go down to the pit;*

We will find all kinds of precious wealth,
We will fill our houses with spoil;
Throw in your lot with us,
We shall all have one purse,"
My son, do not walk in the way with them.
Keep your feet from their path,
For their feet run to evil
And they hasten to shed blood.
Indeed, it is useless to spread the baited net
In the sight of any bird;
But they lie in wait for their own blood;
They ambush their own lives.
So are the ways of everyone who gains by violence;
It takes away the life of its possessors. (Proverbs 1:8-19 NASB)

The Lord of all says: "I have seen My precious little ones slaughtered, and their blood cries out to Me every minute! I have heard the foolishness as well. 'My body, my choice' – but they don't kill their bodies! This practice of shedding innocent blood is performed as a sacrament to Baal, and there is <u>no</u> excuse for supporting it; <u>none</u>! As the Proverb says: *'This violence will take away the life of its possessors.'* The time for repentance is drawing to a close now.

I, the Lord, declare that there is another practice that I AM exposing! This practice creates 'medicine' which is intended to take lives, instead of preserve them! Fear is the bait for this, but I say that this baited net is being exposed, and it will no longer work because the Winds of Change Angel is blowing the lid off of this deception. I say, says the Lord, that those who participated in this will be snared by their own trap, and their fate will be worse than those that they intended to trap!

The Great I AM also says: I <u>also</u> see the politicians of the nations! These who can do nothing good in My sight; these who feign support for their people! These who cheat the people at the polling places! These who open their mouths and spew out lies! These whose only real intention is to oppress, cheat, use, yes, and to kill! Wailing and gnashing of teeth shall arise from these as they are dragged by their feet to justice! Are there <u>ANY</u> who are good? <u>Now is the time</u> for you to separate yourself from the evil ones, or you will be considered to be one of <u>them</u>! The time is very short <u>now</u>.

The lies and secrets, as well as the societies and associations are being exposed <u>now</u>. The time of the Winds of Change Angel exposing all of this is just about wrapped up. Then will come a time of justice and retribution that will make the whole world gasp, become wrath, and finally be satisfied. It will be during these last phases that love and restraint will be needed so that justice doesn't go too far.

My People! Get ready to celebrate! The whole world will rejoice at My Goodness! Amen."

Love as Jesus Does – June 3, 2022

"This is My commandment, that you love one another, just as I have loved you. Greater love has no one than this, that one lay down his life for his friends. You are My friends if you do what I command you. No longer do I call you slaves,

for the slave does not know what his master is doing; but I have called you friends, for all things that I have heard from My Father I have made known to you. You did not choose Me, but I chose you, and appointed you that you would go and bear fruit, and that your fruit would remain, so that whatever you ask of the Father in My name He may give to you. This I command you, that you love one another." (John 15:12-17 NASB)

Jesus is still saying, "Love one another just as I have loved you!" The Lord has not said love one another by your definition of love! Love the way Jesus loved is NOT to pull from the Bible all the verses that you or someone else thinks look like love. This would still be love as defined by man. What Jesus did say is that the Holy Spirit, the Spirit of Truth, will lead us into all Truth. This is love then, that you lay down your thoughts, lay down your life, and follow Him. The Spirit of Christ in you! Yes, die to self and live to Christ Jesus!

Jesus had needs! Sleep. Food. Clothing. But He did not minister to people to attain those things. He did not demand a tithe to support His ministry. His life was not His own. He said that He could do nothing of Himself, but only did what He saw His Father doing. He trusted the Father to provide for His needs. He had truly laid His life down. Yes, He had died to self!

It has been said that to die for Christ is easier than to live for Him. You die once and are buried. But to live for Him is to take up your cross daily. Yes, to wake up and die to self each day, every day. Give up your thoughts in favor of His. Do what He desires you to do. Go where He says to go. Forgo those things you think will make you happy, and follow the still, small voice instead. Will doing this make you look foolish, rude, arrogant to those in your family, etc.? Probably. But, and this is a very big BUT, you will never be happier, more fulfilled, and feel richer than when you are doing life exactly like Jesus! Dead men cannot be disappointed, offended, poor, sick, or frustrated!

The concept of living life as Jesus did is simple then, but living it out is very, very difficult. But worth it! Amen.

All are Struggling, but God's Word WILL Prevail –

June 14, 2022

"Kirk, look around. Are there any Spirit-filled believers that you know who are <u>not</u> struggling? Fighting sickness, demonic oppression, religious persecution? Yes, I tell you, your enemy is desperate, in a rage, and doing everything he can possibly do to embarrass Me! He will have his little hissy fit.

Do not take your eyes off of Me. Do not give in. Do not begin to look at yourselves! Have I not told you what is to come? I tell you that not one of My words will fail. I Am the LORD! Re-look at those words that were spoken! Look at the lies which were uncovered, as well as the liars! What did My Trumpet say? What would happen if he were not elected? I, the Lord, will tell you! He said there would be inflation, fuel prices would increase, there would be shortages, political unrest, wars, etc., etc. How did he know this?

Therefore, look at how things are falling apart for the Luciferians. Kill, steal, and destroy are not merely words by which they live! These things are things that happen by default. They don't have to try to kill, steal, and destroy. Things just fall apart in their hands. This is because these are My words regarding them, says the LORD!

Pay attention then, says the Lord. Pay attention to the words I have used regarding those I love! These words will prevail for them. Words of hope and a future, words of prosperity, words of health and healing, freedom, and favor! Amen."

The Bible vs. My Church – June 20, 2022

The Lord says: "My Church believes what the Scriptures say. They know what it means when I say that My sheep hear My voice. They know Me and will not follow another. These things accompany My Church: In My name (Jesus), they cast out demons; they speak with 'other' tongues; they deal with serpents; and if they drink deadly poison, it will not hurt them; they lay hands on the sick, and the sick recover!

My Church has been built on the foundation of the Apostles and Prophets, and Jesus Himself is its Cornerstone. In My Church, I Myself choose the leadership, even the Apostles, Prophets, Evangelists, Pastors, and Teachers! In My Church, there is <u>Unity</u>, because there is one body, one Spirit, one Lord, one faith, one baptism, one hope, and One God and Father of all, Who is over all and through all and in all!

When I say faith comes by hearing, My Church knows what that means! It has nothing to do with words on a page! My

Church knows what it means to be conformed into the image of My Son, and they have faith that they will do what He did and greater things will they do! My Church understands that it can do NOTHING in its own strength, and that it can do EVERYTHING in the power of the Spirit of Christ.

My Church doesn't put much emphasis on knowing about My Son. They sincerely and desperately want to KNOW Him! My Son died and sent the very Spirit of God to live in men. My Church understands the importance of this! My Church is made up of overcomers. They overcome by the blood of the Lamb and the word of their testimony, AND they do not love their life, even when faced with death. Each morning, they wake up and then die to self so that they can live for My Son. To hide out, sitting on a pile of provisions and waiting for the rapture is below them! To waste their time performing religious 'duties' is, again, below them! My glorious Church knows what it means to live for Me! And I will open the warehouse of heaven to supply their every need!

Will they be tested? YES! But this testing is so that they understand what and who they are and what they stand for! I AM is not opening the heavens for the latter rain for their entertainment! There is work to be done, and My Spirit longs to work with My Church, and He will. Amen."

The Spirit Poured Out in Greater Measure –

June 21, 2022

"Tiffany, do you know why I'm pouring out My Spirit in greater measure? Because these latter days are greater than the former. A greater outpouring is needed for a greater harvest, for greater works, and the greatest manifestation of My Son through His Church – the Church that knows Him and is like Him. These we love and My Spirit is eager to come on them. You need greater power and glory for greater times and greater days."

The Outlook – June 24, 2022

Today the Lord wants to show us the outlook for the United States and the world.

"Are your eyes open," He asks. "Look around you. Look at the economy... do you see winning policies in place? <u>NO!</u> As I have told you: kill, steal, destroy is not simply something your enemy does, or even something he wants to do, necessarily. He can't help it! Things fall apart in his hands because these are the words that I, the Lord, have spoken about him. My words are powerful and creative in nature.

So, $5 or $6 for a gallon of gas is an indication of failure. Shortages are another indication of failure. Inflation equals failure. Food and other product shortages – failure! Is there anywhere in the economy where there is a success? Is there success in the area of family maybe, or religion, politics, education, media, arts? Where are those grandiose promises now? Where is that success and welfare for all that we were promised by the Left? What about the lynchpin ruling for child sacrifice? How is Roe v

Wade doing? And what about the model for gun control in New York? How is that working out?

This is just in the United States and is a microcosm for what is happening around the globe. The failure of the Left (Cabal, Luciferians, Globalists) is in plain view for ALL to see now, and it becomes more and more obvious with each passing day.

Now the question is this: what will you do about this? Will you, My People, simply stand by and let it happen? Or will you show up when My Spirit comes upon you to do something? Again, open your eyes! My Prophets have brought you a picture of the future, and it is Grand! This is the future that I, the Lord, have desired for you! Did you think it would just happen with no involvement from yourself? You will be required to show up! When you simply follow My Spirit, you cannot lose! This, then, is My Word to you, and again, it is creative and powerful, and it cannot fail. Amen."

"The race is on!"

The Worm has Turned – June 28, 2022

Today, all morning, the Lord has been speaking to me (Kirk) about a turning, a change in the atmosphere, a shift.

He was showing me changes that have been hoped for, waited for, even longed for, among a rather small group of good friends. Well, it seems that the dam is beginning to break! Finally! In a word given to us on June 14, 2022, the Lord asked if we knew any Spirit-filled believers who were <u>NOT</u> struggling? So, as I look today, these promised things are falling into place: healing has happened, paperwork stalled in the government is received after a very long wait, housing and transportation are provided, etc.

So, after He had been showing me these things for a while, I took some quiet time. As I prayed and listened, these words came, "The Worm Has Turned." I had heard this saying before, and the meaning seemed obvious to me, but I felt pressure to look it up. So, I found that this idiom is dated back to the 1500's, and its meaning speaks of change. From the internet site, "Grammarist," here are some examples of its meaning. "*The worm has turned means that someone who has previously been downtrodden has triumphed; someone who has previously been unlucky has become lucky; or someone who has previously been obedient has spoken up. The idea is that someone's attitude toward another or his strength of conviction has changed.*"

I found it so interesting that the Lord had used this particular idiom after showing me the changes in my small group of friends.

As I pondered this, He again showed me the decisions by the Supreme Court of the United States. (overturning Roe v Wade, striking down unconstitutional laws in NY regarding gun control, freedom of religion regarding prayer, etc.) The shift, change, new-found boldness there is breathtaking! Then I remembered the "words" He had given us regarding a snowball rolling down a mountain and of the "cascade effect" He had said would happen. Then a recent word saying, "The race is on!" And all the time, He has told us to keep our eyes on Him, or to open our eyes to see what He is doing.

So, I just asked Him about all of this, if there was anything to add to it? The only thing He said was that I (we) need to look back at some of the prophetic words that had come. The fruit from those words can be seen or will soon be seen. Amen.

Cascade effect - https://youtu.be/QarjmU-FvaI
Snowball - https://youtu.be/0OezCNI9QnM
Event Horizon - https://youtu.be/-2booVB62mQ
Vision of the Ships Part 1 - https://youtu.be/WODfj1HcxAk
Vision of the Ships Part 2 - https://youtu.be/UtUyIvZkYhI
Vision of the Ships Part 3 - https://youtu.be/j4I7MF4O8ZY
Change & White House Imposters Removed - https://youtu.be/xJbqjngAxFo

Warrior Bride – July 6, 2022

Today the Lord wants to speak about His bride.

"My bride is not weak and in need of constant tending in the last days! For My bride is tried and true, and there is no falseness in her at all. As I have said before, both love and faith need to be tested to find their strength. My bride is a warrior, and in these last days, she will be tried, but she will not be found wanting.

Just as a war horse runs to battle, she is also always at the ready to do battle. Yes, but her every move is made in love!

Yes, she is My bride! Her strength as a warrior is not in her ability to destroy, nor her ability to kill, but it is in her ability to love! My warrior bride's strength is found in Me. She has died once to herself, and now only finds life in Me. Because of that, she will never die!

Cowards look for a way of escape, for a way to avoid conflict and tribulation. My bride stands at the ready to charge the very gates of hell at My word! She has no fear at all because her love for Me was perfected when she died to herself.

Spot or wrinkle? No. She trembles at My word, and I love her more than she can even imagine! Amen."

Evil Being Brought to the Light – July 8, 2022

I (Kirk) was asking the Lord to speak to me regarding the times we're living in. What's going on now? And later, He began...

"The Winds of Change Angel has been doing his job well. He is uncovering the darkness wherever it is. He has already blown the lid off of so many things that Satan had thought were never going to be found out. There's more to come, however! Prophet, tell the people that I Am isn't finished yet! Are things good? No! But when I Am is done, they will be!

There are so many more vile and evil things that will be brought to the light. You look at others and think that they are still in the dark regarding the evil in the world. But I Am telling you now that the difference between you and them is minimal. Yes! There is that much more that must come to the light! Evil is hidden in places that <u>you</u> would not, and do not, even suspect at all. There are people close to you, that you interact with, who will be found to be evil. You will need to follow My Spirit closely, or you will suspect everyone!

As the end of this cascade event nears, a flood of deception will be uncovered – a deluge! Do not become numb or overwhelmed. The law must run its course, and the 'small things' cannot be simply swept under the rug!

The Lord has His eyes on the young global leaders, and those who believe themselves to be global shapers, and the power behind these in the spiritual realm will soon be removed, says the Lord of all. Watch for these 'leaders' to go missing, attempt escape, become unstable (maybe mental). Then the end of this charade is very near!"

I ask Him, "Like Boris?" He answers, "Yes, like that. Amen."

Hosting a Movement of the Spirit of God – the Point of SGGM – July 21, 2022

Today the Lord is talking to me (Kirk) about our ministry – Seeking the Glory of God Ministries (SGGM). He is saying that we have a church, house churches, but that isn't what SGGM is all about. We have a video channel for devotionals, but that isn't what SGGM is all about. We have channels with prophetic words on them and we host conferences, but again that isn't the point of our ministry. So, then I asked Him: "Lord, what is the point of SGGM?"

He answered, "The point of SGGM is to host a movement of the Spirit of God."

I answered, "A movement?"

He replied, "Yes, a movement, a shift, a redo of the current church model. One fashioned or modeled after the 'Christ' model of the Church.

In this 'model,' the fivefold ministry will be the government of the Church. Those who govern will be the servants of all, and they will not 'lord it over the congregants' as is done today.

My ministers will look at being paid a salary as unnecessary, and it will have a foul taste for them when they consider it. There will be very few who will need to be paid. Most will have jobs besides being ministers in small churches (house churches). But there may be a few Apostles or Prophets who will need to be paid because of the number of churches they are over.

This is a movement of disciples who go out. This is a movement where Jesus Christ is central and most importantly, where the Spirit of Christ is lifted high! In this movement, FAITH is spelled RISK and risk is spelled ACTION! Working for the Lord, in obedience to the Spirit is normal, and laziness and pew-sitting are very rare indeed.

'What church do you belong to?' This question will fade into the denomination era and will not be used anymore, at least not in the way it is now. People will either be members of The Universal Church, or not. And those who are Spirit-filled will know each other by the Spirit of God.

Again, this is what SGGM is a part of. The Spirit is raising other ministries, other people, the fivefold all over the world to be part of His glorious Church!

211

During this time, every prayer ever prayed for the Church will be fulfilled. All of the saints who ever desired to see a spotless bride for the Lord of All will see their prayers come to fruition during this time! Amen."

Three Branches of Government, One Spirit –

July 17, 2022

The Earth is on Trial Word:

"The earth is on trial. I Am the Judge, and none shall escape My justice. I have said My recompense will be given to those who have done evil, and those who have done good. I have not changed My mind."

(To Tiffany:) "Call for justice. Tell the courts to rule in righteousness and in favor of My Son. Tell them the sentence of death is on the wicked and the reward of life and prosperity, health and wellness is for the righteous – My faithful who have stood and will stand in these trying times when I Am trying the world."

"The New World Order is nothing but chaos and dysfunction. It is utter failure in every respect. The enemy thought he could rule Heaven, and he can't even rule earth. Nothing he does is ever right or even has a chance of turning out right. Those who submit to him will find themselves in the wrong every time.

But My Warrior Bride (He smiles as He says this), she is My delight. I see My Son in her."

Trifecta Word:

People across the world have been seeing numbers in threes. We asked the Lord about this.

We heard "Triple Crown – a real Trifecta. The three branches of government will be in one Spirit." People will vote for those who are of the Spirit or are anointed by the Spirit. As goes the USA, so goes the world. This is why people are seeing numbers in threes all over the world. This word is not just for the United States.

The Lord is raising up Constitutional Republics all over the world, so that when the very righteous Margaret Thatcher comes, she can unite them, but not in a one world government. It will be true unity by the Spirit. The Lord is raising up patterns of the Trumpet all around the world, and they will help form these Constitutional Republics.

(These two words go together because God is not going to force the governments of the world or the people to change. He's going to make them want to. The people will make the decision. It's similar to how the Apostle Paul was given an option to follow the Lord, but it was ridiculous for him to choose otherwise. The people and governments will see the good way and they'll take it – for the most part.)

Have Faith to Set Free Those Rescued from Human-Trafficking Dream – July 19, 2022

I (Tiffany) dreamed that there were a lot of kids rescued from human trafficking. Then I heard that there are going to be so many rescued, that it will take the body of

Christ to set them free. There will be too many to send them to "Deliverance Ministers" or "Healers." The Lord says that we're going to have to have faith that when we pray, Christ will set them free, even rewire their brains and fix memories, etc. And we need to believe this will not take a long time, but that they will be set free at a word. The ecclesia will also need to help adopt, set up safe houses, etc. to raise these children to know God and be disciples of Jesus.

Visit to the War Room – July 21, 2022

This afternoon, I believe that I (Kirk) am supposed to ask to go to visit the "War Room" in heaven. As I ask the Lord for this, He says, "Yes, you will meet Me outside the War Room entrance in the corridor in the rear Courtroom."

Closing my eyes, I find myself there. Jesus is waiting for me. He looks like He has on numerous other times when I've seen Him. But as I walk toward Him, I feel like I'm being washed in love, acceptance, goodness. But I also have something like fear, or deep, deep respect come over me. I fall on my face before Him in love and respect, fear, etc. Just then, He bends low and taps my shoulder, and says, "Son, come. Get up on your feet. We have much to do. He takes my hand and effortlessly brings me to my feet. I feel shaky inside, but we proceed into the War Room.

As we enter, we meet two warring angels who stand to the side at attention as we walk in front of them. They tower over me, and I feel kind of wimpy as we walk by. But I get the feeling that they do not view me that way. We go up the narrow stairs to the "Viewing Area" above the War Room itself. Jesus turns to me, and knowing what has gone through my mind, He asks if I understand how the angels viewed me as I walked by? I said, "No, but they seemed impressed by me, and by You as well. I didn't understand why that was."

Just then a picture came into my mind. It was of a soldier in armor. All his weapons were in their sheaths. The armor itself was dented and dirty. It even looked like there was dried blood on it. The helmet was off and as I looked, the person in the armor turned toward me. IT WAS MY FACE! In the spirit realm, I looked like a true and tested warrior! The vision went away, and Jesus said, "Yes, this is truly you. You just don't realize it yet."

So, we kept walking. (I kept thinking of what I looked like in the spirit, pondering it.) As we looked down at TV screens with 3-D images on them, I noticed something quite different than the last time I was there. Everything was as if it were in "fast forward." Both the "images" and the angels were moving faster. Not in a reckless sort of way, quite the opposite. It was orderly and calculated, planned even, just faster. Then I heard, "Yes, and it will speed up even more as the enemy falls. This is the Cascade Event I spoke to you about."

We walked around a bit. Then Jesus turned to me and said, "Come." In a second, we were standing in second heaven. Up high, but below the clouds. He pointed down and said, "Look." So, I did. There were angels everywhere, and I didn't see any people at all. They were all hidden. He wanted me to see the angels as they did their jobs. Mostly, they looked like regular people! All I could think about was how many of them we must meet each day! Amazing!

Then Jesus said, "Yes, the angels partner with you to work against the demonic. That partnership is complex, but the angels know exactly what they should or shouldn't do. They are also empowered by faith, prayer, and the boldness of the one they are helping. So, have faith! Never cease in prayer! And go in all boldness!"

Then the vision was over. Amen!

Dangerous & Confusing Time – July 26, 2022

Listening for the voice of the Lord just now. "Need to know basis" is what I'm hearing. I'm unsure what He means by that. I've heard it before, and believe it means that, like in the military, only those who have cause or need to know are privy to certain knowledge. Those who do not "need" to know are kept from knowing certain things.

Then the Lord says, "In the world this is true, that many secrets are kept, and knowledge is tightly guarded in almost every mountain of influence. But this is not so in My kingdom. As the Scriptures say, even the deep things of God are available by His Spirit."

I believe He is speaking of these things because yesterday another Prophet said that he had <u>intel</u> (not from the Lord although the Lord bore witness to it) that the SCOTUS had already decided that the 2020 election was fraudulent and had overturned it. And also that Trump was going to be put back in office. So, I was asking about this, and I believe I'm hearing it is true.

Then I heard the LORD say: "This is a very dangerous and confusing time. Dangerous because your enemy cannot give up. It's not in his nature. Confusing because there are so many who are not expecting things on the scale of what will be happening. You need to be prepared to learn of things so evil even the most 'awake' among you will be both surprised and repulsed on a level you haven't yet imagined! Then you need to be prepared to have patience for those who are of the 'woke' culture. They have been on a steady diet of blue pills and will be forced to swallow the red ones. They cannot escape what's coming. No one can.

We're almost there. Time is short. Open your heart in love, and yet the law must be followed and applied to those who are found guilty by it. Look around you. Remember what it was like to be enslaved by the evil one! Look one more time! Because things will never be like this again! Ever!

The 'Church' has become a cesspool of wokeism, and that's a place where there shouldn't be sin! Everywhere else it's worse! But look now... because I AM is on the move and this will change.

Do not go into fear My People! Now is the time of flailing and thrashing of your enemy! He will not go down easily, but he will be taken down. Even his followers will begin to lose heart now. They will be called upon to do heinous things, and some will, but others will walk away from his lies.

I AM says today that these changes are not for one place or one people! I AM on a rescue mission, and it is for the whole world! The United States, yes! But the ripples from what I accomplish there will flow around the entire planet. Amen!"

217

Great Reset Moved Up – August 11, 2022 at 11:00 a.m.

God's Great Reset has been moved up! On Tuesday, August 9, 2022, after the FBI raided Mar-A-Lago, the Lord said He was moving up the time table!

As I ask about these things, He says: "Between now and the end of the year a remarkable change will take place on the earth. I'm speeding things up just as you noticed in the War Room in Heaven (Vision from July 21, 2022). The world is getting used to change. People look each day to see what has happened. But as I speed things up, each day will bring multiple events of great importance.

I have said that you must not be in fear. This is especially true during this season! Evil will be brought to light, and it will not happen without blood. You can sense the desperation in the air now, and you have seen some of this desperation in the lawless acts of the deep state actors. This will increase, but so will the pushback. Blood will be spilled in this conflict, but it shall not compare to that which will be spilled in carrying out justice.

The people in the USA are ready for My anointed to begin his rise back to his rightful place. You will see this happening during this season, and rather rapidly! This too will happen, but not without opposition! Lies, desperate lies, fear in the enemy camp, confusion, and yes, violence! As the train picks up speed, fewer and fewer of the deep state actors will dare to oppose the truth, however. And it will be clearly seen what happens to those who do. As this fear spreads, turning on each other will be raised to an art form.

My people, the ones I love, they will become more and more emboldened in this season! They will clearly see how the institutional church has failed them. And being involved again will be in vogue. Having a yard sign that says, 'Trust the Lord' will be accompanied by real action instead of a simple lament. The nazi-like tactics of the deep state will no longer be impressive or feared because real justice will begin to be applied."

Winds of Change – Great Changes are Coming –

August 24, 2022

I (Kirk) was told to look up to the West. So, I did. The sky was perfectly blue with a few big puffy clouds... I didn't see anything else. I kept looking. Then between a couple of clouds, I saw a glint of light. As I watched, it got closer and brighter as once again, I saw the Winds of Change Angel approach. He looked just like he did before with a large sword and brightly polished armor. And he has the impression of power, partly due to how large he and his horse are.

The Winds of Change Angel came to rest in my front lawn as I was watching out of the window. He had the horse walk up to the house and then right into my house! I could see about half of the horse's legs. The rest was below the floor, and the Winds of Change's head was still right at the ceiling. He came right up to me, facing me. We just looked at each other. I thought I might see his eyes through the slit in his helmet. He is a very imposing figure! I should have been frightened I think, but I wasn't at all. He came a bit closer, shifted in his saddle and continued to look directly at me and I at him.

Then he finally spoke: "Are you called 'End Times Prophet'?" he asked. I said, "Yes, that's what the Lord has called me."

He said, "Good. The Lord has sent me to speak to you of things to come." His voice was very deep and gruff sounding to me, like a warrior's voice I thought. Maybe as one who was used to both taking orders and also giving them. And yet, he had respect for me. All I could think of to say was, "Okay."

Then he kind of blurted out that the reason his armor was so bright and pristine was because no evil dares to get close to him. He doesn't allow it! He apparently knew what I was thinking because I was marveling at his armor in my thoughts. Then he started speaking of things to come.

"The Lord has directed me to tell you that great changes are coming in a very short time span on earth. Indeed, I have been at work revealing evil in all the earth. This revelation of evil will now begin to bear fruit. Your government in the USA will see massive change, but it is only one sphere of influence. The others will also see change like the U.S. has never seen before. This pattern of revelation and change will happen around the earth, and everything that can be shaken will be shaken! If you have been paying attention, these are things you should already know. The prophets have been speaking about these things for some time now. Now, on to the reason I came.

Tell the people of the world to prepare. The saints should have provision for a couple weeks in the U.S. and maybe a bit more elsewhere in the world. Ask the Spirit of Truth exactly what you will need in your particular area.

Be prepared for blood. This must happen, and it will. The vast majority of people will be unaffected. If the Spirit of the Lord moves on you to act, to do something for Him, then do not hesitate. Love your neighbor as yourself. Share. Protect. Be Jesus in the world! Most of all, spread hope! Do not fear at all. The Lord is on a rescue mission! Pray!

Do not worry about 'your' money! The Lord knows what you need. Do you trust Him? Simply follow the Spirit of Christ.

The places of influence in the world lean on government to use and maintain their influence for Satan. When the governmental influence fails, the other places of influence will be ripe for change. Therefore, be ready! Ready to go to work, to run for office, join the school board, on every level, the people, people of God, need to be ready to take back what has been lost!

Tell the people to enjoy watching their enemy as they are exposed and defeated by the Lord God! He desires gladness to spread over the world as those who have been so oppressive are finally brought to justice! Rejoice as these evildoers lose their grip on power, as they squirm, yes as they freak out! Look on the foolish as they continue to trust in their masks with the humor the situation deserves! Vaccinations – yeah that's a great idea! (sarcastic tone) Rejoice with the Lord! He is good! Amen."

Devolution of Technology – August 31, 2022

Today the Lord is showing me His Church from His time on earth until the present. In particular, He wanted to show me what Satan has tried to do to it to destroy it. He showed me what He faced: the persecution by the religious, being tempted, and the division that was sown in His followers and His disciples. I saw His crucifixion. I saw how after the outpouring of the Holy Spirit, these things were intensified.

When Satan saw that this wasn't working, he tried to fold the church into the government, thinking that he would gain control over it and dispose of it through regulation and false promotion. When the church broke out of this scenario, Satan tried simple division based on intellectual knowledge of the Scriptures (Denominations).

In these end times, Satan is using everything at his disposal, all of the above, and now technology as well. Through this technology, he accomplished a deception that could not have happened before. Yes, the entire planet has been deceived!

"But, I the Lord, declare that this tower of Babel will fall as surely as its namesake did!" (Jesus speaking.)

Then I see part animal/human/machine things made to replace humans and human laborers. These are to serve a few who would survive a series of events which would kill off most of the human race. The "humans" left on earth at this time would be controlled by "elites" who are completely possessed by the demonic.

After I saw this, I said, "Lord, this is so depressing!"

Then He said, "This last scenario will never happen, even though it is right on the cusp right now. The 'knowledge' that produces these things is both earthly and demonic. I, the Lord, will not permit what I have created after My likeness and image to be re-created in the image of Satan and the demonic. And just as the Tower of Babel was deserted and went to ruin, so will this knowledge and technology be deserted and never will it be used again.

I, the Lord, will cause a technology devolution to take place just as with the Tower of Babel. I have said that I would 'pull the plug' on artificial intelligence, and this is true. But this devolution will be way more extensive than that.

When the peoples of the earth see what had been planned for humankind and the earth as a whole, they will be completely undone! Museums will house the aberrations and tell of the atrocities on the earth, what had been planned, as well as how close to the precipice mankind had come! Such reckless use of technology will never again be permitted. Amen!"

Time & Technology – September 9, 2022

"Prophet, tell the people about time. A time to live, a time to die. What time is it? In your world your life revolves around time... a time to start and a time to stop. How long did you sleep? What did you do during this or that time in your life? Are you one who looks back in time, wishing for or desiring to live in times past? Or do you look forward, waiting for things to happen, and desiring things to move faster? Do you actually live your life for Me or for time?

I created the environment in which you live, the mix of gases which you breathe, the water, plants, and animals, yes even time. The time it takes for the earth to make a revolution and the time for it to travel around the sun. In the beginning, I gave man dominion over his environment. He was to rule and reign over it. But he was deceived and fell to Satan in the garden. Under the rule of the evil one, he lost the dominion which I desired him to have. Because of My great love for those whom I had created, I won back dominion for them through the work of My Son, Jesus. I provided a way for those who would come to Him to be born again into the dominion I have always desired for them. Now Satan has been very successful in his deceit, and his lies have turned things around from what I desire for men.

He, Satan, is always after control. To rule and reign as I do. Can you see that everything that involves technology and invention has not served to make life better or easier for man, but instead has been used to enslave him? The promise of technology is always to make things better. Are things better? Or is mankind now being trained to serve technology? Who, or what, keeps track of where you are? What about your time, is it tracked and controlled by you? Are you 'off the clock' during your days, or are you always available? Technology is exerting more control in the lives of people faster than ever before, and this control is directly opposed to what I have desired for My people!

I have called the communication in the world 'The Tower of Babel,' for it represents one language, which is being used in rebellion against Me and My desires. And in fact, is one of Satan's attempts to come against Me. I have also said that 'Where the Spirit of the Lord is, there is liberty, or freedom.' My Spirit has been poured out on the earth. Is there freedom? There will be! I, the Lord, have spoken!

My Son has said, 'The Spirit of the Lord is upon Me, Because He has anointed Me to preach the gospel to the poor. He has sent Me to proclaim release to the captives, And recovery of sight to the blind, To set free those who are oppressed, To proclaim the favorable year of the Lord.' My Son will not fail to deliver on all of these promises!

These earthly things that oppress My people will be walked back! Technology in the hands of a few will not be allowed to rule in My place! And NOW is the time that I will intervene to begin the devolution of this evil which is now in the world. Amen."

Warrior Bride – Army of the LORD –

September 16, 2022

"Prophet, speak to the people. I The LORD Am raising up an army, My army! I have spoken about My Bride, and she will be glorious! She is a warrior! She shall form into and function as My Army.

As she forms My Army, she shall die! Yes, My Army shall die as it's formed, for everyone in My Army will have died to themselves and only live for Me!

There will be no such thing as fear for them, therefore. For what could an enemy possibly do to them to generate fear? And I will arm them with every weapon in heaven's arsenal. I will not deny them anything that they ask for. Satan will have lost control over them because they only find life in Me.

My Spirit will be upon them heavily, and signs, wonders, and miracles will be so commonplace for them that recording them will be very difficult indeed. Love will be their calling card as they go to war, and their boldness will be the stuff of legends!

My Son will lead these, and His generals, the Apostles, shall be very highly respected because of their ONE desire which is to please Him! Their wisdom in battle and leadership in the fight will only be eclipsed by their humility and ability to be the servant of all.

My Church is My Army. Cowards who only look forward to escape, and weaklings who only dare to say the name Jesus in a building once a week will not be tolerated. My Church will be known for its strength and power!

My warriors desire to go OUT! Yes, there will be a gathering of the saints to equip and train so that they can go OUT! My Church will no longer be a career option for those who have been 'educated' for a position. I, the LORD, will call those who I have decided to call, and the only diploma required will be the witness of My Spirit upon the person. These shall minister in power, and not from earthly or demonic 'knowledge' at all.

As the second outpouring of My Spirit happens during this time, those who 'minister' out of the powerless, old way will quickly and easily be found out and rejected by My faithful. In previous seasons, the religious have been the persecutors of My people, but no more! My Church, My Army will overcome all opposition and shall occupy the high ground. And Satan and his religion, the doctrine of demons, shall be on the run, not My saints!

Reject the previous way of thinking, My People! Have I not said that we will overcome? Stop cowering and hiding. Rise up My Warrior Bride! I AM is blowing the shofar and it's time to assemble for battle! What is there to fear My Church? I AM the Giver of Life itself. Come on, rise up in the newness of life that I AM giving you! Rise Up! Amen."

Word of Judgment to "Leaders" of Nations for Hebrew New Year September 25, 2022 – Given September 23, 2022

This word was published September 24, 2022 because the Hebrew Calendar New Year begins Sunday the 25th at Sundown...

"Prophet of the End Times, speak this to the nations! I, the LORD, have been speaking to My Bride and indeed, My Army, and I have made them ready. I declare that today My Army is ready! So, Prophet, today I Am is speaking to the Nations. Yes, the 'leadership' of the free world. I Am has been very gracious and has granted time for repentance. That time has come to a close.

As the New Year begins, My patience has come to an end for you! All of you! As the sun sets tomorrow (September 25, 2022), your time is also up. Yes! I'm speaking to YOU.

If you are in a position of authority, I'm speaking to you! From the Presidents and Prime Ministers of countries to the military and even to the local sheriff. Fall on your face now before the great and terrible day of the Lord! You have been like smoke in My nostrils and a stench on the earth. And when My hand moves, there shall be no mercy for you at all. For the 'great men' of the earth shall beg and weep, and their pitiful looks shall find no pity. The 'powerful' will be on their knees begging for the bread of mercy, but they will instead find the thorns of judgment. My mercy shall be exceedingly rare among those to whom I have given authority and then misused it according to the will of the evil one.

They think that because of their 'high' office with Satan they shall escape! (I see the Lord laughing here.) These fools who think their plush bunkers and their reserves of gold and silver will save them, HA! says the Lord of Hosts! The very things they depend on to save them will cause them to be hunted down and destroyed! Nations will pursue these members of the WEF Cabal relentlessly, and they will have no rest in this world or the next!

Did I mention a New Year begins tomorrow? Amen!"

Spiritual Israel – Isaiah 43 – September 28, 2022

Isaiah 43:1-13 NASB

But now, thus says the Lord, your Creator, O Jacob, and
  He who formed you, O Israel,
"Do not fear, for I have redeemed you;
I have called you by name; you are Mine!
When you pass through the waters, I will be with you;
And through the rivers, they will not overflow you.
When you walk through the fire, you will not be scorched,
Nor will the flame burn you.

For I am the Lord your God,
The Holy One of Israel, your Savior;
I have given Egypt as your ransom, Cush and Seba in your place.
Since you are precious in My sight, since you are honored and I love you,
I will give other men in your place and other peoples in exchange for you;
I will bring your offspring from the east,
And gather you from the west.
I will say to the north, 'Give them up!'
And to the south, 'Do not hold them back.'
Bring My sons from afar and My daughters from the ends of the earth,
Everyone who is called by My name,
And whom I have created for My glory,
Whom I have formed, even whom I have made.
Bring out the people who are blind, even though they have eyes,
And the deaf, even though they have ears.
All the nations have gathered together so that the peoples may be assembled.
Who among them can declare this
And proclaim to us the former things?
Let them present their witnesses so that they may be justified,
Or let them say, 'It is true.'
You are My witnesses, declares the Lord,
And My servant whom I have chosen, so that you may know and believe Me
And understand that I am He.
Before Me there was no God formed, and there will be none after Me.
I, even I, am the Lord,
And there is no savior besides Me.

It is I who have declared and saved and proclaimed,
And there was no strange god among you;
So you are My witnesses, declares the Lord.
And I am God.
Even from eternity, I am He,
And there is none who can deliver out of My hand;
I act and who can reverse it?"

"Can a Nation be born in a day?
Can the dead be raised to live again?
Can the lesser defeat the greater?
Can the Word of God ever fail?

My people answer these questions from their heart and will not ponder them before they answer! My Spirit within them rises up and answers, but not by the world's wisdom, but according to My Spirit. They (those who are Mine) have been grafted in and are Mine, a remnant who is a Spiritual Israel. My people who are chosen by Me. My Word, even My Son, is a Redeemer, and the branch which has been grafted is now one with My people Israel.

Now, read this testimony (do it again!) which My Prophet Isaiah has written, and see if the Lord your God has also written it for YOU! Amen!"

("I want My people to know I've done it before, and I'll do it again!")

Drawing a Line Between the Holy Spirit and the Antichrist spirit – October 5, 2022

The Lord says that the spirit of religion and the antichrist spirit are one and the same. They work against Jesus and His way of the Spirit of God. He is saying this plainly, and drawing a line between His way of the Spirit and any other way that might be taught or followed. Do not be fooled by the term "Christian Church," "Bible Church," or any other name that may be given to a denomination or church building.

"If there is no witness of the Spirit there, if there are no gifts of the Spirit on display, or if the fruit of the Spirit is missing, then leave that place because it is not from Me, says the Lord.

See! I Am telling you plainly! I Am One, and I Am Three! Who has given you the right to worship the Father, but not His Spirit? Or the Son, but not His Spirit? I Am not divided. I Am One. Either eat the whole Lamb, or it will be of no benefit to you! Worship Me or not. I Am not divided.

It has been said that worship is not the one you sing to. Rather, it is the one you obey. I Am being very clear today. Worship in spirit and truth. No more of this doctrine of demons that claims to worship and believe in Me but has no power. I Am power itself. There is no power outside of Me. Have I not created all things? And are not all things held together by Me?

I have said that My bride and My army are one, and they are. And they are ready! They are ready for this message. They will recognize the Truth in their spirit. Religion apart from My Spirit is dead. No one can be holy without the Holy Spirit.

Have you noticed that My Son called His disciples not in the normal way of His time, not from the 'wise' or educated, as the Jewish leaders and sages of His day did?

He chose as the Holy Spirit directed Him! Have you also noticed how the Apostle Paul, being a Pharisee himself, had to throw away what he had gained through scholarship and then he called it 'rubbish'? The Apostle Paul had to be retaught by Jesus through the Holy Spirit too!

I have not changed, says the Lord! I will have My spotless bride, says the Lord God! She will be chosen because she has walked with Me and talked with Me, and My Spirit and her spirit are One with Me. I know them and I love them. Amen."

Which Prophetic Words Come From the LORD? – October 14, 2022

Today I (Kirk) see death and destruction, FEMA camps, innocent people imprisoned, hunger and thirst. This is the USA, it is the UK, it is Australia, it is every continent and land. Every nation on the face of the earth is in poverty and decay. Machines govern over the enslaved multitudes, and heartless men control the machines. Death seems the most merciful escape from this form of hell, and those in authority are all too willing to provide it. As I look at these "camps," I wonder why humans have been kept alive at all?

I see machines at work in every industry – farming and manufacturing – everywhere I look. There are even machines making machines and doing repair on machines. Everything I could imagine is accomplished by Artificial Intelligence and robots. Some of the robots look like humans, and act like them. Others look like a mix of human and animal, like a biological robot. Whatever the form, they are all tightly controlled by an elite group of "humans" whose hope is to be made immortal through the technology they have command over. In this world system, there is no love at all, no mercy, no kindness – only a hellish existence in a world of fear, indifference, lust, enslavement, and extreme cruelty.

This is <u>NOT</u> a prophetic word! I am not prophesying that this will happen at all! This is not the Lord's plan! I want to be clear about this!

I have been behind the enemy lines: a spy. I have seen his plan. Prophets, immature Prophets, sometimes see these things and believe they are a prophetic word from the Lord. They are not. It is a travesty to count things from the demonic as having been from the Lord.

The Lord is a Redeemer! Do you see any redemption in this account? The Lord is full of goodness and hope! Do you see goodness and hope? The Lord is love! Do you see love? Therefore, words of gloom and doom that come with no hope, no love, no goodness, and no redeeming qualities are not prophetic words from our Lord. Repent of believing something from Satan is from the Lord! Forgive immaturity in the Prophetic, for the Lord is raising up many Prophets who haven't completely understood His ways! Above all, don't be fooled and go into fear! Amen.

Time and the Prophetic – October 24, 2022

Time (One More Time)

"Prophet, I want to speak about time again.

When I speak to My Prophets, and when they prophesy about an event in the future, I have taken them out of their time paradigm and then placed them back into it in a different moment. They view the event, and then go back to where they left off. For this reason, it is difficult for them to timestamp a future event, unless I tell them, they see something which has a date on it, or some other means by which time can be evaluated. They travel through time in the Spirit, and it only takes an instant to happen.

There is another aspect of time I want to show you. I exist outside of the constraints of time, and I have created time for you. As such, you only exist in the now. The past is, of course, passed, and you cannot go back to it. The future is only reachable if you exist when it arrives. So, you live in the now, and even that is in the past as you think of it! The 'now' cannot be captured and held onto either.

So, reach forward for the future! I AM has put a desire within you for the future. Prophets look forward. The Spirit of Christ shows you things to come. He leads you into (meaning future) all truth. The Lord has set heaven in front of you. You have a future and a hope! Do not look at the past without the lens of the Holy Spirit! If you trust in your intellect or memory, Satan will show you all of your short-comings and lie to you about anything he can. This is exhausting, depressing, and a waste of time!

Fear is the mark of hell and the beast! Are you in fear of acid rain, the Ozone hole, overpopulation, the rising oceans, the inability to produce enough food, global cooling, global warming, Y2K, Covid 19, and on and on? Always, there is something to fear that, of course, needs money to 'fix' it. Have any of these produced the promised devastation? No.

Love is of God, for God is love. Love is His mark. Perfect love casts out fear. Therefore, spend your time looking forward, yes, dreaming with God! There is an election coming for the U.S.; believe for the good! In the UK and in Europe as a whole, yes it looks like a cold winter, but God's plans are good. Australia, Asia, Africa, India, Canada, South America, God has good plans, and His timing is perfect! Amen!"

Judgment Beginning – October 28, 2022

Today the Lord is showing me some things pertaining to His judgment. I see the veil or curtain in the second temple torn from top to bottom as Jesus died on the cross. The veil was the very thing that kept sinful men from entering the Holy of Holies, and this veil was a constant reminder that men and God were separated under the Old Covenant. And then I saw that after the veil had been torn, God would never dwell in a temple made by human hands again! God the Father had judged sin and death. His very Son, Jesus, had become sin and had born the Father's judgment for us, so that anyone who would come to Him would be counted by the Father as righteous, even the righteousness of God in Christ Jesus.

This, then, is judgment itself: if one is in Christ, he is already judged! If not, then he is judged already. Jesus is the only door into heaven. There is no other way. We are free to choose His gift of redemption or not.

After speaking to me about these things, the Lord said: "Now look, Prophet. Look at the world." He opened my eyes, and I looked at the world. It looked like I was watching people. I didn't understand what I was seeing. I could see through structures, the earth, and any solid object. I saw some people who seemed to glow with light and others who didn't.

Then the Lord said to me, "Do you see the sons of light?" I said, "Yes, I believe I do, but there are so few, Lord!" It looked like only about a tenth, or maybe less, of the people had the light.

Then the Lord spoke again. "Yes, those are My chosen ones who will begin to bring in the harvest of the last days."

I thought, "How will so few bring in so many?" I was thinking of the billion-youth harvest.

The Lord spoke to me about my thoughts. "Prophet, most of the ones that you see as having the light will be supporting those who are going out. It will be a huge task! But My Spirit is with you!"

Then I saw another judgment of the Lord, and my eyes were opened to see the earth's wealth. To my eyes it appeared to be like water. There was a flow to it, and reservoirs of it, both big and small. Then I again saw the people who were glowing with light. As I watched, the reservoirs seemed to get leaks in them. The leaks were just a trickle at first, but they got to be a fairly large and there was a constant flow from the reservoirs to those who were glowing with light. As this happened, those who were glowing did not store it or keep it. Smaller streams of the wealth/water poured from them to those who were not light. As I watched, this process seemed to start out at a rapid flow and then slowed to a constant, but smaller, flow.

236

Then the Lord spoke again. "My people shall be blessed and not cursed any longer. For the wealth shall flow from the darkness into the light, and those of the light shall be an example of what love and wealth should look like."

I kept watching, and I noticed something else. The people who were not of the light seemed to clamor and be in great distress. Not all of them. In fact, maybe around a tenth of them did this. Then I noticed that their light, which was darkness, was also snuffed out. And they were gone from my view.

Then this vision stopped, and I heard the Lord's voice once more: "The last shall be first and the first last. Watch for My judgment. Behold, it is beginning. Amen."

Judgment for the Judiciary – November 4, 2022

"Kirk, prepare the people for a judgment that is coming!

When the founders of the United States gathered, I Am was there! And when they wrote the Constitution of the United States, I AM was there! When the framers of the three branches of the U.S. government marked off each branch's boundaries, I AM was there!

Today I want to speak to you regarding the Judiciary. Prophet, tell the people: There is going to be a shaking in the Judiciary! One branch was given a specific task, which was to keep the other two branches within the framework of the Constitution – not to be partial toward anything, except the Constitution. Some of the Justices understand this and still do their best to uphold the principles set forth in this document. This warning, or word, is not directed toward them. Quite the opposite!

I AM will no longer tolerate the Justices who have made a laughingstock of the Law! Therefore, I AM initiating a purge in the Judiciary! Yes, the Federal! Yes, in the State. Yes, in local government! From top to bottom, the justices' <u>records</u> will be held up against the Constitution of the United States. Those found wanting will be removed from their positions, and those who are found to be traitors to the United States will be fully prosecuted, and the very law which they attempted to subvert will be applied to them without remorse. Yes, the Congress will act! And yes, the highest court in the land will support the President as he applies the Law.

Money, influence, threats, and any other kind of subversion will no longer plague the judiciary! Even judges who serve for life will know that serving 'during good behavior' has teeth! I AM has spoken. Amen."

A Rebuke from the Lord – November 16, 2022

"Are you disappointed regarding the mid-term elections? What about Donald Trump's 'announcement'? (Given November 15, 2022 – that he's running for President in 2024) Did that disappoint you too? Or maybe it's the 2020 election results/cheating? Are you still disappointed because of that?

What about My Prophets? Have you heard some very bold 'words' which you have decided will not happen, or maybe these 'words' aren't happening on your time schedule? Or maybe you've decided to stop listening to My Prophets because you did at first – after the 2020 election – but what they prophesied hasn't yet come to pass! And hey, it's been two years after all! These 'Prophets' could be false prophets you know... (Even though what they have said came to your heart with a witness of the Spirit of God).

I, the Lord, find no pleasure in My sheep who wander from Me. Who look for greener pastures as soon as faith is required. Who hear My voice and decide in their hearts to leave Me. Will you only follow the Good Shepherd as long as the grass is green and plentiful and water is near?

My eyes roam to and fro on the earth. Where will I find faith? Sheep need no shepherd when everything is going wonderful for them. But, when things become difficult and dangerous, that is when the sheep <u>need</u> a shepherd!

So then, where do you find guidance? Where is the source of your faith? Who can you believe? Who knows where you are, what's around the corner, where is the good way? The mainstream news? Ah! You're a thinker, so you know where to find the truth on the internet! Or maybe there is this really knowledgeable patriot who knows all and tells all .... Look, My people! Even a broken clock points to the correct time twice a day! I AM is not broken!

My Prophets are chosen by Me. I AM responsible for them, and I AM capable of raising them up or casting them down. You will know them by their <u>FRUIT</u>! Not by their popularity, or even by their accuracy, but by their fruit! A Prophet's fruit will be known and demonstrated by their unbending devotion to Me. Their only desire in life is to lift up the Son of the living God by following His Spirit. They have died to themselves and live only for Me! Money, fame, ministries, comfort, detractors, supporters, reputation, none of these things matter to those who are Mine. Only My approval, direction, and a relationship with Me matter to these who are Mine.

Therefore, answer Me! Where do you get the news that you believe in? And where do you put your faith? Amen."

Faith for the End Times – November 25, 2022

"End times Prophet, take up your pen, and I will speak to you.

I Am has spoken regarding these end times in which you are living since ancient times. Yes, and from the dawn of time I have spoken about and thought about this season of time.

The ancients desired to be alive during these times, not because they saw ease and comfort, but because they foresaw the reward for faithfulness would be great. And truly, they are still excited and amazed at those who will be faithful during this season. Truly, heaven is abuzz with excitement to hear the testimony that will come from those whose faith does not fail them!

All of heaven knows that the Lord is the victor! All of hell knows this too! Even Satan knows who the victor is! It is all settled, except in the minds of men. So then, this battle rages on, just like it has from the time of Adam and Eve. I Am tells all men what He holds for them and what He has given them freely, and all they have to do is believe. Meanwhile, Satan tries to get their eyes off of My words and blessings, speaking to them of earthly things, things they could hold and see, things which are being withheld from them. Therefore, do not listen to him. He is a liar and a thief and full of death and destruction. My people, if you believe him and follow him, there is no end to the deaths you will die!

Look, I Am fully aware that you desire to be spoon-fed, to have what you want now, to be told exactly what will happen in the future and when! I Am, however, requires faith! This is not up for discussion. FAITH is required. Yes, you must trust ME! This faith is not a 'one time' confession! It is an everyday, die to self, live for Me thing!

So now, do you still wonder why My Prophets are sometimes vague, sometimes seem to disagree, and always say, 'Do not fear'? It is not My intention to make things crystal clear to you. These prophets of Mine are not soothsayers, readers of the crystal ball, or diviners! They are Mine, and they say what I tell them, in the tone and volume that I direct them to.

Do you think you can cajole Me into doing something by saying, 'Well, I just don't believe the prophets anymore; they have been speaking grand things for so long and I just need to walk away from them'? Do I really need to tell you that your faith is being tested?

I have put forth My anointed one who will lead you. I have exposed things that you, in your sleep, never even thought of. I Am bringing down Babylon in a way that only I can do. I AM bringing My faithful into a very bright future and blessing them in ways that have never been seen on earth. DO NOT FEAR! HAVE FAITH! Amen."

Wake Up! Run to the Battle - December 9, 2022

Today the Lord is saying, "Wake Up!"

He's asking me if the people understand what's going on. And because He's asking this, I don't feel very hopeful. I answer, "Lord, you know...".

Then He says, "Some do. But by far, most do not. Most people think that there's a political problem – like those on the far right vs. those on the far left. Still others blow it off as simply a process of ideological change. Others correctly see that the world is in a battle of good vs. evil but have no clue that this is a spiritual battle. It's not simply evil men vs. good men. There are demons who are literally fighting in this battle. There are also angels literally fighting in this battle for the world.

The people see things that 'just don't make sense,' things that cause death, things that cause energy to be more difficult to obtain or cost more, farms being shut down for no good reason, good distribution systems being tampered with maliciously, and medical organizations that seem to be more about killing than preserving life, etc. Let the reader understand that these things are driven by the demonic whose calling card reads, 'Kill, Steal, Destroy.' No, it's not the Green New Deal to save the planet from 'Global Warming.' It's the Demonic New Deal to provide cover for Kill, Steal, and Destroy!

Open your eyes, My People! Your enemy isn't even hiding anymore. He openly creates fear of something – anything – and you go along with it? Have I said there is such a thing as global warming? What happened to global cooling, acid rain, the ozone hole, Y2K, the sea level rising? Is the sky really falling? By now you should have learned something about this fear mongering! It is demonic. I Am says, 'Do Not Fear!'

All of these lies have an agenda – to generate fear and to cover something else that is furthering the demonic agenda.

Now then, isn't it true that I Am has said that in the last days there would be false teachers and false prophets? That some of these would even come in My name? (These are the ones generating fear!)

Therefore, stop persecuting those who bring the Truth and the Gospel! The demonic is right out in the open, spewing lies and prophesying lies to generate fear. Call these liars, cheaters, and agents of the devil out! You think it is safer to call out those who are Mine, says the Lord. But I Am is telling you cowards who do this, that it is not safer!

I Am the Lord! Is there something I have not seen? Something I don't know about? NO! I Am is calling My Own out of the darkness and into the glorious light. Come, My faithful. Fight with Me and the heavenly hosts! I Am on a rescue mission, but I desire all those who will to do My will to enjoy the victory that will be the result of this fight! Throw off the lies and entanglements. Run with Me to the battle! I Am a warrior! Fear not, because I AM able! Amen!"

Made in America – December 10, 2022

I (Tiffany) heard the Lord say, "Made in America." We prayed about it, and Kirk heard that God's Great Reset will be Made in America. There are other nations rising up, and sometimes it looks like they may lead the way, but it won't be so. This Great Reset the Lord is doing will be

Made in America. This nation will lead the way and the Trumpet is at the helm. For it is true that the world will be known as Before Trump and After Trump. Amen.

War Room Situation Update – December 16, 2022

Today, as I (Kirk) was praying, I asked the Lord if I would get a "word" or vision or something today. I heard, "Yes, are you ready right now?" I answered, "Yes, I'm ready." The Lord then said, "Okay, meet Me in the Courts of Heaven."

I closed my eyes and was immediately in the spirit and in the rear area of the Courts of Heaven. I looked around and then walked toward the Court. As I approached the main walkway that runs the length of the seating area, I saw Jesus and walked toward Him. As I approached, He turned toward me, reached out His hand toward me, and said, "Hello, friend!" He seemed so glad to see me, and I also reached out my hand like I thought I would shake His hand. But, as He took my hand, I realized that He intended to keep hold of my hand as we walked.

On other occasions when I have met the Lord in heaven, He towered over me. Today we were about the same in stature. We walked to the front of the courtroom and proceeded up the stairs, past the judge's chair, and went through a door in the back, which led down the corridor, or hallway, where I had visited the War Room before in a different vision. As we walked, we also talked. Surprisingly, He loves to hear about my life and asks questions regarding whatever I may be doing. The conversation seemed so relaxed and informal.

We got to the War Room, and angels were entering and leaving. It was very busy today, even busier than when I had seen it in its "speeded up mode" during a prior visit there. We again went up to the viewing area above the area where all the planning and where all the angels were studying the future events on the TV screens. (I'm not sure exactly what to call them. The angels watch events play out in 3-D and plan for future events.) What was really different this time was the number of angels and saints and creatures all up on the observation area. And there were even some that were floating in the air above the War Room area!

I asked Jesus what was going that there was so much excitement today? Jesus answered: "It has been like this for some time. All of heaven expects a great event to happen on earth. So, all of these are excited for what will happen and are watching to see what will happen. No one wants to miss it! Aside from My appearance on earth, it will be the greatest event of all time! Each day brings fresh excitement on the run-up to this event, and heaven gets evermore excited to see it."

I asked Jesus what exactly was going to happen? He smiled a sort of sideways smile and answered, "God knows exactly what will happen."

And I then realized that no one in all of heaven knew what was to take place. That is probably what some of the excitement was about and also why the War Room was so busy. Maybe a sneak peek could be had on one of the angel's viewers? So, after thinking about that for a while, I asked Him if I could know when this mysterious event might happen? He then turned to face me and said, "I understand your curiosity, but no one but God knows exactly when 'the event' will happen, and indeed, that's the way it must be. We are in the season, and indeed, very close to the time, however."

Some time passed as we walked and talked. Then once again the Lord Jesus turned to me and stopped. He just looked at me for a time. Then said, "Kirk, My Prophet, go and tell the people that what they have been hoping for is on the way. Tell them that they <u>must</u> go through some things on the way... lies, perhaps unpleasant things. A time of awakening and perseverance, an eye-opening experience is needed by all.

This time of My Great Reset is not a small bump in the road so that you can get back to the way things were. A real awakening – one that will not be forgotten – needs to happen in order for the actual reset to take place. I, even I AM telling you that some will become impatient, but it will be to their own detriment. Be patient! I Am working a work that no one can stop! No amount of whining or cajoling will speed it up either! Keep your eyes on Me, trust Me, and do this thing with Me! Above all, do NOT fear! Amen."

Vision of Kari Lake & Donald Trump holding up a wall –

December 17, 2022

I (Kirk) see Kari Lake and Donald Trump holding up steel – like a dam. Looking over the top of the steel, I see water and debris as it slams into the steel wall. Kari Lake and Donald J. Trump are holding it up. Their hands are over their heads, and they have dug in with their feet, and are actually holding back the flood. I see them looking around as they work and yelling for help.

Help does come, slowly at first. And then suddenly, there are people everywhere helping. I see the people who came to help wearing ball caps. Some said "MAGA" on them. Others said, "The American Patriot Party." They hold the line, and the flood does not breach the blockade.

Fierce Love of God – December 23, 2022

"My love is so fierce, Tiffany. In all things I Am motivated by love. Love will not allow Me to turn a blind eye to evil. I Am love. My justice will be meted out completely, nothing left undone. The earth has never seen such justice as will happen in My Great Reset. I will not rest until it is done. I said, 'Give Me no rest until I make Jerusalem a praise in the earth.' Neither shall I rest in this great work I Am doing.

My Son shall be exalted in the earth. My Spirit shall be honored in My people, in My Church, My True Church, the one that truly bears My Son's name. He is highly exalted in Heaven, and My people bear His likeness on earth. The earth will be in awe at this."

Movement of Apostles – December 23, 2022

The coming of the apostles is not a denominational thing. It is a movement. It's like when the International House of Prayer came about. There's no denomination about prayer. It's simply a movement of prayer. Now is the time of the Prophets. This isn't a denomination either. It's a movement of prophets. It will be the same thing with the apostles.

This move will be organic, by the Spirit. The apostles will seem to just pop up, and they will be in authority. This isn't organized by men, though men will participate and those apostles over apostles will help facilitate. Even so, this is a move of the Spirit.

The time of the prophets is winding down and the time of the apostles will begin. The prophets will never be discarded, but they'll have a different role where they'll lift up their apostles. It will be a change in the church. The prominence in the kingdom will move from the prophets to the apostles so that the apostles can lead the church in these end times.

God has not Changed His Mind (DJT & God's Great Reset) – December 30, 2022

Today as I (Kirk) am in prayer, I heard the Lord say:

"Prophet, say to the people: I AM has not changed His mind! Donald J. Trump is the one I have chosen to lead My Great Reset. My words through My Prophets have not been wrong! Donald J. Trump did win the 2020 election. The Trump Train is running and will continue to run on time! The shot heard around the world has been fired. Is there anyone in any country who still believes that 'they' have free and fair elections? Open your 'eyes' and 'see' the truth of My words. Has the world changed since My wrecking ball was elected? I AM telling you it has, and the change is still accelerating. And it has a way to go yet.

Do you really believe that the wagging tongues of the impatient and faithless unbelievers will stop when Donald J. Trump retakes the Official Presidency? No – their offense and demands will not be satiated until they repent of their unbelief and turn to Me. Don't give them the time they so desire. Trying to answer their unbelief will only cause them to look at something else. Their arguments and logic are earthly, demonic.

Conversely, those who are Mine, the ones I love, have kept the faith. Indeed, their faith has risen up during this time. It has become stronger and stronger with every challenge. These are the ones I have seen as worthy. These are the ones I have chosen for these last days! And yes, the latter rain will surely fall on those who have stood the test and have bested all of the enemy's tactics and trials.

Now, My people, look to the future with great anticipation and joy! Your God is love and He is good! Can evil ever really win? Could Satan really challenge Me? It is said on the earth that this upheaval is not political or cultural, but that it is spiritual. In particular, it is good vs. evil. Or maybe God vs. Satan. But I tell you, NO! This notion assumes that there is a chance that I AM could lose! There is no such chance.

The chaos that you see is My love at work. It is a rescue mission that I AM undertaking in a sovereign manner. I AM inviting My saints to participate in this because I wish to revel in the great victory that they will have! We are using

Plan A. There is no fallback plan, no secondary plan, such as Plan B. My plan is perfect and cannot fail.

The result of this great victory will change the earth forever. I have detailed these changes in other 'Words' and Prophecies. Amen."

2023

The Letters – January 13, 2023

Today in prayer, I (Kirk) see a group of people at work. They are working at a machine that prints letters and stuffs envelopes. They are preparing a large quantity of envelopes. There are many plastic boxes full of them. I'm wondering why I'm seeing this – the workers and everything else look pretty normal.

After watching for a while, I noticed one of the letters on the top of a stack in one of the boxes. I don't know how, but I was able to zoom in on the front of this letter. It was addressed to a "Judge Green." I kind of scanned all of the boxes and most of the top letters that I could see all seemed to be addressed to people involved in the law. Words like "judge," "magistrate," "clerk," etc. were common. This didn't seem out of the ordinary either. I supposed that these people received many letters from the government.

I began asking the Lord what the meaning of this vision was. In my spirit, I heard, "It's the next wave." Right then I saw Mar-A-Lago. Then it was over.

Vision of Hell – January 20, 2023

Vision given to Kirk.

The Lord said, "Come up here." I said, "Where, LORD?"

I began to see all of the different places in Heaven. Some I had seen before and some not. The Courts of Heaven, animals, horses and dogs, the clear water and fish, stars and the earth, the two trees in the Garden, the Throne Room, all of these things and much, much more flashed before my eyes.

Then I came to a place. The area was very light to my right but completely dark to my left and filled with smoke. At times I would get a whiff of the smell of hell and death, just like the demon smelled in the natural when I smelled one in a room in my house years ago. It was an awful, dry smell, a stench that made me wince. I moved forward, and I started to hear voices, then suddenly a blood curdling scream! Talking, yelling, cursing, confused speech, moaning, and all kinds of human voices. As I got closer, I realized that all of the voices were in some kind of response to the terror these people were experiencing.

Then I began to see something that looked like a conveyor belt, but it was quite wide and almost full of people. The stench of death was very strong here. It was very dry and felt depressing and hopeless. The "conveyer" transported those on it toward the darkness and completely out of sight. The darkness almost seemed alive to me as it swallowed those transported into it. Of those on the belt, some looked tough, rebellious, and violent. Others looked like thinkers, studious and confident as they came from the lighted end and headed toward the darkness. By far, though, most of these people looked like good people from all over the world and were dressed in their normal clothing from wherever they had lived.

I was there in the spirit and kind of up above and to the side of the conveyer. Without exception, all of these people looked toward the side I was on, seemingly looking beneath me. As they did, their eyes would grow wide open and some would drop to their knees, young and old alike, their eyes open, and some would say, "They were right" or "I should have listened to them." (There were no children at all, but quite a few young adults.) And I realized that they were all receiving a witness of the Lord of what their fate was. I understood that all of these had been either exposed to the Lord in some way and had refused Him or had become entangled in religion and did not represent the Lord, but only had a form of religion.

I again looked and saw all of these disappear into the darkness. For all eternity, forever, darkness! I asked to come back. Amen.

The Time is Near – January 27, 2023

The Lord says, "Until now things regarding My Great Reset have been quite subdued in the USA. That is about to change. There shall be a series of events that shall take place that will divide the wheat and the chaff. Yes, these events will indicate to the intellectual mind that the world is coming to an end. Those whose anchor is not from Me will be in a panic, and they shall do things that will show that this is the case.

DO NOT LISTEN TO THEM! You have the truth. You have heard the Prophets. You know Me. Do not fear! There will be signs and there will be great wonderment that will make men faint in terror, but you will not pay attention to them. Your eyes will be fixed on Me. There will be signs in the heavens and on the earth and darkness."

[As I write these things, what I see is that some (or all?) of these things will be our enemy having his last gasp – like events in the water, maybe the ocean, which cause destruction generated by man-made means. It's not a supernatural event, even though it may be made to look that way. The fire or signs in the sky could be something that was made for warfare but is being used to create fear and maybe even death. The darkness too – it didn't seem literal as if the sun went away. And my thoughts went to electrical communication, black outs.]

"These events must take place to wake up the peoples of the world, to jar them from their stupor. And I Am shall allow Satan to have his little hissy fit. And I shall use it for good. His attempt to frighten the world into submission has, and will, fail. I mentioned the USA. However, these sorts of things shall happen around the globe, and especially in the areas where people have been waking up. The U.K., Australia, South and all of North America, and Asia.

Apostle Tiffany, let the people know what the Prophet of the Lord has said. Amen."

Great Reset Blessing Decisions – February 3, 2023

"What will you do with the blessing that you receive?

The GREAT reset has begun. This is no secret. Everyone around the world can plainly see evil being uncovered and exposed to the light. This is a dangerous phase because of what evil men might be led to do. This phase will overlap the next phase, which is the 'involvement' phase. Or it might be called the 'personal involvement' phase because this is the place in time when the saints will need to get involved in the seven mountains. There will be ample opportunity for involvement, too!

Justice will get into full swing during this involvement phase and will be present for a great while as the total extent of the corruption is uncovered and dealt with. During the involvement phase, wealth from the darkness shall begin to flow to the light and will usher in a period of blessing for those who have stood in righteousness. I AM has gone to war with His saints, and there shall be plunder – very much plunder! The treasures of darkness will flow like a river into the light!

I AM wants to speak regarding this flow of treasure and also the fortunes that will be made in all of the seven mountains of influence. This will be a time of great prosperity around the world.

The Lord is asking you, yes, you personally! You! Not your neighbor or your relatives or anyone else, but you! He wants to know what you will do with this wealth that is coming. Will you hoard it like those of the world do? Or spend it on yourself perhaps?

Following is easier for those who are not rich; their choices are limited. But for the rich, it is easy to depend on their riches. I AM asking you now – will you still follow My Spirit? Or will you begin to depend on your newfound wealth? Make up your mind today! Determine to teach your children! More wealth will not solve your problems. This wealth transfer is a blessing, but real blessing is found only in Me. Do you really think after My reset there will simply be the 'easy life'? Is that what you're looking forward to?

Remember, I AM has said that work will again be viewed as honorable! My people's calling card will be their work ethic, love (commitment to Me), and generosity! Banks will be for saving! The medical industry will be for people's health! Schools will be for learning! Entertainment will be wholesome! And so much more.

All of these things will take a lot of work to keep in line with My Spirit. Remember this is MY reset! Amen."

Separation is Found in the Knowledge of Christ –

February 5, 2023

"From the beginning of time man has desired to know the mysteries of God. Man has even aspired to be God for the sake of knowledge (I see Adam & Eve). As you know, all wisdom and knowledge is hidden in Christ. Therefore, only those who humble themselves will be given the insight into the mysteries of God. Only by saying – I lay it all down that I may have the Son – may one be found to be in Christ and to know His mysteries. No knowledge attained another way will profit man. Knowledge will do no good to anyone on the Day of Judgment, except to know Me through My Son. For those who know Me through My Son, all things are added to them. There's nothing that I will withhold, for their desire is for Me and My Son. All of this knowing comes through My Holy Spirit.

Can you see how one must humble oneself then? To submit to My Spirit is to know and do outside of one's own strength. This is difficult, at best, for those whose identity is in what they have, or can, accomplish.

Those who follow My Spirit are full of grace and truth because they are filled with My Son. His life is in them. They've chosen to eat His flesh and drink His blood – to partake of the whole Lamb and die to themselves, that they may truly live.

What I Am doing and am about to do on the earth truly will separate the wheat from the chaff and tares. Those who truly love My Son will not hesitate to be filled with and to follow His Spirit. Those who do not, will not. The separation will become more clear and more distinct so that even those with eyes that do not see will understand there is a difference.

Power? Are you wondering if it is power that shall be the separation? (I [Tiffany] was wondering...) The separation is those who know Me and those who don't. And as the

Scriptures say – those who know their God will perform great feats (Daniel 11:32). Yes, there will be power, such as the world has never seen yet. The power of a life in Christ will be a source of wonderment to the world. Amen."

His Government & the Harvest – February 10, 2023

Isaiah 9:2-7 NASB

The people who walk in darkness
  Will see a great light;
Those who live in a dark land,
The light will shine on them.
You will multiply the nation,
You will increase their joy;
They will rejoice in Your presence
As with the joy of harvest,
As people rejoice when they divide the spoils.
For You will break the yoke of their burden and the staff on their shoulders,
The rod of their oppressor, as at the battle of Midian.
For every boot of the marching warrior in the roar of battle,
And cloak rolled in blood, will be for burning, fuel for the fire.
For a Child will be born to us, a Son will be given to us;
And the government will rest on His shoulders;
And His name will be called Wonderful Counselor, Mighty God,
Eternal Father, Prince of Peace.

There will be no end to the increase of His government or of peace
On the throne of David and over his kingdom
To establish it and to uphold it with justice and righteousness
From then on and forevermore.
The zeal of the LORD of armies will accomplish this.

The Lord says, "This then is the prophecy of My servant Isaiah. Some of the events he spoke of have come to pass. Behold, the field is white for harvest, but the tares must be removed first, and burned with unquenchable fire. Amen."

Vision of Streams in the Desert, War, and Wasteland – February 24, 2023

Today the Lord came to me (Kirk), and said, "Come with Me. I want to show you some things."

He took me to a high sand hill that overlooked a desert. I could see nothing but sand hills as far as the eye could see. We were in an extension of the Sahara Desert called the Arabian Desert. As I looked, the Lord asked me if I thought this desert could turn green with life. I looked around again. It was very dry there. But I knew who I was talking to, so I said, "Yes, Lord. I believe You could make it green and fertile."

Just then He raised His right hand and flattened it. He then slowly rotated in a half circle. "Look again," He said to me. So, I looked. I could see the whole Arabian Peninsula now.

As I looked north, it began to turn green. Along the Red Sea there was more green. There were fields, crops of grain, groves of fruit, and all manner of produce where desert had been. I looked at Him in amazement. He looked back at me and said, "Yes, streams in the desert shall be one of the effects of this Great Reset."

Still standing on the sand hill, the Lord again stretched out His right hand. As He did, what appeared to be something like a huge movie screen opened up in front of us. I saw what looked like a war-torn area, buildings and homes all broken and in disrepair, smoke coming from some of them. War machines like tanks and other vehicles rolled down empty streets. People, adults and children, hid themselves where they could, and only came out to search for food and water. I could smell death and acrid smoke. It was awful.

We both watched the scene in front of us. Then the Lord spoke. "Why did this happen? For what reason did this people rise against their neighbor?" After a minute, I replied that I didn't know.

Again, He spoke. "Was it jealousy? Anger? Mistrust? Did someone have something to gain? Or was it just a desire to kill?" Again, some time goes by. Then, "I tell you, it's foolishness that brings this on, demonic foolishness!"

And again, He turns to me. "What would happen if those who listen, yes worship the demonic, were removed? Those who fund – removed? Those who pit one against the other – removed? And what if those who would benefit from warfare were removed?"

I answered, "Well, I guess the endless wars would stop."

"Yes!" He said.

He again raises His hand, pointing to the scene in front of us. He flicks His wrist, and it changes. Now I see the sky filled with black smoke and fires on the ground. (It looked like the video of the train derailment in Ohio.) Then I saw lakes and rivers – all polluted, discolored, and deadly. I saw cities all over the world that were deserted and empty. To live there would mean certain sickness and death! The scene changes, and I see private aircraft and the "elite" of the world meeting together. They think highly of themselves and speak of global temperatures and environmentalism.

The Lord speaks to me again. "Do you ever see these fly in to clean up a disaster? Or maybe fund the cleanup? I say, NO! They are a facade and do not care about the earth or its people! They work for Satan himself." The scene before us closes.

Then the Lord stands looking off into the distance. As He looks, He begins to speak: "Yes, this is a rescue mission, and I will do it. I know there are those who believe that it must get worse. The blind lead the blind. But you see! Don't bother with them. What will it take to convince them? A clever argument? Starvation or torture? No. Even these will not convince them of their folly. I AM says follow Me and don't bother to chase after them. They will distract and bring nothing else to the table. Do not fear! Keep your eyes on Me. Amen."

Anger of the Lord Aroused – March 1, 2023

This day the Lord says, "Do <u>not</u> touch those who are called by Me, and do <u>not</u> speak against My anointed ones! Do <u>not</u> slander or hold in contempt My chosen ones, those who have answered My call and obey My voice! Yes, My Apostles and yes, My Prophets, and the rest of My ministers as well. Remember the Korah rebellion, you mockers and rebellious ones! Therefore, the very Book you hold dear and yes, worship, stands against you and testifies against you! You religious zealots, put your Book away for a moment and look up!

I AM very near, but you will not come to Me. I have loved you, but you don't even know Me. You persecute those I have called and elevate those who have graduated from your own schools. You make worthless the very Book you say you believe. You have a form of godliness but NO power. You claim to have power because of your studies and the titles that you bestow upon yourselves, but these are based on earthly knowledge and wisdom. Yes, I said EARTHLY! Earthly and demonic! You claim to 'know' Me, but you do not.

And the Father who sent Me, He has testified of Me. You have neither heard His voice at any time nor seen His form. You do not have His Word abiding in you, for you do not believe Him whom He sent. You search the Scriptures because you think that in them you have eternal life; it is these that testify about Me; and you are unwilling to come to Me so that you may have life. (John 5:37-40 NASB)

So, look at this then. The very words that you say you believe testify against you! I AM says that you are responsible for the revelation that you were given, and you were given MUCH! Therefore, do not come to Me and expect mercy! I AM has given you the Prophets and the Fathers, My very own Son, and you have the Scriptures! My Apostles, Prophets, Evangelists, Pastors, and Teachers speak, but you do not listen.

Repent and come to Me. I hold out My hands all day long. I've been waiting, but I Am not waiting much longer. Amen."

The Apostles – March 3, 2023

The Lord says, "Look at this mess! Even My fivefold ministers look like the blind leading the blind! This should not be! I AM has called them, and yet there is infighting among them as if they were of the world!

Look! You see My Teachers and Pastors, yes and My Evangelists are easy to spot, just as My Prophets, again easy to spot! But where are My Apostles? Oh, there are those who believe that they are Apostles. They have been given much grace as an Evangelist or Prophet, or maybe even a Pastor. Then people start to call them 'Apostle,' and they believe it. But there is One who calls. Only One!

It is written that the gifts and callings are irrevocable, and this is true! If I Am calling you as a Prophet, then that's what you have been called to. It is irrevocable. Don't you know what this word means? It means this: Incapable of being recalled or revoked; unchangeable; irreversible or unalterable. So, it does not matter what the person in the office desires to be or thinks they are. It doesn't matter what they are called by others. I AM calls you to your office, and He has decided that it will not change! Once He has called you, you are what He has called you to. You will <u>not</u> someday graduate to another office.

In the case of a Prophet, you must be called to the office of Prophet to have the office of Prophet. If you have the <u>gift</u> of prophecy and use it to an amazing effect, and you tower over those in the office of Prophet, you are still not a prophet with an office of Prophet. And if you, as a Prophet in the office of Prophet, tower above all prophets in accuracy and authority, you will neither ascend to the office of Apostle nor exceed an Apostle's authority. Those in the offices of the fivefold ministers are irrevocably chosen by Jesus Christ, and that is the one and only way to a fivefold minister's office.

Apostles then are leaders in the fivefold. They are charged with authority over the other offices. Prophets prophesy – Evangelists evangelize – Pastors pastor churches – and Teachers teach. (This is simplified.) The measure of success is measured in this way, but the Apostle's measure of success is how they lead. If the other offices under an Apostle are very successful, then the Apostle is successful.

My Church is a mess because usurpers and charlatans have called themselves Apostles, but these have no real power, only persuasive words of men's wisdom. The Church is about to be <u>rocked</u> by real power and authority that comes from the Lord Himself. The authority and power seen in the first few chapters in Acts as the new Church is established will look like child's play. My church in these last days will again be filled with Power and Authority as exemplified by My Apostles. They will come on the scene in much the same way, except that the power will be released by My Spirit in <u>greater </u>measure.

Watch for the Apostles then. A few will come on the scene to call the rest of them from their normality. They know who they are already, but they need to be released. Amen."

The Spiritually Sick and Weak – March 3, 2023

The LORD: "You're weak without food, aren't you?"

Tiffany: "Yes."

The LORD: "What about those who never hear My voice?"

Tiffany: "They're dead. *'You have neither heard His voice at any time, nor seen His form.*'"

The LORD: "Yes, and there are those who hear Me only for what they want. They think My gifts and callings are the same as My approval of everything they are doing. They point to the number of followers they have and every external thing to determine they're in the right. I AM rebuking them. They're weak, and they don't even know it. They're sick and not able to see it. They are "*wretched, miserable, poor blind, and naked*" and do not know it (Revelation 3:17). Tiffany, the gap is widening."

Tiffany: "Why?"

The LORD: "Because the revelation of My Son is rampant on the earth, and yet people choose to ignore it."

A Vision of the Apostles – March 10, 2023

I (Kirk) was taken to a place where I stood with Jesus in the middle of a huge group of Apostles. At the front of this group were the first Apostles – the "Twelve." I also saw Paul, Junia, and others I hadn't heard of before.

As I walked with Jesus, it was like walking through time. The Apostles we saw were dressed according to their ethnic dress of the day and time period. All of these had been called by Jesus as His ministers and as Apostles. He didn't speak to me, and as we walked on, I noticed a greater and greater number of Apostles which He had called. As I looked at them, I started to try to pick one out of the group to look at. And as I did, his name would come to me. I had not heard of any of these! Finally, I asked Jesus why I had not heard of any of these Apostles except a few of the very early ones.

He said, "These are truly My great ones. They have ministered before Me in purity and devotion. They were virtually unknown by men, however. And most never served in the 'church' of their time. Truly, these Apostles were the forgotten ones. But I remember each one! The 'church' wanted nothing to do with these, and in fact 'got rid' of a great number of them. 'The church' did not want true followers of Me, nor did they want My Spirit. They wanted control. All of My ministers were persecuted, tortured, mocked, or ignored during this season. None more than My Apostles and Prophets, however."

We continued to walk. I started to notice modern dress among the Apostles, and then I saw kids! Little ones! I asked Jesus if these too were Apostles? And why were there so many of them? Jesus answered, "These are My End Times Apostles, and yes, there are a great many of them! Some of these little ones already know that they are called as Apostles. Others will be brought forth later in their lives. There are a very large number of them, and indeed, a great number of all the fivefold ministers, because this is the season of the end times harvest. The 'church' the way it is now could never handle this influx of people. In fact, not enough buildings could be built of the modern 'church' type to house them. They will be overwhelmed, confused, and ineffective. The move to house churches is of necessity."

We walked further, and suddenly there were no more Apostles, and we were standing alone. We turned and looked back at the crowd we had just walked through. Jesus' face lit up and shown with light. He was so in love with these men, women, and children who had been chosen to be His Apostles. He turned to face me, and said, "Prophet, tell My people the time of the Apostle approaches. Embrace them. They are My chosen ones who will lead My Church, the true Church. I AM going to release power in this season too, and it's for anyone who is willing to carry it. But none will receive more if it than My Apostles. Amen!"

The Stench of Vermin – March 17, 2023

Today the Lord brought back to my nostrils a smell, actually a stench. I (Kirk) grew up on a family farm. We raised cows, sheep, chickens, and some of the feed crops that they would need to eat. The smell of fresh grain of whatever kind always had a rather good and sweet smell to it. However, the harvested grain was always an attraction for vermin, mice, rats, racoons, etc. And whenever these were present, the good smell of the grain was tainted. Even if you didn't actually see the pests, the stench would tip you off to their presence. An effort to eradicate these vermin would ensue in order to prevent the spread of sickness and disease and tainting of the grain, not to mention the theft and wasting of the grain.

The Lord is saying that this is the stench that has come up into His nostrils in Heaven. The vermin of hell have gotten into His granary! They taint everything they touch.

"Yes, My people's food is contaminated, as is the water they drink. Infectious agents are toyed with and released with nefarious intent. Then an antidote to the infectious poison is trotted out and touted as the cure! But the cure is more deadly than the sickness! Variations of this evil are used in all of the 7 mountains of influence (Family, Religion, Education, Media, Entertainment, Business, and Government). A problem is created, and then a solution is rolled out, which has no chance of working for My people, but only benefits the vermin.

The detection of these vermin in the world is in full swing now. More and more will be revealed. This season of detection, along with the exposure of these pests takes time, but the removal of all the vermin is predicated on their detection and exposure. Wisdom in these matters says that the elimination of a few of these scum without finding out the depth of the full infestation is foolish. The elimination phase has nevertheless begun. Remember the Wheat & Tares Parable!

Yes, I the Lord have heard the shouting: 'Hopium, hopium' (false hope) and 'When is something going to happen' and

'False Prophet!' Do not listen to these at all. Their words are <u>not</u> Mine. Their words only aid those who are against Me.

Remember, My people, I AM inviting My church to participate in the great victory that is coming! It will be the story of the ages and a great testimony for those who stand. It will also be a great shame for those who step back, are impatient, or are cowardly. Therefore, come to the front line of battle. That's where I AM. Is there a better or safer place than to stand with Me? Amen!"

The Throne Room of God – March 24, 2023

I (Kirk) asked the LORD if He had anything for me today – a vision, word, or if He might just speak with me. He said He had two visions for me today. Then He asked if I was impatient. I answered: "Yes, frequently." Then He asked, "Well, what about today, right now?" And I answered that I was.

Then the Lord said, "Kirk, go up to heaven." I asked, "Where in heaven, Lord?" He said, "The throne room." So, I went there.

I saw that there were many there in the throne room already. They all looked like orbs of light, and there were perhaps millions of them. But it didn't seem crowded at all. As I looked, I saw three thrones there. The one to my left was the throne of the Son of God. In the middle was the Father. And to my right was the Holy Spirit. Jesus looked pretty much like a man, as did the Father, although I couldn't see His face. And the Holy Spirit also looked like a man, but He had no face. There was an altar with burning coals in front of the thrones, and the smoke from it filled the place. (The smoke came up in puffs, and I had an understanding they were prayers.) There were creatures that flew above all of this. They were made out of fire, and their circling of the throne area made the smoke fill the area.

I was confused by all of this because I had been to the throne room before, and this was so different from the other times. As I thought about this, a voice came from the thrones. It sounded like thunder, and lightning flashed and rolled out from the thrones, and everything shook. (It wasn't like Father, Son, or Holy Spirit spoke individually, but like they spoke as One.) The voice said my name: "Kirk, come forward."

I guess I was one of the orbs of light too, but I went forward. Then, as I approached the thrones, I became or turned into the form of a man and stood between the altar and the thrones. For a moment I thought that I should be in fear or something. I didn't know what to do. As soon as this thought came, the voice from God said, "Do not fear." And even though I had thought about fear, I wasn't afraid to be there. So, I simply stood there for a time.

Then the voice thundered again asking, "Prophet, do you know why you're here?" I answered that other than being asked to come, no I didn't. The voice said, "We wanted to show you where you are meant to be, and to reinforce your faith and patience."

Again, the voice thundered, "You're wondering why this place looks so different. The appearance of things here changes based on countless things or desires. Do not concern yourself with this because I AM does not change."

I said, "Lord, I will be patient. Please help me with my impatience!"

Again, the voice of thunder: "Prophet, you will do everything I ask, as will your Apostle. Be patient. I Am good."

Dare to Dream (With God) – March 24, 2023

The Lord says: "I'm doing something different on the earth, as I've said before. Don't look at history to find the old patterns and ways. I'm doing something different! You have not come this way before, and this change is a global change. It will affect the entire planet in ways never before seen. I AM has given clues to the Prophets regarding the changes that will take place, but these clues are only clues and generalities. The extent and what all the countries and nations will look like in the future has not been imagined by man yet. The changes are of a magnitude that would impress Noah!

Imagine the 7 mountains of influence reduced to 3. What might those 3 remaining mountains be? What could take away the influence of these mountains? Prophet, tell the people to be ready to change their thinking in ways that will bring forth a new freedom that has never been seen before!

Imagine the freedom to be righteous and act righteously toward everyone and expect the same from others! This is normal, says I AM, and it will be the NEW normal. Do not expect the old system with a makeover. The old system is headed to the trash heap. It's over and done!

Think about religion thrown out in the trash heap too. All of its ways and rules and ideas – all thrown out! That church with all of its earthly ideas, rules for holiness, places where men claimed to represent Me but never did... I AM spewing it out of My mouth. The stench in My nostrils was awful, but the taste is worse!

I Am trying to get <u>you</u> to dream with Me! Get rid of the lament, and the belief that your brothers and sisters are basically bad! Those who are filled with My Spirit are bad? Skepticism and mistrust are NOT virtues! Faith and trust are from Me. Don't believe the evil one anymore! Come, dream with Me! I Am Good! I Am the way, and I Am the truth, and I Am the life. Come!"

Fear and Praise – March 31, 2023

Today the Lord again says, "Do not fear!" And He goes on: "I Am has spoken to you regarding fear many, many times in the past, but these are perilous times, and there will be even more and greater shaking! You see My anointed threatened by corrupt men, and your enemy tries to bring fear. He is My anointed. This is true. But don't you think I AM could raise up another if that were necessary?

Am I so weak that I have to depend on a man, or am I so strong that I can use a man to change the world? I AM the Lord of Hosts! Nothing surprises Me; nothing is equal to Me; I Am never a failure and have never considered being so.

Do you see a leaf shaking in the wind? Or do you see the whole world shaking? Which is more difficult for Me to save? They are the same! My power does not run low, nor is My battery able to run down. My power is infinite and will be forever.

Do you see the desperation in the world right now? Do you see a cornered animal lashing out in desperation? Do you see the masses rising up to challenge this evil plight in the world? Do you see the tares maturing along with the wheat? Yes, your enemy will try to look mean and strong, but like a caged animal, his days are coming to a close.

Therefore, it's time to blow the shofar! It's time to raise a hallelujah! It's time to sing praises! The end of the Cabal grows near! I Am not wringing My hands in worry. Don't wring yours either!

Did you think that this current world system could topple without some shaking? My Prophets have been bringing words regarding this shaking for a long time. Trust Me. I Am good. Amen!''

As this word ended, I saw a vision of more shaking: threats and rumors of wars. I see those whose trust is in the government and the military, those who have no faith... they are breathless with fear. The fake news gins up and exaggerates the fear as their system collapses. The nations of the world create friction as things are in a flux, some by looking to gain advantage, others knowing the plan. The militaries of the world's great nations stand at the ready, and indeed come close to a great war. As I watch though, I don't see it actually happen...

Great Reset Well Underway – April 4, 2023

"Tiffany, the Great Reset, My Great Reset, is <u>well</u> underway. Today My Trumpet was arrested. I allowed him to feel that pain. And yet for him it is all joy. He knows the end, and he knows it's dangerous, but he's willing to take the risk. I have given him the heart of a lion. He will be unbending in delivering and meting out My justice.

I will remind him of this day when he's tempted to do otherwise. I will remind him of the J6 prisoners and their families. I will remind him of those falsely accused and imprisoned because they spoke truth and stood for righteousness. I will remind him of the lying media, the traitorous politicians, and the satanic cabal. I will remind him of the blood of children and infants crying for justice. (Pray for him.)

He will accomplish all that I have for him to do. I have assigned many good people to him to help him. I have assigned intercessors and prophets to decree and declare. And I have assigned My saints to go into the mountains of influence and gain the victory for Jesus Christ. All of this is by My Spirit and <u>not</u> by the power of man. My angels have been working, and they will be working until Kingdom come. They have been rejoicing, and I desire My people to rejoice with them."

You have been thinking of plagues in the Scriptures. Do you see how plagues only affect those without faith? This is how it is with My judgments. Blow the Shofar and Raise a Halleluiah is still the theme!"

A Request of the LORD for Judgment – April 5, 2023

Today, at the LORD's request, and as Apostle and Prophet of the Lord, representing His church and the nations of the world, we do hereby release the Lord to bring judgment in every part of His Kingdom.

This release is <u>not</u> because He needs our permission, but rather, that He has desired to partner with us, and has asked in that regard for us to agree with Him and release Him in the spirit of partnership to do as He desires. And this we now do.

At this time, the LORD has desired to bring a summary judgment. And as His representatives, representing the True Church, we agree with this assessment regarding a summary judgment. We see that His anointed has been touched, His people wronged, and our adversary has crossed the line.

Therefore, we are in agreement with the LORD, and also with whatever remedy seems good to Him.

So be it.

Planet of Scrolls – April 7, 2023

I (Kirk) was taken in the spirit to a large planet. As I approached it, I thought it was completely made out of scrolls. That's how it appeared to me. Then, suddenly, I was on a path through a wooded area. On the trail itself, I noticed words. I studied them and realized that the words were from Jesus, words that He had spoken. I looked around and started to notice that everything here had words on it, all were words that Jesus spoke. I saw tree trunks with words; the leaves of the trees had words on them, everything had Jesus' spoken words on it!

I bent down and lifted a blade of grass. On the underside of this blade of grass, it said, "and God became flesh." I was thinking that I could spend forever here and not be able to read every word. It was beautiful and also a bit intimidating because, well, having read the Bible and having taken in the words of Jesus in red letters, what I had read was less than a drop of water in the oceans of the earth. Untold numbers of Bibles could be written, and the word of God, Jesus, keeps speaking. It is very difficult to wrap my mind around.

As I was pondering how beautiful it was and looking around, Jesus came toward me, walking on the path. Love washed over me, and as I looked at Him, I noticed His eyes. They were so deep, so full of love. This time, He was as I imagined He was when He was on the earth as a Man. As He approached, He held out His right hand and said, "Come. There are some other things I want to show you."

When our hands touched, it was like we turned into light and shot away so fast that everything turned into a blur. When clarity came again, we were standing in a place where there appeared to be something like outdoor movie screens everywhere I looked. There were people and other beings, angels, etc., watching these. I wondered what they were watching. Just then, Jesus spoke:

"You can watch whatever you wish here – how God formed the earth, anything in all of history is available, detailed things regarding Our intervention in everyone's life, the angels' work through the ages, etc. These are the testimony of God, and they cover all time – the past, present, and future of the earth and everything in it.

Prophet, you have wondered what there is to prophesy. There are so many Prophets who have prophesied already.... Do you understand what I AM showing you?"

I said, "I think so. You're saying that there is an infinite amount of prophetic words and revelation. There's no real limit to the prophetic."

Jesus said, "Yes, that's it from your point of view." (I understood that my view was infinite. His view was not.)

Again, the Lord speaks, "They have touched My Anointed and desire much worse for him. Next comes judgment. I Am not pleased, and the fate of those arrayed against My Trumpet will be even worse than they could imagine. For those who have touched him, even though they are completely ignorant, their fate is already sealed up. And for the ones who have put them up to this and financed this sham, they are completely evil, unredeemable, and damned. So be it says the Great I AM."

The End is Near – Feel the Wind of the Spirit –

April 9, 2023

"Tiffany, the end is near. Can you hear the sound of My trumpet? Can you feel the wind of the Spirit? Can you see

He's being poured out? Can you feel the pressure? Soon, He will be poured out in full force upon <u>all</u> flesh! All who desire Him shall carry Him to the farthest parts of the earth.

The rocks split open, and dead people came to life at the death and resurrection of My Son. How much more shall the impossible occur in these last days with the outpouring of My Spirit – what is termed 'the Latter Rain'? I Am not holding back when He is poured out full force. The earth shall shake like never before as darkness flees, justice prevails, righteousness is established, and love is expressed through faith! Amen."

Muslim Women Pregnant with the Gospel Dream –

April 9, 2023

In a dream, I (Tiffany) was seeing through the eyes of a woman, who looked as though she used to be Muslim, or I had the idea she used to be Muslim. She was with a man, and she had a pink sheer scarf/veil thing that had writing on it, and she kept wrapping and unwrapping her face with it. Then she and the man wrapped their heads together, with her back to his front side. He put his hands in front of her and she kissed them. Then he touched her waist, and they knew they'd get married. After this, they had to give the new church-starting manual to someone else. I had the idea the "someone else" would be the Amish.

The Holy Spirit says the Muslim woman in the dream represents all Muslim women. The man represents Jesus. He touched her, and she's pregnant with the gospel. The Muslims are going to turn to Christ through the women.

I also understood that the Amish would follow close behind.

Psalm 91 Today – April 21, 2023

Psalms 91

He who dwells in the secret place of the Most High
Shall abide under the shadow of the Almighty.
I will say of the Lord, "He is my refuge and my fortress;
My God, in Him I will trust."
Surely He shall deliver you from the snare of the fowler
And from the perilous pestilence.
He shall cover you with His feathers,
And under His wings you shall take refuge;
His truth shall be your shield and buckler.
You shall not be afraid of the terror by night,
Nor of the arrow that flies by day,
Nor of the pestilence that walks in darkness,
Nor of the destruction that lays waste at noonday.
A thousand may fall at your side,
And ten thousand at your right hand;
But it shall not come near you.
Only with your eyes shall you look,
And see the reward of the wicked.
Because you have made the LORD, who is my refuge,
Even the Most High, your dwelling place,
No evil shall befall you,

Nor shall any plague come near your dwelling;
For He shall give His angels charge over you,
To keep you in all your ways.
In their hands they shall bear you up,
Lest you dash your foot against a stone.
You shall tread upon the lion and the cobra,
The young lion and the serpent you shall trample underfoot.
"Because he has set his love upon Me, therefore I will deliver him;
I will set him on high, because he has known My name.
He shall call upon Me, and I will answer him;
I will be with him in trouble;
I will deliver him and honor him.
With long life I will satisfy him,
And show him My salvation."

"Prophet, this Psalm, written so long ago, was written for you and others like you. It is prophetic in nature, as I saw you and the others who would come to Me during this time. I Am has loved those who would take the name of My Son for themselves and live according to His Spirit. His great love cannot be separated from My love; it is one and the same. All of the Law and the Prophets and the Fathers looked forward to His time. Truly, all of heaven has looked forward to the time when My Son would claim His prize, and when Satan would inevitably receive his.

Some ascribe much complexity and wisdom to Satan. They analyze and indeed put much thought into his plan – how he knows things, technology, time, and other supposedly mystical things. I Am says: Do not waste your time on these things. Satan is a loser whose end is the lake of fire forever. Whatever you learn about him is a waste of time and will not be credited to your account.

There are other things that will be counted as weed, hay, and stubble. They are fear, worry, accusations, human judgment, and all of the 'wisdom' of the world. I Am has never advocated these things! This 'wisdom' is earthly and demonic!

How many times do I have to say, 'Do not fear?' Therefore, do not listen to those who try to gin up fear! They do not speak on My behalf! I Am a Redeemer! I take the bad and cause it to work for good for those who love Me and work according to My purposes – remember?

What narrative are you following? Do you really believe that I would send My only Son to reconcile the world to Me, send My Spirit to live in you, give you every advantage that I can give, YES, I said every advantage, and then allow Satan to completely undo all that I had done? If that's what you believe, then you have bought into a theology of the 'end times' that is a doctrine of demons.

I Am providing for redemption, salvation, healing, and deliverance! I Am good, My people! My strength is unequaled! I Am able to create anything or destroy anything with a whisper! Why have some among you bowed down to a created being? A liar and thief, one who ruins everything he touches? Why? Amen."

Angel Over Russia – April 28, 2023

I (Kirk) was taken to a place in the heavenlies today, a place far above the earth. I stood in midheaven with the Lord and looked down on the earth. The Lord had called me to come there with Him. It seemed like we were waiting for someone.

As I looked at the earth rotating below us, I must have been moving as well. I saw the Atlantic Ocean. Then Europe came into view. After that, Russia. Then, when Russia was fully in view, I saw a great angel coming. He was on a reddish horse and wore a white robe with a red sash. He appeared to have great authority. I have seen Michael and Gabriel a couple of times, and this angel looked to be equal in authority to them.

When he had stopped near us, I turned to the Lord and asked, sort of in disbelief, if this great angel was over Russia (in authority). The Lord said, "Yes," that he was. I said that I had never heard of anything good that had come from Russia. Not any of the prophetic voices speak well of Russia either. Some have alluded that Putin may not be as bad as he is made out to be, but that's about as close to a compliment as I've heard.

The angel spoke, "Prophet, if that's what you believe, you are believing a lie. It may be attractive as far as patriotism goes, but it's a lie."

I turned and looked over at the Lord for confirmation. He simply nodded in agreement with the angel.

The angel spoke again: "Reality is quite the opposite of what you have been told or led to believe. Russia has been, and is currently, <u>knowingly</u> working for the good of the United States."

I was simply astonished, and just said, "No way!" We're being told exactly the opposite! I looked, and the Lord confirmed what the angel was saying!

The angel again spoke up: "Prophet, look at who is opposing the globalists, and look at who they hate and abuse. Don't be fooled by propaganda, even patriotic propaganda." He continued, "It is true that Russia is acting in their own best interest as well, but also on behalf of the United States."

There was a pause, and the angel again spoke up. "Prophet, I have been busy in Russia and the surrounding countries. They have been greatly responsive to my work. In a short time, they will be committing to bring teams of missionaries over to the United States to help complete the Great Reset."

By this time, I was believing what he said, but wow! I then heard the Lord say, "Come, this is enough for now." And I was back at the office. Amen.

Vision in Time of God's Great Reset – May 12, 2023

I (Kirk) am taken in the spirit forward in time.

I see fields that all have partially grown crops in them. They look very beautiful. There are rows upon rows of various kinds of plants. As I looked, I wondered if these crops were bio-engineered or not, or maybe they were sprayed with herbicide or pesticide? They looked so perfect – all green, no weeds or other variations – just beautiful! Then I heard the Lord's voice, "Prophet, look what can be done without poisoning the water, ground, or food that people will eat."

I just blurted out, "But how Lord?" And I looked to my right, and there was the Holy Spirit in the form of a man.

He then said, "All the crops of the world are now grown under the same guiding principles. The first being that whatever is produced must be healthy for consumption and also be grown in such a way as to benefit the earth."

Then my mind went to how much oversight that must take to monitor all the produce of the world! Again, the Holy Spirit spoke, "There is very little monitoring that is required. The people of the world have escaped from the lust for more riches, ever more and more. Farmers now grow and produce for the benefit of all. That is their mindset. But as a result of that, they actually produce more and of better quality, and are paid better than ever! Their customers look for quality and are very concerned with they and their families' health and welfare. They are willing to pay more for what they desire."

The next thing I knew, I was standing outside in the parking lot of what looked like a repair shop. I looked around, but I seemed to be alone. There was an overhead door open, and I felt compelled to walk towards it. As I stepped inside, I saw a number of vehicles. They looked quite different from what I was used to. They were very sleek and even sporty looking. A voice said, "Can I help you?"

I said that I was just admiring the vehicles, and that I wasn't very familiar with them. An older gentleman stepped toward me and stuck out his hand. I shook it, and we struck up a conversation. He said that the vehicles that were in the shop were very different from older technology ones. He could see that I was interested, but that I had no clue about what I was looking at. In a very kind and patient manner, he described to me how transportation had changed so much. He said the driving force of this change was honesty. All I could say was, "Really, how did honesty change a whole industry?"

He said, "Well, honesty has really changed the whole world, but as far as transportation is concerned, people now look for a product that suits their needs and is produced in an ethical and healthy way. It is not merely economics or pride that governs what people purchase. The object is to benefit others (from the raw materials to the finished product), and gently use what the earth gives us in the way of materials to work with."

Next, I was standing outside a hospital. It was of a medium or smaller size than I was used to. "I doubt you could get lost inside," I thought. I was all alone again. I walked up to the double doors and walked in. There was a person just inside the door who greeted me and asked if I needed help finding someone. I said, "No, but I've never been here before. Could I look around?"

She said, "Sure, I would like to take you for a tour then." So, we walked further into the building, and as we did, we were walking past all kinds of equipment for fitness: weights, stationary bikes, treadmills, etc. I asked if there was a health club that was located here too.

She said, "No," that the "patients" were expected to exercise while they were there. It was standard procedure. (She acted like I should know this.) As we walked on, we came to a room, walked inside, and she turned toward me and simply stated that this was a standard patient's room. I looked around. There was a bed toward one end of the room, a very nice couch and a couple of armchairs. It had the appearance of a very comfortable living room. She said that they also had extra beds in case someone would like to stay the night with the patient. I was so impressed at how inviting and relaxed the atmosphere was there!

I inquired about the staff, like where was everyone? Susan (her name) answered with a question: "Who were you expecting to be here?" So, I asked where the security people were? Doctors and nurses?

We stepped out of the room, and she pointed to a doctor. She also pointed out a number of the staff and said what their specialty was. But they all wore street clothes, and unless you read their I.D. tags (which were very inconspicuous), you couldn't tell their profession. Then she said that they had no need for security personnel.

I asked a few more questions. From what I gathered after my questions, there were actually very few hospitals, and the ones that existed were lightly used because people rarely needed them.

Suddenly, I was standing in a grocery store, apparently in the produce section. As I looked, I was thinking how HUGE this produce area was! Most of the grocery area was taken up by the fresh produce! As I walked around, some of the things I noticed were that the people there were polite and unhurried, and I didn't see any cell phones.

The processed food area was different too. I didn't see anything that was familiar to me. Some of the names on the packages were familiar, but the packaging was different. Nothing said, "Organic" or "Low-Fat" or things like that. I picked up what I thought was a package of soup. I looked for the ingredient list. All it said on it was the contents of the soup, like "potatoes, beans," etc. There were no strange chemical names or any preservatives named at all.

I kept walking and I noticed an area in the store where people were sitting and talking and had cups in their hands. It was a coffee and tea bar, and there was no charge for it.

So, I asked the person working there for a cup of tea. There were many kinds, so I just pointed to one that looked kind of plain. I took it and went and sat down. I was looking around and feeling out of place, not uncomfortable or anything, but everything was so different.

Just then a young lady walked up to me and asked if she could sit at the table I was sitting at. I said sure, and she sat diagonally across from me. I thought it strange that she would even think of doing that, me being a man and older than her. She then asked my name, and I asked her name. Hers was Joy. We started to talk, and I was surprised how relaxed she was while talking to me. It was like we'd known each other or something. So, I asked if she was a follower of Jesus. She answered, "Well, yes of course," and she looked at me kind of like, "Where are you from?" I didn't think I should tell her that I actually lived in the past, so I said that I had been in a remote area for a long time. Could she tell me what had happened while I was away?

She asked if I knew of Donald J. Trump? I said yes, that I knew of him. She continued, "Well, the world is spoken of as 'Before Trump and After Trump.' He brought a great change to the world. He was God's anointed servant to bring the change to the world that Jesus paid for. This change is called God's Great Reset, and it was so dramatic that people all over the earth were changed because of it. Honesty and Justice will never be taken for granted again. People are still studying what exactly went on, and they are still shocked to find out how corrupt, unjust, and cruel people were to each other back before the reset. But they all understand that it was Satan who was behind it all. We all, all the people in the world, have decided never to let that happen again. When all of the evil ones were removed, that decision was easy." Amen.

Trump's DOJ – May 16, 2023

I (Tiffany) dreamed Trump's Department of Justice was all one and cohesive between departments.

Interpretation from the Holy Spirit:

This is how it will be. Trump takes things that are complex and makes them simple. He clears the table and starts over and makes it simple. There won't be a bunch of groups like TSA, DHS, FBI, CIA, and on and on. It will be the DOJ, or whatever name Trump may name it, but it will be one.

Everyone Waiting for the Apostles & Prophets – May 17, 2023

"All of heaven and earth are waiting for My glorious ones to arise. They will look like common workers because they'll serve everyone, and they'll choose the least likely people to help them, just like God does. Everyone has been waiting, and it looks like the Apostles and Prophets have arrived late, but they haven't. They're right on time to make and deliver the food from the Lord."

Everyone Must Choose – Tree of Knowledge of Good & Evil <u>or</u> Tree of Life – May 19, 2023

Today I (Kirk) see Jesus in a vision. He's holding out His hands to me and saying, "Come." I go towards Him, and He takes my right hand. As soon as we touch, we are walking in a grassy field with sparse trees. As we walk, the Lord turns toward me and begins to speak. "Prophet, I Am has been giving you 'words' and visions about the future and also regarding decisions that people must make. Those decisions have been the same since the world was populated with men, since Adam and Eve." ·

As He spoke, we approached a more wooded area. We walked into the woods and followed a trail. After a short way, there was an opening. I was thinking that I had been there before, but it looked a little different. Just then, Jesus again spoke. "Yes, you have been here before, but as you may have noticed, We like change. Nothing here in heaven dies, but it does change. The vegetation grows; things change."

Just then I saw a familiar tree in a rather open area. The big and low hanging fruit gave it away. And the Lord said, "Yes, you are correct. This is the Tree of the Knowledge of Good and Evil, the very one you have seen before." The fruit of this tree was just as tempting as I remembered, very large and bright red. It looks perfect and good, but I know not to eat of it.

Jesus again speaks, "Yes, Prophet, you know not to eat of it, but there are others who see how easy it is to pick and how beautiful it looks. They believe in themselves. They think, 'Well, just one bite, or one of the fruits, and then I'll walk away from it and not eat of it anymore.' But this fruit is so tempting, chasing knowledge and learning becomes a habit that once developed draws away even those who have My Spirit within them! It is very dangerous, a slippery slope indeed! Knowledge then is like a drug which one becomes addicted to, and ever more is needed. Then when a load of knowledge is attained, this person begins to believe that they know what is good and what is evil, but they do not."

We walked on past the Tree of the Knowledge of Good and Evil, through the forest, until we came to the Tree of Life, just like we had in another vision. Jesus stopped, as did I, and we looked at the tree. It wasn't nearly as attractive either as a tree or because of the fruit. The fruit was a green color and was out of reach and much smaller than the fruit of the Tree of the Knowledge of Good and Evil. Once again, I became hungry as we looked at the Tree of Life. The Lord said, "Go ahead and eat, Prophet."

So, I struggled up the tree as best I could and picked one of the fruits. The climb back down was made more difficult because I was holding the fruit, but in time I made it. As I bit into the fruit, the memories of being there and eating this fruit came back. Again, it took a lot of chewing, and even then was not easy to swallow at times. And I started to feel full after eating only a portion of the fruit, but I also knew that I had to eat the whole thing to gain any benefit from it. After I finished, I felt better in mind and body than I ever had! Wow! And I was very satisfied!

Jesus again spoke, "How do you feel, Prophet?" I answered that I felt amazing!

Jesus answered, "Faith is required to eat this, My fruit, because it doesn't have the apparent goodness from its appearance, and it is not low hanging and easy to attain by man's own strength. One must be led to desire it by My Spirit, but He is a Gentleman, and will not force anyone. He, the Spirit, desires everyone to eat of this fruit, but many choose to follow lies instead of the truth, which is freely available. Others put it off so they can have fun. But in procrastinating, they have made their choice. Still others are fooled by religion and trust the fruit of the Tree of the Knowledge of Good and Evil. My Spirit calls them, but the attractive, low-hanging fruit that can be attained with their own effort is all they can see, and they are angered if someone tries to tell them differently.

Therefore, everyone MUST choose! In not choosing, they have chosen. The way to destruction is easy, and many choose it. My way is less attractive and more difficult. Few find it and fewer choose it." Amen.

Easy Cure for Many Diseases Dream – May 24, 2023

I (Tiffany) dreamed there were a couple of boys who had measles, so they took off their shirts and went out into the sunshine. Within 4 hours, they were healed. The sunshine had killed the measles.

Interpretation from the Holy Spirit:

It's not necessarily that exposing measles to sunshine would kill them, but it's that I have been thinking there are easy cures for a lot of diseases, and the Lord is saying that I am right. There are easy cures for a lot of diseases. These will be brought to the light during God's Great Reset.

Vision of Ritual on a Sandhill – May 26, 2023

Today I (Kirk) asked the Lord if He had any "words" or visions for me. He said He did, and then gave me specific instructions of things I should do to prepare for it. This was strange to me and involved talking to Him first and then getting ready by again listening to what He had to say to me to prepare for the word/vision. After a while, He asked me if I thought I was ready. I said I thought so, but wondered if I really was because of the strange preparations.

I then found myself in a kind of a desert at night and alone. I felt I should begin walking. The sand wasn't easy to walk in, but I didn't feel like I was in a hurry, so I just kept going up and down the sand hills, until I started to see trees, familiar kinds of trees – oaks, maples, and a few pine trees too. It was still sandy, and I wondered if the "desert" was actually beach sand, but I didn't see or hear water or waves. As I looked around, I noticed faint light coming from between a couple of the sand hills. I slowed my pace and stealthily looked over the top of the hill into the valley.

There was a fire and people around it. Some were close to it, and others formed an outer ring of people, as though they were watching a ritual or something. I backed off a bit and made my way closer so I could get a better look. As I did, I noticed that there were guards, and they looked to have uniforms on, like military uniforms or something. I snuck closer, and they didn't see me at all. It was like I was invisible to them. I came to a vantage point that was quite close, and I looked down at the goings on.

As I watched, I suddenly knew that this was some kind of satanic ritual. Some of the people wore strange robes. Others were completely naked. They were doing unspeakable things involving a baby, and there was also a young woman who was bound. I knew who a lot of the people were too. The Clintons and Obamas, to name a few. But there were others that I wouldn't have suspected as being satanists there, and they were participating too. A lot of the people I recognized, but don't know their names. I cannot write what they were doing. It should be enough to say that "kill, steal, destroy" was in full display! I couldn't watch anymore. I walked away.

As I walked through the sand, suddenly, the LORD joined me. I was crying because of what I had seen. I walked toward the Lord and threw my arms around Him. He was crying too, so we held each other and wept for a time. After a while, we loosened our grip, looked at each other and began to walk hand-in-hand. I let everything I had seen and heard just pour out of me. He took it all with nods and other small gestures without saying a word. After a few minutes, I realized how much better I felt, like a burden had just been lifted from me. I looked at Jesus and saw a tear in His eyes. I suddenly had the realization that He had born all of mankind's sin – all of it!

We stopped and turned toward each other. I looked up at Him. This time when I looked, His eyes looked like a blue flame, and He spoke and said, "Prophet, I AM sorry you had to see this. You and the people have to know what they're up against, however. You must tell them what they are being saved from."

Then as He continued to speak, I felt the anger rise up in Him! I felt the searing hot blade of the double-edged sword, sharp words that pierced heart and soul and reached the very depths of my being! He was speaking about His recompense and the judgment that would fall on the wicked! But these sharp words passed right through me. There was no place for them to land because I was covered by His blood – righteous and holy unto the Lord of All! Amen.

(It turns out the preparations beforehand were necessary because of the difficulty of the vision.)

Meaning of Life – May 27, 2023

"I AM Life itself, and apart from Me you cannot find life. Those who search for the meaning of life apart from Life will never find it. Those who look for the meaning of life in Me have already found the Way, the Truth, and the Life, and they need not look further.

Those who look for the meaning of life apart from Me only find what their warped minds fancy most. What are these things compared to eternity? And if there is no eternity of life, then they have located something temporary to begin an eternity of death!" Amen.

Sin and Religion – May 27, 2023

"Why do men, especially religious men, make such a big deal about sin – defining it, mapping out how one arrives at each sin, making laws, rules, and principles to keep from sinning, forming a belief system around a perceived sin, and splitting the church to avoid participation in a practice that has been deemed sinful? Has the I AM not shown them that this practice of following the 'Law' does not work? Have I not said that the Spirit will lead them into all truth (righteousness)? Is not the Law fulfilled in those who walk not after the flesh, but after the Spirit?

So, why is it so difficult to leave the Old Covenant and simply follow My Spirit? It is because Satan is a legalist. Without the Law, there is no trespass, no accusation, no guilt, or condemnation. It is for that reason the enemy must keep the law of sin and death alive. For when the Spirit of God sets men free, the enemy is limited in what he can do.

Therefore, when religion (Satan) creeps into your 'church,' it is being set up for failure by your enemy. Do not fall for the quick and easy way of laws, rules, and principles! It is the Spirit of Christ that brings life! Freedom! So, walk in the Spirit and live by faith!" Amen.

The Great Delusion – June 2, 2023

"Prophet, write: As soon as Jesus said, 'It is finished,' and Satan knew it was true, that he had been beaten, *it* began. First, he tried to snuff out the new 'church.' When that didn't work, he incorporated it into religion. From there he began work on the Great Delusion. So, this Great Delusion involves the organized church, but that alone is not the big picture.

In the organized church, or religion itself, Satan has used mainly deception to bring it to where he has desired it to go. This deception uses mainly the Bible to accomplish his goals. It is true that the Bible contains truth; its words were inspired by God. Satan is a legalist, however, and just as a skilled lawyer intent on evil can warp and mold good law into something it was never meant to be, Satan also set out to do this with the Scriptures. He has inspired the scholars using a little truth to write things that seem right and logical on the surface but lead to things that the Lord never meant to be.

Satan has been very successful in guiding doctrines and theologies away from the true Christ, away from hearing the voice of God, and has even led the organized church into believing that one cannot hear God's voice and should not try to. A relationship with a book (the Bible) is promoted as 'the way,' and knowledge is the key. So, study the Bible forever and don't engage with the crazy people who hear God and practice signs and wonders! Satan is still promoting the Tree of the Knowledge of Good and Evil. This, then, is the Great Deception of the Church.

Now, onto the Great Delusion! The Great Delusion works in conjunction with the deception of the church. It is in its most base form simply knowledge. There are other things involved, however, and these in the simplest terms might be called wisdom, human wisdom. For this delusion to work, people need to believe that they are basically good. This belief stands in opposition to the words of Scripture that say, 'He who believes in Him is not judged; he who does not believe has been judged already, because he has not believed in the name of the only begotten Son of God' (John 3:18 NASB).

Satan's brand of human goodness questions God's intentions towards man. 'Well, if God is good, how could He see me as bad?' Or 'How could a good God allow this bad stuff?' In doing this questioning of God, this belief system has no need for God and dismisses Him and decides man is then the ultimate goodness on earth.

Enter woke thinking! Now, the adherents to this begin to make all kinds of claims about what everyone must believe is truth! And what people have known and understood from the dawn of time is thrown out.

Man is now in control of what is truth. Churches that cannot hear God's voice now pick up this 'logic' in small or great degree because they are no longer established by the chief cornerstone, and Apostles and Prophets do not bring revelation or prophecies to build a good foundation with Christ as the centerpiece.

But the Lord is saying today: 'Open your eyes, and you will see Me dismantling everything Satan has done. EVERYTHING! The Delusion is ending NOW!'" Amen.

Jezebel – June 9, 2023

Today the Lord says: "See, I have shown you the Great Delusion and the Deception in the Church. Now, I AM desires to show you the spirit behind this – in the world and in the church.

She dresses herself up to make herself appear desirable, surrounds herself with false prophets, and makes bold promises. She even threatens those who will not agree with her, and she will attempt to seduce men or women who might give her more control. She has a claim on authority, but it is through someone else. She is always greedy for more influence and power, but never through acceptable, forthright means, always through deception and seductive means. She is always perverse, opposing the good and righteous. She is very ambitious and gets others, through their agreement with her, to be ambitious at carrying out her desires. She is ruthless and cruel and changes her appearance (2 Kings 9:30) to try to get what she wants.

This, then, is the Jezebel spirit. It is one of the main players in the church and in the world today." This is one of the spirits we war against!

A Vision as this is written down...

I see the wife of a former president of the United States, and I see two other women who I believe I have seen before. I see them in secret meetings following the behest of malevolent spirits. There are flashes of rituals in high places. I also see scenes flash by of others who are high up in government doing things for these three.

Then things change, and I see fear in the eyes of these three women. They meet, but not like before. They are no longer bold and laughing and looking joyful because of the evil they are planning. They appear, or maybe I just have a knowing, that they are trying to protect themselves. Then there is another meeting between them, but only two show up. The ex-president's wife is missing from the meeting. The two that meet look horrified and scared.

Then after a little while, I see their pictures and names on a newspaper front page. I struggle to read what it says, and all I can make out is one word: "Executed." That's it. After I read that word, I realized that the spirit of Jezebel had been broken. She (it) was beaten!

I just sat, thanking the Lord for breaking the power of this evil spirit, praising Him, and blessing the work He had done!

Another quick scene came after this in which there were people who were confused, and some were angry. Most were looking for help. The alphabet people realized they had been duped and were looking for help wherever they could find it! And the Lord said, "Time to go to work!" Amen.

Mystery (and word regarding End Times) –

June 23, 2023

Today the LORD is speaking about mysteries.

He says, "I AM not the God of mysteries. I AM constantly making Myself known, making My plans known through the Prophets, raising up My Church in truth, bringing revelation to the Apostles and Prophets! I AM the Lord Who Speaks. Is there any other beside Me? I Am the Lord, and there is no other.

I AM recorded in the Scriptures depicting the end times simply and succinctly, and yet men whose desire was to mislead and confuse have raised up mysteries, complex and confusing as being the truth. Are the Scriptures not clear?

God, after He spoke long ago to the fathers in the prophets in many portions and in many ways, in these last days has spoken to us in His Son, whom He appointed Heir of all things, through whom also He made the world. And He is the radiance of His glory and the exact representation of His nature, and upholds all things by the word of His power. (Hebrews 1:1-3a NASB)

I AM not the God of confusion! I do not use 'double speak,' and I AM not a man that I should lie!

Therefore, when I AM spoke in parables regarding the end of the world, will it not be so? (Matthew 13:24-30, 36-43, 47-52)

But men are given to much chasing of the wind, trying to fit something into their ideas or imaginations that they are given over to: lies from the enemy and fantasies, even though these things have already happened, just as they had been prophesied to. (i.e. They try to fit the book of Revelation and other end time Scriptures into their ideas or imaginations, and they have fantasies about tribulations and a rapture.)

So, when you see a great deal of study, confusing details that simply cannot be remembered, things that generate fear, fantasies about escape, then go back to the simple way that I AM has spoken in the Parable of the Wheat and Tares or the Parable of the Dragnet. Can you see how I, the Lord, speak? Simply and pointedly. Great knowledge and study are not needed or desired by Me! "

...[T]hat their hearts may be encouraged, having been knit together in love, and attaining to all the wealth that comes from the full assurance of understanding, resulting in a true knowledge of God's mystery, that is Christ Himself, in whom are hidden all the treasures of wisdom and knowledge. I say this so that no one will delude you with persuasive arguments... See to it that no one takes you captive through philosophy and empty deception, according to the tradition of men, according to the elementary principles of the world, rather than according to Christ. (Colossians 2:1-4, 8)

This is Paul speaking to the Colossians, but the application is clear. <u>The preeminence of Christ cannot be overstated in the way we think and what we accept as truth.</u> He is the Way and the Truth and the Life. Amen.

"If you believe I'm all about mystery, that's all you'll see, but if you believe I'm all about revelation, that's all you'll see." Amen.

The True Church – June 30, 2023

Vision given to Kirk.

I'm taken in the Spirit to a place where I find myself seated in what appears to be a theater. It's dimly lit, and I believe I'm all alone there. I sit quietly waiting for something to happen. Then, in front of me, curtains spread open. There is a movie screen there. A movie begins, and a narrator comes on the screen. He either appears as an angel, or a thought comes to me that he is an angel. The movie shows the rise of Christianity around the globe. The narrator starts from the beginning (Judaism) and goes through the time of Jesus being on the earth. It's interesting, but I'm feeling like I really desire to see something more relevant, like a time when I could have an impact on what's going on.

As the speaker continues, I realize that this isn't about religion. This is the true Church, the one after the heart of the Lord! As I watch, it comes into the 1900's and quickly moves into the 2000's. But the data presented is skewed. It doesn't look like what I'd learned. By the 2000's, the population of Christ followers elsewhere in the world looks much larger than in the USA.

The presenter then begins to show future growth of Christ followers. Dots appear where new followers are. The spread looks like a matrix where there are so many of these "dots" that the area is almost solid in color. Also, the spread starts slowly but builds so quickly that it's amazing! And what's really amazing is that there are very few places on earth where the "dots" are spaced far apart. I believe I was being shown churches, so how could there be so many?

Just then, on the screen, there are videos and videos of churches! Five, 10, 20 or so people meeting together in huts, houses, apartments — all over the globe! House churches!

Suddenly I found myself at a table, like a kitchen table. As I cleared my eyes, I saw the Lord Jesus! He was making coffee, and the room was filled with the smell of the coffee! It smelled — well, heavenly! Just then He turned around and came to where I was sitting. He set two cups of coffee down on the table, pushed one over to me, and began to sip on the other.

"Kirk," He said, "I've been excited to see you again!"

(In my mind I thought, "Wow! What a greeting from the Great I AM!")

Before I could speak, He said, "Oh come on now, you love Me, and I love you We are able to sit and talk."

Yeah, He knew what I was thinking. In a kind of nervous voice, I said, "Yes, of course," and began to cry because of Him. Just then He reached over and touched my hand. My head cleared, and the tears stopped. Great peace came over me, and I could speak without quivering in speech. We spoke of some private matters, and after a bit, moved into what He really wanted to say to me.

He said, "I want you to tell the people that the Great Reset of God is very near. You just saw a video regarding how it will work. The House Church Movement seems weak, but I AM assuring you that it is not! My strength is perfected in weakness, and this movement is of My doing! My church will have My government. The fivefold ministers will be that government. And their only desire will be to follow My Spirit in everything they do.

This movement, My movement, will seem to be in weakness because none of the temptations of the institutional church will be present. There will be no getting rich on the backs of My sheep, no career clergy. I AM will be the Head of this Church, not men. And because of that, the power-hungry will also be thwarted. I Am giving an Iron Scepter to the Apostles and Prophets, and they will rule over it in righteousness and love because I AM giving of Myself to them.

I AM beginning down this road today, and I AM not stopping until I have created the greatest army of believers that nothing can stop. This then IS the beginning of the End Times Harvest. Amen."

Expectations – July 7, 2023

When you expect something one way, or at a particular time, or even within a length of time, and it doesn't come, there is the possibility of disappointment, frustration, doubt, or anger. This is a good place for unbelief to sneak in. This is because you haven't learned to divorce your expectations from your faith.

In other words, you would never think of forcing God to do what He does according to your demands, right? Yet, this is exactly what expectations do! You are telling the Lord that He better do this or that according to your expectations, or you won't believe anymore!

This isn't the way it appears to us. We feel we are perfectly justified in our expectations. We feel they are actually faith, but they are not. And this approach to faith will not work! God has to be God. He will do what He will do according to His good pleasure.

The Lord doesn't want our expectations to outweigh our faith.

Trump Judging as Commander in Chief – July 7, 2023

I (Kirk) see a courtroom, and there are proceedings in progress. This courtroom is arranged differently from what I've seen on TV or elsewhere. In the front and center of the room is a desk. To the right of the desk is an elongated table, and to the left there are defendants. The desk in the center has what appears to be a very decorated military man sitting at it, and the table to the right has military people seated at it as well.

Just then a defendant is escorted to the center table. A brief description of the charges is read, and corroborating evidence is produced. Questions are asked by those at the table on the right.

Just then Donald J. Trump walks up to the table in the center of the room, bends slightly, and speaks to the man at the desk. There is a brief discussion between those seated at the desk. Then the man at the center desk picks up the gavel, slams it down, making a loud noise. The defendant, with his head hanging low, is led out. This scenario happens over and over in very rapid succession.

Donald Trump is involved in some judgments, and others not. I understood that he was acting as Commander in Chief, and as such had considerable influence regarding what was going on.

Each case took a matter of minutes to decide.

Vision Tears of Blood Over the Nations – July 14, 2023

I (Kirk) see Jesus crying as He watches the world below Him turning. It's the children, the mistreatment of the children that grieves Him. Tears form in His eyes and fall from His cheeks. I see the tears fall to earth. One falls on China, right in the middle of the country. Another falls on India. One falls on the United States. Another falls on Africa, right in the center of the continent (Democratic Republic of the Congo) and another on Kenya.

My attention is drawn to Africa, and I see that the tears are of blood. The blood from His tears begin to "soak in" or be absorbed by the land and kind of disappear. As I watch, I see that the very earth, or soil, of these countries is turning reddish. This coloration spreads, and slowly the whole of Africa itself is turned reddish in color. I lift my eyes and see that the other places where the Lord's tears had fallen have also turned a reddish color.

Looking back at Africa, I see newness of life and joy in all the people there. I see a new prosperity and peace where there had been conflict. Roads and infrastructure had been built, and travel was going on where it never had before. The Lord had used outsiders, including China, to help with these things. They didn't know that they were serving the Lord's purposes, and in fact believed that they were serving their own interests.

 Other countries similar to China joined in partnering with these "Christian" countries where the tears of blood had soaked in and spread, some of which were also freshly stabilized countries in the great continent of Africa because of the redemptive blood of Christ. The people of this continent enjoyed a great surge in their standard of living, and the entire world was blessed because of all of this.

The world, the entire planet, had found Jesus Christ and was blessed beyond measure because of what had happened. Amen.

Rescue of Children in Arizona – July 21, 2023

Today as I (Kirk) was praising and preparing to listen and pray, I caught a whiff of Heaven. Now as I sit here it comes again in waves, almost disappears, then comes strongly again. I ask the Spirit of God why I am smelling this. He replies, "You will bring the fragrance of Heaven with you wherever you go."

I ask, "Will Tiffany too?"

The Spirit answers, "She will bring power. You will bring the fragrance."

Suddenly I was driving a tour bus. I was in Arizona near the Mexican border somewhere, I think. I drove off the main road and onto a dirt road. I went about 6 miles and then turned onto a two track and went another mile to a turnaround big enough for the bus to navigate. I drove about 100 yards back the way I had come from and parked the bus.

I opened the doors and stepped out. Wow! It was hot outside! I walked away from the bus, south, I think. As I walked, I bumped into a cactus. I quickly pulled away, but it didn't hurt. I looked my arm over, but there were no wounds or spines in it at all. I stepped back to look at the cactus I had brushed my arm against. It was full of spines! I reached out to touch it in a spot where there were no spines. My finger passed right through it! I tried this with my whole hand. My whole hand passed right through! I could walk right through any cactus and couldn't even stub my foot on rocks. They passed right through the rocks! I walked maybe 10 minutes marveling at this miracle I was walking in.

Just then I heard something like a voice. I walked towards it. It was whimpering. Maybe it was a child? A few more steps and I came upon about 20 kids, mostly girls, but a few young boys as well. When they saw me, they were afraid, but didn't run. I think they were too tired and thirsty. One of them spoke a little English, and after a time, I gained their confidence. I told them that I was there to rescue them. (I didn't really know, but I thought that's why

I must be there.) I helped them as much as I could to come toward the bus, trying not to walk through anything that might scare them. They might have thought I was a ghost or something if they saw my body pass through objects.

When we got to the bus, I found that it was stocked with tons of water and packaged food! So, all of us ate and drank, which made the kids happy. I had them all get on the bus. The air conditioning was amazing! I made my way down the two track and dirt road back to the main road. I didn't really know exactly where I was or where I was going. It almost felt as though the bus was on autopilot even though I was driving it. Something else strange is that on the bus everything seemed normal, like my hands and feet had normal touch and didn't pass through anything.

I drove a couple of hours and saw a town coming up, but before we got to it, I turned off into the desert again on a dirt road. I came to a house with a pale barn and parked in the driveway. Some people came out, and I told them what had happened. They were overjoyed to see the kids and told me that this was what they did. They re-united kids with their parents. They said that they had nothing to do with the government and were privately funded.

I felt my part in this was over, so I got back in the bus and drove back down the dirt road. I don't know what happened to the bus, but I suddenly felt myself back at the office.

Amen.

Vision of Jesus with Iron Scepter and Two Witnesses –

July 28, 2023

I (Kirk) was taken to a place, and I saw the Lord of All sitting on a lone throne. His hair was white. His eyes were a flame of fire alternating to normal brown eyes, like between wrath and love. He did not look old, but vigorous and strong. In His right hand He held an iron scepter. It had a handle at the bottom and a cross at the top. On His left stood the archangel Gabriel, and on His right stood the archangel Michael. The very air was charged with power, and there was a rather serious tone. The Lord Jesus sat as a statue holding the scepter.

Then when the time was right, He spoke. Lightning flashed in all directions from the throne, followed by thick smoke rolling behind the lightning. The whole place was filled with smoke. I did not understand what He said, but as I watched, two people solemnly walked up to the throne before the Lord of All.

These two represented the Apostles and the Prophets. As they approached, simultaneously they knelt on one knee before the Lord. They stayed this way for a short time. The Lord rose up from His throne and stood before them. Gabriel and Michael stepped forward and stood on the sides of the two who knelt, as if to steady them. The two kneeling faced the Lord. The angels and the Lord faced the Apostle and Prophet.

The Lord raised the iron scepter, holding it in both hands by the handle and laid it first on the Apostle's head. As He lifted it back up, a flame of fire was burning on, or perhaps above, the Apostle's head. He then stepped to the side of the Prophet and Gabriel and did the same thing. Fire was also left on the Prophet's head.

The Lord and the angels then stepped back, and the Lord again sat down and spoke. The lightning and smoke rolled out from Him, and the power of Him charged the room! I could not understand what He said because of the thunder.

The Apostle and Prophet then stood to their feet, looked at the Lord for a few seconds and then turned around and walked forward, away from the throne. The flames of fire on their heads remained on them as they walked. Amen.

Tree of Knowledge, Churches, & Wisdom –

August 4, 2023

I (Kirk) was taken in the Spirit of the Lord to the garden again. I again walked with the Lord on the now familiar trail that went past the Tree of the Knowledge of Good and Evil and on to the Tree of Life. This time I felt more prepared and didn't really get tempted as we approached the Tree of the Knowledge of Good and Evil. We again stopped and gazed at the Tree of Knowledge with its low hanging fruit, big and so attractive and easy to pick too, due to its low hanging nature.

Just then the Lord speaks: "This tree challenges men because of wisdom. The fruit of this tree is larger, more attractive, more abundant than that of the Tree of Life. It can be easily picked and tastes better than the Tree of Life too. Therefore, in an earthly way of thinking, it would be wise to choose this tree over the Tree of Life.

Have you noticed the enemy's way is to imitate My ways, but make his ways more attractive, easier, and his ways involve no responsibility? Love, for example, involves commitment and many other virtues, including giving up of oneself for another. Satan's way of 'love' involves taking, using, and pleasing oneself with no commitment.

The 'church' that calls itself by My name has chosen the path of the Tree of the Knowledge of Good and Evil. Its 'fruit' is the fruit of men's efforts. It does 'give,' but to itself. There is no real love, only comparing oneself to another member, of whom the one doing the comparison is always better. The so-called 'fruit' of this 'church' is earthly, demonic. This church is full of pride and deceit, and I AM standing against it.

My Church chases after Me! My Church is not lazy but chooses to do the work that I AM laying out before them. Only showing up for an hour or two a week is abhorrent to them! My Church has eyes only for Me and doesn't worry about what others are called to do, unless they need help, in which case they are more than willing!"

Then He paused for a moment before speaking again: "A 'church' which follows a doctrine of demons is very easy to spot. It will be self-serving, self-centered, self-absorbed, have programs to entertain itself, the members will speak of 'the church, the church, the church,' or 'the pastor, the pastor, the pastor' ad nauseum, but My name will never come up! Great emphasis will be put on tithes and offerings because this is the source of everything that this 'church' does! I AM not attending these 'churches,' and you shouldn't either!" Amen.

Fivefold Active in Government – August 9, 2023

The Lord: "What causes men to sin?"

"I guess it's a desire outside of You."

The Lord: "In My Great Reset men won't desire things outside of Me like they do right now. They will desire Me and what comes from Me. This isn't something that will happen instantaneously. My fivefold will be very active in teaching My ways, how to follow My Spirit. They will be active in government, especially My Apostles and Prophets, because they will help to lay a right foundation in the governments of the nations of the world.

Sin will be frowned upon, and the way of the Spirit will be taught. What I AM about to do will change the world forever. For I AM bringing to light those things hidden in darkness. And I AM revealing things long hidden that will benefit the world.

Religion is oppressive, but My Spirit brings freedom. Religion has oppressed the truth and actively sought to destroy it, but haven't I proven that death is defeated? Is there anything that can stand against Me then? So then, you will see the goodness of God in the land of the living." Amen.

The Deal – August 11, 2023

I'm taken in the spirit to a place, a room with a long table that seats maybe 20-30 people. At this table are military generals. These generals are plotting a coup. Some are objecting and suggesting another way. I hear one of them speak up saying, "Well you all know that he's a deal maker. I believe we could propose a deal. And I don't think he could resist it!" Most of those present seem to agree. The meeting goes on for a while as discussions regarding the details of "the deal" are worked out. The meeting then breaks up and the room is empty.

Then I see what I believe is the same room, and a series of meetings with a handful (or maybe a few more) of those same generals. These meetings also include Donald J. Trump. Some of these meetings are just with Trump. Others also include members of his family, particularly his sons. The deal that is worked out is risky, and all of the participants acknowledge that. To fail would be certain death, but to succeed would be the greatest coup the world has ever seen and an overthrow of evil like no other time in history. The deal that was reached would be particularly rewarding to Donald Trump as well, even though the risks were very real and quite high.

In the end, a deal was reached, promises were made, and it was on! Trump's first presidency was assured. The cheaters would be cheated out of their plan for Hillary. And the actual presidency would be an amazing success, as well as being a setup for what was to come.

In 2020, Donald Trump was going to lose the run for presidency no matter what. He had to! This is what the plan called for, and it <u>would</u> happen! During these four years (2020-2024), DJT was to maintain his presence and popularity, but also be the bait in a high stakes cat and mouse game, drawing out the deep state by being seemingly powerless and inept in the legal system.

Nevertheless, Donald J. Trump was to keep taunting and saying things that are a <u>real</u> threat to the deep state so that they could not resist coming after him in every way imaginable.

The meetings and the words stop at this point, and I'm asking, "What comes next?" What comes next is rather funny!

I see a giant rat trap. It's the old kind with a wood base and heavy wire, which is lifted and pulled to the opposing side of a small pocket in which to put cheese. I see DJT where the cheese is supposed to go, and there are many, many rats trying to get at him. Just then I hear: "The trap is set and will be sprung over and over. None shall escape!" Amen.

The Plumbline and Iron Scepter – August 18, 2023

"I AM says, Kirk (Prophets) take up the plumbline! And Tiffany (Apostles) take up the iron scepter.

The Prophets have set in place the perimeter of the Holy City! It has been laid out using the Plumbline of the Lord, to a perfect dimension. This plumbline is the Holy Spirit of God, and the layout itself is perfect because I AM perfect, says the Lord God of all.

Now I AM giving the Iron Scepter to My Apostles, and they shall judge and make judgments within My Holy City, according to (meaning within) the boundaries set by My Prophets. They will work together in harmony, one holding the plumbline and the other the iron scepter.

During this time and this season, no deception or ruse shall ever bias My anointed ones who will rule My Holy City in justice and love. They will only follow Me and do what is in My heart because I AM giving of Myself to them. If any evil tries to enter My City, I AM giving My angels power to make it as nothing.

The peoples of <u>all</u> nations and from the farthest islands shall come to My City and they shall live as a holy people in the land of their Father, and there shall be great peace and love there. None shall be poor or hungry there because I AM has spoken. Amen!"

Take Up Your Authority – August 25, 2023

Today the Lord is speaking about authority.

He says, "No one can, or could, give Me more authority. There is no one who is higher in authority than Me. Therefore, all authority flows from Me, and I can retain it or give it out as I desire to do. I gave authority to Adam. Foolishly, he lost it to Satan after being fooled in a clever scheme. Because of love, I won it back, and once again gave it to the sons of men.

Men have authority. It is theirs because I AM has freely given it back to them. Since that day, using the only tool he has, Satan has been trying to blunt that authority with lies. The sons of men have never really understood what they have been given, but Satan knows and is fully engaged in a thousand schemes to convince men that this hard-won authority which they possess is not worth much, is weak, doesn't exist, is still his, doesn't work, etc.

But I AM telling you right now that if God thought it worthwhile to wrestle back from Satan, it is NOT worthless! If mountains can be cast into the sea by a command from one who believes in his or her authority, what can stand in their way?

Therefore, TAKE UP your authority which has been given to you, and use it! I said, 'ALL authority in heaven and on earth has been given to Me, therefore GO!' So, what are the limits of your authority? Do you see any? Don't be fooled! All authority in heaven and on earth has been given to you as one who is in Me! Don't believe the deceiver any longer. Reject the lies and believe!

There is so much more to the New Covenant which I have made with you than you can see right now. Be bold. Have faith. And fully wield what I have won for you! Amen."

Visions of Great Deception – September 1, 2023

Today the Lord is showing me (Kirk) vision upon vision.

In one vision, I see a huge black rock that rolls through the towns, cities, and even the countryside. As it rolls, it leaves destruction in its wake. It rolls over and crashes houses, crushing the fortunes and dreams of the inhabitants. They see what has happened, but mostly do not understand it. They are angry and shake their fists, but at what?

Then I see a second vision in which people are working, doing difficult tasks and in return for their labor, they receive paper with numbers printed on it. It has no value in itself; it's merely paper and ink, but people receive it gladly. I see them going to buy food with this paper, only to find that it takes more and more of it to do what they need to do. I also see those who print this paper with the numbers on it. They are evil and have an amazing scheme worked out where they print this stuff and then sell it to governments. The governments then pay them for the raw materials to make it, and a fee for its use. The governments in turn charge the people a fee to pay for their paper with numbers on it. The more things cost that the people need to buy, the more paper must be printed, and the more that needs to be collected to pay for this paper with numbers by the government. It is very lucrative for the evil ones.

I then see a third vision in which there are places for "education." The evils ones have been at work here too! The goals are ever changing in these places. I see one common theme, though. It is "programming of the students," not their education that is important. The particular kind of programming needed is determined by those same evil ones in the previous visions – programming to chase a "dream." These dreams are manufactured, of course. They're made of things that are not really necessary, and mostly foolish, in fact. And no mention is made of the suffering and pain that others suffer to bring these things to those who need them. There is always a crisis for the educators to instruct on, too. These generate fear and an urgency to solve! But the actual solution really only involves two main things: 1. Compliance and control. 2. Wherever there is a population with a high standard of living, this population must pay for the solution. These things are drilled into the students throughout their instruction. This instruction becomes very much like a religion. Comply, or else! No free thought is allowed, even on a student's clothing!

Then I saw the religion of the urgent – a constant emergency and compulsory adherence to the doctrine of fear. There are too many people on the planet! Global warming – people will die! Global cooling – an ice age is coming! The ozone hole – too much ultraviolet light causes cancer! Acid rain – the crops will die! Y2K – the power grid will fail! Too much CO2 (where do those carbon credits go?). This goes on and on.

But the Lord says, "Break free from all of this! I AM exposing it all, so that even a simpleton without My Spirit in them should be able to see what is going on here! My people! You have to desire the truth in order to see it. Stand up and speak the truth. Don't be subordinate to lies and liars anymore! Rise up! Come to the front lines! Will you settle for a lie? I AM saying, NO! Rise up and be counted, or die a coward, never standing for Me or anything else! Amen!"

All Authority in Heaven & on Earth Vision –

September 8, 2023

The Lord called me (Kirk) up to Heaven today, to the Courts of Heaven. I was in the back, or the foyer, of the courts where the accused are prepped to walk up to the front where the Judge sits in the ornate chair in the front of all of those gathered there. As I looked around, I saw that there were actually some proceedings going on. The seats were full of multitudes of onlookers, and the warrior angels were lined up on both sides of the walkway and up the stairs leading to the judgment area.

As I watched, suddenly, there were two women who walked past me, hurriedly. They were headed toward a door, but as they approached, two very large and fierce looking angels stepped in front of the doorway. Other angels came to apprehend the women as well. These women were in pure panic and horrified of this judgment.

There were others there who seemed to enjoy the judgment! When called upon, they would go forward, sometimes whistling! It was like they couldn't wait to be put on trial.

Just then, I looked to my right and there was a man standing close to me, like right in my space close! He slowly turned toward me, and I saw that He was the faceless man that had shown me around Heaven before. We talked a little while, and then I asked Him why some of the people going before the Courts of Heaven seemed so relaxed and even enjoyed being there. He turned to face me more directly and began to explain. Then He asked me, "What do the Scriptures say, Prophet? How much authority does Jesus have?"

I answered that He had all authority in heaven and on earth. The faceless man answered, "That is correct." Then He asked, "Prophet, how much of that authority did He give those who are in Him?"

I answered, "All of it."

Again, "Correct, Prophet." Then He asked, "Does all authority in heaven and on earth supersede the courts of heaven's authority?"

I drew a breath, considering my answer. I said, "I believe I'm seeing that it does!"

The faceless man answered, "You have seen correctly, Prophet."

I then asked Him, "When someone is accused and claims that their only defense is in Jesus Christ, then the court no longer <u>can</u> convict them because the courts do not have the authority to do so, right?"

He said, "You have spoken well, Prophet."

Amen.

New Year – 5784 – September 15, 2023

"Today a new year begins," says the LORD!

"This year will be different than last year. This year, as it has been prophesied, I AM rolling out My recompense for the just and the unjust. The Winds of Change has been busy uncovering things that were unimaginable for most people. Some people are still sleeping, but that sleep will end, and all – yes ALL – will see the strong arm of the Lord as I AM working.

There is still more evil to uncover, and that will continue to happen. There is no evil that shall escape being brought to the light. There will also be more violence and loss of life. The evil ones will be evil to the end. But the end is near, and not far off as some suspect."

As the Lord's voice trails off, a vision begins. I see those who have misused the law becoming fearful. Indeed, they are trying to plan for an end which they never thought would happen. Those who had taken or "won" elections and laughed at the righteous and used the law to go on the offense – to persecute and to punish the innocent –

yes, those who were so well insulated against the righteous that they thought they would NEVER be caught.

The people lower in status who were to provide a covering for their higher ups were losing interest in covering for them because they were trying to cover their own deeds. Truly, those who had been on offense were now on the defense. I saw them trying to use the law, just as they had done when they used it against the innocent, only this time to protect themselves, but it did not work. The people had become very, very bold and were demanding action and results! Nothing else would do! I saw military tribunals in action. Yes, finally!

I saw two attempts at pandemics. Two different sicknesses from two different areas in the world. But the people would not comply with mandates and the globalists this time, no matter the consequences. And real and inexpensive remedies were found and used instead of the deadly "medicines" being promoted.

I also saw that through all of this, the Lord was bringing His people along in their understanding. They were seeing all of these things as good! The theologies of the past, such as teachings on the rapture and the idea that the victorious church would lose were relegated to the trash heap. People were looking forward to a better world, and they were understanding what a good God they served.

I saw angel armies being deployed in numbers that I had a hard time imagining. I saw them working out in the open, helping people, beating back evil and rooting out even the deeply hidden spirits in family lines, in the seven mountains, places you wouldn't even imagine had evil spirits! Amazing! The angels were doing battle with the spirit of religion too, exposing the lies of the institutional church and those who governed it. The spirits behind personal sin were being dealt with too. Lust, greed, Jezebel, fear, etc. Every spirit that could be named, and those who weren't named as well. None would escape the uncovering of the Lord.

"Freedom is on the horizon! Do not give up! Amen."

Dream Disconnect with Time – October 11, 2023

I (Tiffany) dreamed I was in a church and was watching Eric Clapton sing. I and the people I was with were moving chairs so we could see better. When I woke up, I heard the lyrics in my head, "And that's why they call it the 'blues'. Time on my hands could be time spent with you." I looked up the lyrics and found that the song is actually sung by Elton John. I don't listen to his music or Eric Clapton.

Interpretation from the Holy Spirit:

The Lord says there's a disconnect between what I was seeing and what I was hearing. This has to do with time.

How did Jesus say, "*Before Abraham was, I AM,*" when He came as a Man? How did He tell the story of Lazarus and the rich man as though He was there if He was a man? How could He physically go to the temple and stand on the pinnacle of it when He was in the desert?

The Lord says we need to be open because He's going to show us more. There's something here regarding having all authority. Time is created. We have authority over it.

Two days later, the Lord brought understanding through the following prophetic word ...

Mastery of Time – October 13, 2023

Today, I (Kirk) was praying, and the Lord said: "Why is time your master, and why are you a slave to time, Prophet?" I answered, "Lord, I am here in the flesh for a limited time, for so many days, hours, and minutes."

Then He said, "Prophet, are you not Mine then? Do you serve another master too?" I answered, "No, Lord! You are my Lord and Master. You alone!"

Then the Lord said, "Prophet, divorce yourself from this created thing that has mastery over you then!" I asked, "How, Lord? I am inescapably tied to time, right?"

He answered: "Listen to this prayer, Prophet. 'Our Father Who art in heaven, hallowed be Your name. Your kingdom come, Your will be done, on earth as it is in heaven.'" He stopped there and asked, "Prophet, is there time in heaven?" I said, "No, I don't think so."

He answered, "Correct. Therefore, the earthly things are the master of those who are earthly. Prophet, what do the Scriptures say? *'But the court will sit for judgment, and his dominion will be taken away, annihilated and destroyed forever. Then the sovereignty, the dominion and greatness of all the kingdoms under the whole heaven will be given to the people of the saints of the Highest One: His kingdom will be an* everlasting *kingdom, and all the dominions will serve and obey Him.'"* (Daniel 7:26-27)

I asked, "But Lord, how can this be?"

And He again answered, "You are My End Times Prophet. Therefore, tell the people that receiving back the dominion that Adam lost actually means something. And when the Scriptures say that you are seated with Christ in the heavenlies, it means something, and it's not simple poetry or something! All authority in Heaven and on Earth doesn't mean something besides what is obvious. I AM giving My saints dominion over the things which I have created. Time is one of these things. Try to name others. Come, and test out your authority! Amen."

Africa is My Sweetheart Too – October 13, 2023

"Prophet, I AM telling you things that have been hidden for ages! Yes, both of your angels (Tiffany's and Kirk's) have served in Africa. And yes, they both have an affinity for the people there. Yours especially.

But she is My sweetheart too! I chose Israel, the United States chose Me, and I tell you, ALL of Africa will choose Me too! Africa has been lied to, used and abused, she has been poor and hungry, and has suffered greatly! I love her so much, and this is why Satan has brought his steal, kill, destroy to her. But she has shrugged off all of these things! Africa is turning to Me! And I AM going to <u>end</u> her torture!

Rise up, My beautiful one! Rise up and look at Me! I AM turning My affection toward you, and I AM never going to let you down! I AM making streams in the desert. I AM making roads in the wilderness. I AM bringing forth resources in Africa that I have hidden until now. I AM cutting off those who have used My beautiful one for so long. I AM bringing prosperity to the ones I love in Africa. Amen!"

When Fear Speaks – October 17, 2023

Praying now, and the Lord shows me (Kirk) the conflict between Israel and Hamas, the brutality and the bodies. He shows me Ukraine and Russia in conflict too. Again, more loss of life and piles of rubble where houses and buildings had been. He shows me the Lunatic (Biden) and his handlers, how with brutality and destruction they rule the news cycle, turning the attention of the world wherever they desire. They grab the good people of the world by their heartstrings, manipulate them to send money wherever (it really doesn't matter), and then it flows through various means right back into the coffers of the political machine that had started the conflict in the first place. Kill, steal, destroy! Does that have a familiar ring to it? This is how <u>fear </u>speaks. And this is how the Cabal stays in power. If one war doesn't work, try another!

"My people," says the Lord, "don't be fooled anymore! Your goodness, your desire to help, is being used against you! Can you see that the goal of the Cabal is to kill, steal, and destroy? Therefore, who will win these endless conflicts? Do those who start these conflicts fight them? Who loses their life or property in these wars, and who walks away richer, having lost nothing? Wake up!"

I ask the Lord, "What about the U.S.? Will there be an attack here too?"

He answers, "Prophet, there has been, and there is a plan to attack the U.S. from within. It has been in the works for many years. It is a coordinated plan using several of your enemies. This plan will, however, fail. Your enemies will once again underestimate the resolve of the American people. Amen."

Warning to Posture Yourself for what is Coming – October 30, 2023

The Lord: "Prophet, have you postured yourself for what's coming?"

Kirk: "I'm not sure what You're speaking of."

The Lord: "The Great Reset. Have you postured yourself for the change? Or will you go into fear?"

Kirk: "Lord, You've been speaking of the things to come for some time. I believe I'm ready. But what posture should I assume? I'm not sure what you're saying."

The Lord: "Kirk, there are some events coming that have the potential to cause fear in My beloved ones. Tell the people to take a posture of <u>faith</u>. Tell them to re-look at the words of the Prophets in order to keep their eyes on Me. In this way, their faith will not be shaken."

Kirk: "Lord, what will this look like in the natural world?"

The Lord: "War, rumors of wars, some real bloodshed, some fake or staged and designed to create fear, world events, violence and threats of violence that will be so real that even My saints will be tempted to go into fear. But tell them (the saints) that in this chaos I AM will have His finest hour!

As the dust starts to clear, all eyes will see the evil ones fail. It will be magnified when the world sees the Lord's saints rise up with no fear of evil and start the process of meting out justice. This justice, My justice, will come hard and fast. To some it will seem cruel and unbending because the timeline for mercy and tolerance will be over. The law, the real Constitution, will be followed to the <u>letter</u> and will not be deviated from. There will be <u>NO</u> plea deals, no political class exemptions, and those Soros DA's and lawyers who have made a mockery of our justice system will be the ones who will be convicted of treason, etc. so that they will not have any effect on this process either! So yes, it will <u>look</u> rather ruthless because of what law and order should look like when people are treated equally according to the law."

Kirk: "When will this happen, Lord?"

The Lord: "Prophet, this is the season where this matter of justice has risen up before Me, and I AM is not slow regarding these matters. Watch DJT's language to understand the timing on this. Amen."

The spirit of the Law – November 3, 2023

Such confidence we have through Christ before God. Not that we are competent in ourselves to claim anything for ourselves, but our competence comes from God. He has made us competent as ministers of a new covenant—not

of the letter but of the Spirit; for the letter kills, but the Spirit gives life.

Now if the ministry that brought death, which was engraved in letters on stone, came with glory, so that the Israelites could not look steadily at the face of Moses because of its glory, transitory though it was, will not the ministry of the Spirit be even more glorious? If the ministry that brought condemnation was glorious, how much more glorious is the ministry that brings righteousness! (2 Corinthians 3:4-9 NIV)

Today the Lord is opening up these verses in 2 Corinthians 3. When Paul wrote this, he was obviously speaking of the Jewish religion, including all of its laws and the Ten Commandments, which were "engraved in letters on stone." He was calling it a ministry of death. But just now the Lord is saying that the Jewish religion is just an example of religion in general.

Religion does not, and indeed cannot, follow the Spirit of Christ. Instead, it takes up the model of following the letter. Even if the New Testament is read and "believed," it is looked at as new rules to be followed. This offers no hope to the followers, of course, because they cannot follow the Law any better than the Jews did in Jesus' time. Therefore, to the religious, the New Testament also becomes a ministry that brings death. Why is that so?

It is because the people are not able to follow the Law. As soon as laws are given, people begin to find loopholes and ways to work around the Law. Then more laws are needed to control and cow (coerce) them into following the original laws. This process leads to totalitarianism because lawless people will not obey laws unless they are pressed into it by force.

But, where the Spirit of the Lord is, there is freedom! Spirit filled believers have a bent toward righteousness. In fact, they despise lawlessness because it is not from the Spirit of God. Few laws, rules, etc. are needed for those who follow the Spirit of the Lord. And there truly is freedom in this lifestyle.

All of this is background for a look into the world of today. The Lord is showing us why He has decided to intervene. I see all the laws that worked well for years now being corrupted by the lawless: judges, district attorneys, and lawyers who have no interest in being fair or law abiding at all. Their unfair and illegal antics make the communist countries look good and fair by comparison! And the Lord says that only good people can be truly free, and it is the Spirit of Christ who makes people good and righteous. Amen.

Vision of the Beginning – November 10, 2023

Today the Lord called me (Kirk) to come with Him to a place which, according to the Lord, few, if any, prophets had seen. He took me in the Spirit, and we went to a place where there was nothing! No light, no sound, and the darkness was so complete that it felt thick and endless. I couldn't see anything at all, and I couldn't even see the Lord. Feeling His presence was the only thing that kept me from crying out. It was so desolate that I cannot express it.

We were floating there for some time. It could have been a few seconds or an eternity. There was nothing by which to mark time. Then I felt a hand touch mine. I couldn't really tell, but I thought that Jesus might be positioning me, like to face a particular direction or something. I felt, or thought, that we were maintaining this orientation for some time, but I really couldn't tell because the only sensory input I had was His touch on my hand.

Then, in the distance, I saw a point of light. It looked so small in the vast nothingness. I barely had time to think this thought before the light had grown to a size that took up everything in my field of view. Then it washed over me and Jesus. There was not feeling or jostling when it overcame us, but I felt as though we were inside an explosion. Fire and smoke, light and dust, all different colors and shapes rushing past us...

I thought, "Is this the creation of the universe or something?"

I turned to look at Jesus. He was smiling, and He said as a thought to my mind: "Before time and space and everything in them was, I AM."

He continued speaking to my mind and said, "Prophet, tell the people that everything that they see and what they don't see was spoken into existence. It is a small thing for order to come from disorder, for justice to come from injustice, for good to come from the bad. I AM has been since the beginning and shall be to the last. My promises are good and shall be forever. Do not go into fear, therefore. Keep your eyes on Me. Trust in Me, and you shall see things much greater than this! Amen."

I AM Truth – November 17, 2023

A s I (Kirk) pray, the Lord begins to speak to me...

"Very few people on earth know the truth. There are those who have an abundance of facts at their fingertips, more knowledge than at any other time in history, but they still don't know the truth. There are very intelligent people who understand science. They have a 'big picture' view of things that surround them, and they amaze people with their knowledge, but they don't know the truth. There are those who would rule the world with artificial intelligence, machines which can solve problems, learn of their own accord, and even mimic human emotions, but they don't know the truth. There are those who, because of their wealth, family name, or supposed status, believe that they should and will dominate the world. These are the most deceived of all and have exchanged the truth for a lie.

I AM Truth (says the LORD God). Apart from Me there is no truth. I AM the Creator of all things. And therefore, I AM the One who determines what truth is! I AM the One who was since the beginning and will be forever. I open doors that cannot be shut and close doors that cannot be opened. I speak and a thing is established or torn down. I create with a word. I give life or take it away because there is none like Me! I have lived and will live for all of eternity, and nothing or no one can lengthen My days or shorten them. Quite simply, I AM.

Therefore, will the computer or AI become equal to Me or outsmart Me? He who sits in the heavens laughs! Will another tower of Babel be built that I AM incapable of short circuiting? The evil one will never become My equal, even though his attempts go on and on. This latest attempt of his looks even more feeble than the tower of Babel, and in time, I shall draw a breath and blow it all away.

My people, who are called by My name, you shall rise up in these last days and become what has been dreamt of through the ages! Yes, you shall know the Truth, and <u>He</u> shall set you free! Truly free! It shall be known what the Scriptures mean when they say, 'Who the Son sets free is free indeed!' My power will be poured out in these last days, and all the knowledge and wisdom which has been hidden in Me shall be poured out as well. The wait is almost over. And in fact, My Spirit is right now being poured out on anyone who desires to carry Him!" Amen.

2024: The Transition – November 24, 2023

The Lord speaks to me (Kirk) today. He says: "Prophet, lift your eyes and see. I AM would show you some things."

He continues, "Prophet, tell the people that I AM has a plan. One plan. Plan A. And it will be carried out on the earth. And tell them that My plans are good!

Now, about your enemy. He too makes plans, but his plans are destined to fail. Then he must formulate back up plans and regroup to carry them out. What will he do? Is there anything he wouldn't try to do? To what extreme would he go to keep his grip on the world? Therefore, prepare yourselves then for this coming evil. Do <u>not</u> go into fear! But plan on seeing some of the enemy's tactics displayed. Kill, steal, destroy – yes, this will happen. But do not back down or shy away. Remember, Plan A is still in effect. When the religious become downcast and want to give up, remember they were never with you anyway. When tempted to panic, remember I AM is still in charge!"

I'm taken in the Spirit to an unfamiliar place. There are many machines at work, earth moving equipment, and scores of workers. Some are at work making new roads. There are a lot of engineers and surveyors laying out a great project. I asked in my mind, "What is this?" The voice of the Lord says, "The capital city will no longer be separate from the states it governs over. It will be in and among the states and the people, for it will be under the same law and the same standards as the rest of the country over which it governs. It cannot be separate any longer."

I continued to look over this great undertaking, and, in doing so, I came to a building which was completely finished. It was big and white and had very broad steps leading up to it. There were people gathered everywhere. It was very crowded. Being in the spirit, I drifted over the top of this crowd and looked at the top of the stairs to a place where a podium stood. As I waited, I saw a man step up to the microphone and begin to speak. I couldn't hear what he said, but he only spoke a few words, stretched forth his right hand, and ushered the next speaker to the mic.

Donald Trump then took his place before the people and began to speak. I still couldn't hear what was said, but I watched, and when the first words came from him, the crowd went totally crazy hugging each other, throwing things in the air, crazy! In my mind I wondered what he might have said to get that reaction. Again, the Lord spoke: "He just took back his rightful spot as President." WOW! I too felt just beside myself!

President Trump spoke for some time, then turned his back to the crowd, stretched out his right hand straight in front of himself, and began to slowly turn in a circle with his hand completely stretched out in front of him. He did a complete 360-degree circle. Again, the crowd went crazy!

I lifted my eyes right then as he swept his hand, and I saw everything that was wrong made right. Trash disappeared, the broken things were restored, the air cleared, the downcast were raised up, etc. I thought, "How weird. How could this happen?" Then I again heard the Lord: "I AM a Redeemer." Amen.

People will Flock to the Military – November 25, 2023

"When the Trumpet's back, people will flock to the military. It will be honorable again."

Kenya – November 29, 2023

"My people! I AM totally in love with you! I have been with you in your tribal times. I have been with you as you have begun to come out from under oppression. I have been with you as you have come from many directions and tribes and clans to form a country as one people. And now I AM calling you to become as one people reborn in My Spirit, independent of the world and totally dependent on Me!

Come to Me! For I AM, and I really do reward those who diligently seek Me! I AM a giver. It is My nature to give FREELY (Hebrews 11:6). Those who have My Spirit are also givers of whatever I AM giving them. If money, then give money. If strength, then help those who need it. If food, then food. In My economy those who give do not have less because I bless them with MORE! This is because I AM love, and love never fails!

This then is how I, the Lord, see Kenya: A prosperous country, ridding itself of evil and crime because My people are taking their places in government, in schools, in places of leadership throughout Kenya. Not because of their own strengths or skills, but because all wisdom and knowledge is hidden in Christ Jesus, and My people can do anything in Him! Amen."

The Four Winds – December 1, 2023

Today the Faceless Man, the Holy Spirit, took me in the Spirit, and we went far above the earth below us. The Faceless Man was dressed in pure white light, and His head and arms were a whiter white than His clothing (robe). We looked down at the sphere below us. I could see oceans and continents, etc. As I looked, the Faceless Man pointed to an area above the northern region of the earth.

I saw a small dot where He was pointing. As I was trying to see what He was pointing at, my eyes started to "zoom in" on this dot, and I could see that it was a great angel. He didn't have a horse or armor or anything, but he was dressed in white with great wings. The Faceless Man then directed me to look to the southern region, and high above the earth in that area there was another angel just like the first. There were also angels standing in the heavens above the eastern and western regions of the earth.

The Holy Spirit began to speak to me. "Together, these are called The Four Winds. They have been given charge over the spiritual winds on earth. Satan is always trying to thwart what these are doing because they stand against him and his ways. The Four Winds moderate, or hold back, destructive wind that he would generate to steal, kill, and destroy. The spiritual wind controls the natural.

Prophet, today prophesy to The Four Winds! Prophesy to the winds a new power! Prophesy an overwhelming wind of the Spirit of God upon the nations! Prophesy a wind of destruction upon the wicked and a refreshing and welcome wind at the back of those who are of the Spirit of God!"

So, I prophesied as I was told to do. As I did, I was given a vision inside this vision. I saw a series of very quick visions of the evil one trying, through those who followed him, to accomplish things, but everything they tried was very difficult for them, full of mistakes and failures that exposed them even more. Everything they did worked against them!

Then I saw another series of short visions. The righteous ones had the wind of the Spirit behind them in everything they did. Doing good, thwarting evil, bringing justice was easy and efficient. They made no mistakes and were empowered in everything they did. These visions then disappeared, and I was back with the Faceless Man.

The Holy Spirit then spoke to me again: "The spiritual controls the natural, and so the onset of this change will come in the form of strange winds that will be noticed on the earth." Amen.

Rapture for the Cowardly – December 8, 2023

"Kirk, you are My End Times Prophet. You have been wondering about the rapture of My Church just now. I want to plainly tell you: There will be no rapture of My Church! My Church doesn't want a rapture. Those who are fully in Me have already died to themselves and now live for Me. Their hearts' desire is to do everything I desire them to do. They are My warriors and would think nothing of dying for Me or My sake. They love Me to the death and are completely fearless and will be to the end.

Those cowards who only think of preserving themselves and escaping in that day also have a destination, and it is not paradise, but rather, as it is written, they have a date with what they fear most. Yes. The Lake of Fire. Amen."

Vision of the Universe & Diversity –

December 15, 2023

(Kirk) was praying, and I heard the Lord say, "Come up here, Prophet."

So, I went. I went so fast that very quickly I was passing the farthest star in the farthest galaxy, and as I did, I saw a door standing open. I zipped toward the door and went through it. As I did, Jesus joined me, and where there was almost complete darkness before, His light was now brightly shining. His clothing was pure white and very bright. His hands and feet were even brighter than His clothes — like lightning. But even though there was unbelievable brightness because of the Lord, there was nothing to reflect back the light. I wondered, "Where are we?" as I looked for something, anything!

Then I heard Jesus in my mind saying: "Prophet, we are at the limit of the Father's creation. Through this door there is nothingness where nothing exists. Even though His creation expands continually toward and into this zone, beyond there is nothing, like before the creation of the worlds."

I wondered if He had made other universes in the nothingness. The Lord said, "No. There could only be one."

We went back through the door and stood at the edge of the universe, looking at all of the stars, more numerous than all the sand grains of all the seashores on earth. And yet, we traversed it like nothing almost instantaneously from one end to the other. I was just thinking of these things and that I was there looking at it with the One who had made it! Then I wondered if there was another planet somewhere with people on it as well. Again, His gentle voice comes into my mind.

"No," He said. "Have you noticed how We like to make things that are one off? Like each snowflake is different from all the others. Or in people, each is different from every person who ever lived. Each tree, flower, rock, none are the exact same as another. We love diversity and never tire of it. You too, then, should embrace diversity. It is from the Creator, from Me."

That word, I thought, that word "diversity." It carries a meaning in my mind... Instantly, He spoke again in my mind.

"The oceans have their limits. As you have seen, the universe also has limits, as does every other thing in creation. There is only 'one' who is evil and desires to corrupt what has been created. Those corrupted things We hate because they're evil and have been done against Us. This too shall pass, however. Your enemy's days are numbered. Amen."

As He spoke, I could see that His diversity was good, but what the enemy has pushed on the world calling it diversity when it is really sin is evil. Then I was back praying again.

Message of Hope – December 15, 2023

Philippians 3:13b-14 (NIV) reads,

But one thing I do: Forgetting what is behind and straining toward what is ahead, I press on toward the goal to win the prize for which God has called me heavenward in Christ Jesus.

Who can go back in time anyway? People, as they age, seem to look back with fondness and forward with disdain. But we are not of those who shrink back or look back. We are always called forward – from glory to glory!

The Holy Spirit gives us grace to see a glimmering, bright hope in our future. Even when surrounded by desert and dryness, when we are straining, we go forward in hope and His joy.

Our hope is a living hope that springs up inside us! Our hope and joy are not dependent on our circumstances. On the contrary, it transcends this world and its limitations and systems. Our living hope lives within us, the same Spirit who raised Christ from the dead! The Hope of Glory! The Spirit of Jesus Christ Himself! He is our hope and our salvation!

Relationship with the LORD – December 22, 2023

The Lord begins to speak to me today...

"Kirk, you know that I love you, right?"

I answer, "Yes, Lord, I know that You love me!"

The Lord says, "Kirk, there are so many who do not know this. They are true believers too! Today, Prophet, prophesy to My people who are called by My Name. Tell them to come to Me and ask Me if I love them. Tell them that I Am desiring to answer them! And I will!"

I answer, "Yes, Lord, I will do this! Is there anything else you desire me to say to them?"

The Lord replies, "Prophet, tell them that I will surely answer them, and this question will be the starting point of many relationships with Me! I desire obedience, not sacrifice, but how can anyone obey the voice of One they cannot hear? Or how can one have a relationship with one who only requires sacrifices continually?

I AM not a dictator or tyrant requiring fear and submission. I AM love itself. I AM a giver of good gifts and a rewarder of those who diligently seek Me. A religious mind only sees what must be <u>done</u> to appease Me and ladders that must be climbed to reach Me.

But those with whom I have a relationship <u>know</u> Me and love Me. They have come into My fold through the gate (My Son). They follow Him and will not follow another. These are the ones I love, and they will follow Me wherever I lead them. These do not have a 'belief system' or 'systematic theology' which they 'believe in.' No, these are My sons whom I love! We have become one, and I have given of Myself to them. They are the overcomers, the victorious church. Yes, truly these are My warrior Bride who has neither spot nor wrinkle! Amen."

The Judgment – December 30, 2023

Revelation 11:11 *But after three and a half days, the breath of life from God came into them, and they stood on their feet; and great fear fell upon those who were watching them.* (NASB)

"Yes, I, even I, will give these of Myself and they shall have authority on the earth, and they shall judge and make judgment just as they hear. And I AM will allow this authority to manifest as POWER such as the earth has never seen before! The earth itself will shake and the oceans will roar, but they will not compare to what I AM releasing to My Apostles and Prophets.

FEAR? When the wicked on the earth see these rise up and realize that the very judgment which has been promised will come as a shout comes from Heaven saying, 'Rise up!' and MY chosen ones will ascend to their places to judge and make judgments in great <u>Power</u> and <u>Glory</u>, yes fear of the inevitable will be like a wildfire throughout the whole earth! And I AM telling you now, this fear will not be unfounded, but as the Scriptures say, 'Anyone who desires to harm them will be killed by the fire that comes from their mouths!'

All of this will come as an earthquake to planet earth, and the dead shall number a tenth of those there. The rest shall praise God because of their great fear, but further judgment will come.

The righteous will be in their glory, praising God and dancing in the streets! My Son shall be glorified beyond all expectations because of how He has partnered with the sons of men to bring His justice and His honor to the whole earth. And every Scripture will be fulfilled regarding His judgment upon the wicked! Amen."

2024

Prayers Answered in 2024 – January 7, 2024

"You will see the end result of many prayers this year (2024). Many prayers. These are things I've wanted to do and have been working on for a long time, in which I have invited you to participate with Me in.

Faith feeds on the testimony of Jesus. Each testimony of My power and working exalts My Son. They are all part of testifying to Him. The faith of My children will rise to levels never before experienced during the time of My Great Reset as My Son is exalted in testimony after testimony.

The fruitless deeds of darkness will be exposed to the most minute detail and judged accordingly by those whose sole persuasion and focus is to live on every word I speak.

Many have speculated on the mark of the beast, but have missed the spirit behind this mark, which is fear. Fear is NOT from Me. It's not a virtue, safety net, or admirable in any way. What people think and what people do will reflect if they are participating with this spirit. What they FEEL is inconsequential. It's what they agree with that matters. (In other words, feeling fear is not the same as agreeing with it.)

My people who are called by My Name do not participate with fear. They are motivated by love because they have chosen the way of the love that they have experienced in My Son. They obey out of love. They harken to My voice always, and I will not let them down. This will be a great year of testimony to the love of My Son and all He has paid for. And it's only the <u>Beginning</u>! Amen!"

Flood the Earth with the Holy Spirit – February 4, 2024

"I will flood the earth with My Spirit – the glory of God. The flood of My Spirit will remove all that offends. Those on the Rock will remain standing in praise to the Lord of all!"

Shortcut Prophetic Word – February 23, 2024

A shortcut is a different way to do something that saves time and effort.

Throughout the Scriptures there are examples of those who were presented with the opportunity to take a shortcut. The serpent told Adam and Eve that they could be like God if they would eat the fruit of the Tree of the Knowledge of Good and Evil, that instead of being obedient to what God had told them, a shortcut to His likeness could be had (Genesis 3). Then in Exodus 33, Moses was presented with a shortcut. An angel would go before the Israelites, driving out the inhabitants of the land and leading Israel into the land of milk and honey. Moses refused this shortcut. And then of course, Jesus was tempted by Satan, and if He accepted the offer presented to Him, all the kingdoms of the world and their glory would be given to Him (Matthew 4:8-9).

In ministry there are also shortcuts. Some are very, very tempting indeed! We are called to follow the Spirit of Christ, and our rewards come from doing just that. But standing before a large crowd teaching or going to a seminary and having instant access to a church and a paycheck is very tempting. And wouldn't God want that anyway? What could be wrong with doing ministry the traditional way, the accepted and well-worn way? Wouldn't God want us to do things that are acceptable to a denomination or religion? Doing things a different way is probably not even acceptable, right?

Matthew 7:13-14 (NASB) reads, *"Enter through the narrow gate, for the gate is wide and the way is broad that leads to destruction, and there are many who enter through it. For the gate is small and the way is narrow that leads to life, and there are few who find it."*

The Lord says, "The broad way and the wide gate please men. Indeed, this is the path set up by men according to the ways of men and the world. These people are not inclined to follow the Spirit of God and in fact, have done things their own way so long that they do not even hear His voice anymore."

Matthew 7:21 (NASB) reads, *"Not everyone who says to Me, 'Lord, Lord,' will enter the kingdom of heaven, but he who does the will of My Father who is in heaven will enter. Many will say to Me on that day, 'Lord, Lord, did we not prophesy in Your name, and in Your name cast out demons, and in Your name perform many miracles?' And then I will declare to them, 'I never knew you; depart from Me, you who practice lawlessness.'"*

The Lord says, "These have loved the praise of men more than the praise of God. They have preached the wisdom of men and have a form of godliness but no power. Their sheep are likewise powerless, and their so-called 'fruit' is not from the good tree, even though it looks 'nice.' These study the Scriptures but fail to even realize that they ARE the current reincarnation of the Pharisees, the high priests, and the teachers of the Law! They are truly blind! I AM has made this so simple! John 17:3 says, *'This is eternal life, that they may know You, the only true God, and Jesus Christ whom You have sent.'* Amen."

Standard of Judgment Against the Wicked the Same as it was for Eli's House – February 28, 2024

I (Kirk) was instructed to go to 1 Samuel 3:14. When I did, I found it was the account of Eli and his two sons. *"And therefore I have sworn to the house of Eli that the iniquity of Eli's house shall not be atoned for by sacrifice or offering forever."*

"Prophet, ready the people for the billion-soul harvest. Ready them also for the recompense of the Lord, both for the righteous and the wicked. Iniquity has its reward, just as righteousness does. Eli's sons had committed gross immorality and injustice, and they were given a chance to repent. But Eli's correction fell on deaf ears, and Eli himself then allowed their evil. Further, I the Lord, had told Eli that his house was going to be judged, but he still did not repent.

I AM going to judge once again, just as I did in the time of Eli. There are those who have again committed gross immorality and injustice against My people. These have also been warned, but like Eli, they have hardened their hearts. For these the recompense will be the same as for Eli's house. For these there is no atonement, no sacrifice, and no offering that can be made for them or their house.

Therefore, because of My great love for those who are Mine, I will repay, says the Lord. Eli turned a blind eye to what Hophni and Phinehas were doing, even though he had the authority to stop it. Therefore, the standard will be the same in the season of My Reset, and Ichabod shall come to an end forever on the earth. Amen."

Note: Eli's daughter-in-law went into labor when she heard that her husband and father-in-law were dead and that the ark of God had been captured. She gave birth to a son and named him Ichabod, which means inglorious or no glory because the glory had departed from Israel. (1 Samuel 4:19-22) The Lord is saying that after His justice and during His Reset, the glory of God will never depart again. Inglorious will come to an end forever on the earth. For the Glory of God shall fill the earth! Halleluiah!

Obedience NOT Sacrifice – Don't Chase After Me – March 1, 2024

Today the Lord is saying that He desires obedience. Not obedience to words on a page. Not even obedience to a man or woman of God. He doesn't desire us to chase after Him either. Instead, He desires simple obedience like Jesus has spoken of: "I can do nothing of Myself; I only do what I see My Father doing."

To chase after the Lord without really following the Holy Spirit is to take what the Scriptures say by making your own judgments regarding what is said in them. This is to believe you are doing His will without really knowing what His will is. It is to do good works listed in the Scriptures without the guidance of the Holy Spirit. Yes, it is spending your money giving to those in need apart from the Spirit of God in order to be nice or to appear nice to those in need by giving them food or shelter without the Spirit of God's leading.

For example, you may believe He approves of "mission trips" to poor countries and so you "support" those who do these things, but you have never asked the Holy Spirit for guidance because you can obviously see that these things are for a good cause. You lean on Scripture verses that seem <u>to you</u> to indicate "giving" means anytime you release something you own to someone else for free it is a good thing. After all, Christians are supposed to be nice! However, making up our own rules about how to give leads to trouble. The account of Ananias and Sapphira bear witness to this.

Also, consider Matthew 6:1-4 below. It speaks of giving to be seen by men, and if you do this, you will have no reward for it. Jesus said,

"Take heed that you do not do your charitable deeds before men, to be seen by them. Otherwise you have no reward from your Father in heaven. Therefore, when you

347

do a charitable deed, do not sound a trumpet before you as the hypocrites do in the synagogues and in the streets, that they may have glory from men. Assuredly, I say to you, they have their reward. But when you do a charitable deed, do not let your left hand know what your right hand is doing, that your charitable deed may be in secret; and your Father who sees in secret will Himself reward you openly."

Therefore, even though you're giving something away to a church or a very good cause, it must be done according to the leading of the Holy Spirit. The tithe that is taught and preached about cannot please God if it is given apart from the leading of the Holy Spirit. We are not under law anymore when we are in Christ. If He leads someone to give ten percent, then they should. If not, then they shouldn't. Theologies, doctrines, pastors, the law, and even Scriptures do not lead us into all truth! If you believe what the Scriptures say then you believe that the Spirit of Truth leads us into all truth, and He convicts us of righteousness and of sin and of judgment.

Yes, the Holy Spirit is God, and Jesus thought Him so important as to say that it was to our advantage that He (Jesus) would leave, and the Holy Spirit would come! As the Apostle Paul wrote in 2 Corinthians 3, we really are servants of a new covenant, not of the LETTER but of the Spirit. For the letter kills, but the Spirit gives life! (2 Corinthian 3:6 reads … *who also made us sufficient as ministers of the new covenant, not of the letter but of the Spirit; for the letter kills, but the Spirit gives life.*) Amen.

Authors' Bio

TIFFANY ROOT & KIRK VANDEGUCHTE bring Jesus to the nations through *Seeking the Glory of God Ministries*. They have a prophetic channel on YouTube and Rumble that can be found under *Seeking the Glory of God*, and they have daily devotionals on their SGGM DEVOTIONAL channels on YouTube and Rumble.

The Lord has said regarding Seeking the Glory of God Ministries:

"The point of SGGM is to host a movement of the Spirit of God. In this 'model,' the fivefold ministry will be the government of the Church. Those who govern will be the servants of all, and they will not 'lord it over the congregants' as is done today.

This is a movement of disciples who go out. This is a movement where Jesus Christ is central and most importantly, where the Spirit of Christ is lifted high! In this movement, FAITH is spelled RISK and risk is spelled ACTION! Working for the Lord, in obedience to the Spirit is normal, and laziness and pew-sitting are very rare indeed.

'What church do you belong to?' This question will fade into the denomination era and will not be used anymore, at least not in the way it is now. People will either be members of The Universal Church, or not. And those who are Spirit-filled will know each other by the Spirit of God.

During this time, every prayer ever prayed for the Church will be fulfilled. All of the saints who ever desired to see a spotless bride for the Lord of All will see their prayers come to fruition during this time! Amen."

Other books in print can be found on Amazon.com. They include: *Trump Prophecies; The Revelation of Jesus Christ and the End Times; Walking With God: 1-Year Devotional; Picking up the Pace One Year Devotional; For God So Loved the World; How Loud Can a Dragonfly Roar? Panda Trouble; and Penguins in the Antarctic.*

Please visit www.seekingthegloryofgodministries.com for more information.

Made in the USA
Columbia, SC
23 December 2024

50394478R00200